VISUAL FACTFINDER

THE
WORLD
WARS

First published in 2006 by Miles Kelly Publishing Ltd
Bardfield Centre, Great Bardfield, Essex, CM7 4SL

This edition published in 2007

2 4 6 8 10 9 7 5 3

Editorial Director: Belinda Gallagher
Art Director: Jo Brewer
Editor and Picture Researcher: Amanda Askew
Designer: Stephan Davis
Reprographics: Anthony Cambray, Stephan Davis,
Liberty Newton, Ian Paulyn
Indexer: Jane Parker

British Library Cataloguing-in-Publication Data
A catalogue record for this book is available from the British Library

ISBN 978-1-84236-679-0

Printed in China

www.mileskelly.net
info@mileskelly.net

VISUAL FACTFINDER

THE WORLD WARS

Written and consulted by:
Rupert Matthews and Brian Williams

MiLes
KeLLy
PUBLISHING

WORLD WAR I 12-213

BUILD-UP TO WAR

Mr. Melvin Millon
2–1571 Coronation Dr
London ON   N6G 5N9

1915: NEW WEAPONS, NEW WAR

1916: STALEMATE

1914–1918: THE WAR AT SEA

1917: THE WAR SPREADS

1918: THE WAR TO END ALL WARS

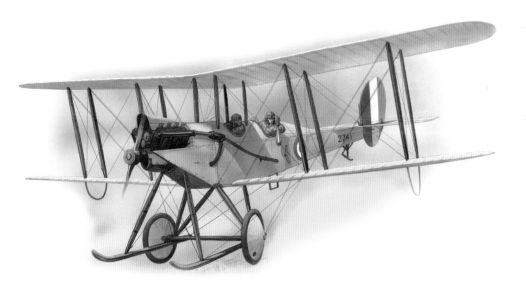

WORLD WAR II 216-415

BUILD-UP TO WAR

1941: STRUGGLE FOR SURVIVAL

1942: BY LAND, SEA AND AIR

1943: TOTAL WAR

1944: ALLIES ADVANCE

1945: THE PRICE OF VICTORY

WORLD WAR I

A Europe of empires

- **Before 1914**, Europe was dominated by three large empires that no longer exist today – the German Empire, the Russian Empire and the Habsburg Empire, which is sometimes called Austria-Hungary.

- **A fourth empire** was the Turkish-Ottoman Empire, which once ruled all of southeastern Europe, but by 1914, only ruled the Middle East.

- **All of these empires** were governed by dictators who took little notice of democracy or the wishes of their peoples.

- **The German Empire** included modern Germany and parts of what are now France, Poland, Denmark and the Czech Republic. It was the newest empire, founded in 1871 when the smaller German states joined together.

- **The Russian Empire** included modern Russia, plus Latvia, Estonia, Finland, Lithuania, Ukraine, Belorussia, Turkmenistan, Kazakhstan, Uzbekistan, Tajikistan, Kirghizistan and part of Poland.

- **The Habsburg Empire** included modern Austria, Hungary, Serbia, Croatia, Montenegro, Slovenia, Slovakia, parts of the Czech Republic, Poland, Italy and Romania.

- **There were several smaller independent countries**, such as Switzerland, Belgium, the Netherlands and the Scandinavian countries. In the Balkans were several new countries that had become independent in the previous 50 years as the Turkish-Ottoman Empire broke up.

- **Some European countries**, such as Britain, France and Germany, ruled extensive overseas empires in Africa, Asia and the Pacific.

- **There was great inequality** of wealth in Europe. Some countries, such as Britain, were prosperous with advanced industrial activity. Other countries, such as those in the Russian Empire, were poor with few factories or good roads.

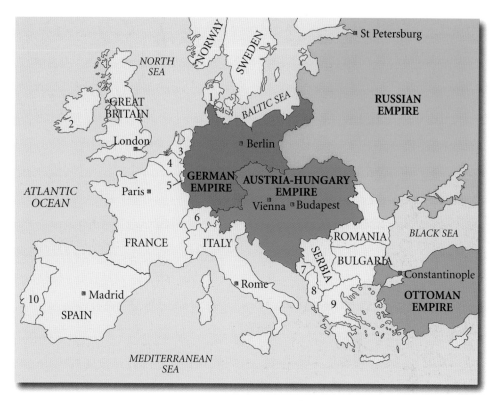

▲ *Europe in 1914. The empires of Germany and Austria-Hungary dominated central Europe, while Russia and the Ottoman Empire stood to the east. France and Britain were dominant in the west.*

KEY

1 Denmark	6 Switzerland
2 Ireland	7 Montenegro
3 Netherlands	8 Albania
4 Belgium	9 Greece
5 Luxembourg	10 Portugal

. . . **FASCINATING FACT** . . .
Some countries in Europe were republics, such as France, but most were monarchies, which had a king or emperor as head of state.

The alliances

KEY

- ▢ Triple Alliance/Central Powers
- ▢ Triple Entente/Allies
- ▢ Neutral
- ▢ Balkan League
- 1 Denmark
- 2 Ireland
- 3 Netherlands
- 4 Belgium
- 5 Luxembourg
- 6 Switzerland
- 7 Montenegro
- 8 Albania
- 9 Greece
- 10 Portugal

▲ *In the early years of the 20th century many countries sought security by forming alliances with other countries. These alliances proved to be particularly crucial in World War I.*

- **For almost 100 years**, Europe had been peaceful. The foreign ministers and diplomats of the different countries met regularly to discuss problems and opportunities. They were usually able to reach a compromise without a war.

- **Since 1815**, there had only been two major wars, and both of these were over quickly. The Crimean War of 1854 set the Ottomans, Britain and France against Russia in a dispute over the Balkans.

- **The other conflict**, the wars of German reunification, saw the German states fight Austria and France and unite to form the German Empire.

- **Even when a war did take place**, the diplomats ensured that the results were reasonable. Neither side fought to destroy the other, but simply to ensure they got their way in a particular dispute.

- **Countries formed alliances** to support each other if a particular event were to occur. Some lasted a short period of time, others for many years.

- **In 1887**, Spain and Italy signed a ten-year treaty agreeing to join their navies together if either were attacked by France. This agreement was designed to counter the power of the growing French Mediterranean fleet.

- **In 1897**, the Habsburg Empire signed a ten-year treaty with Russia promising to block any changes in the Balkans. The small Balkan countries had many disputes with each other, but Russia and Austria preferred peace and stability, rather than letting the Balkan states sort things out by force.

- **By 1914**, Germany and Austria were linked by the Triple Alliance with Italy.

- **At the same time**, Russia and France were tied into a similar alliance.

- **Britain was linked to France** and Russia by various agreements, but had not signed a firm alliance. However, Britain was allied to Belgium and promised to help if any other country tried to invade it.

Great power rivalries

● **In the years before World War I** there were numerous incidents and clashes between the great powers. Each of these was eventually solved by diplomats without a war. However, each incident led to increased tension and mistrust.

● **On 12 June 1900**, Germany announced a 17-year plan to construct the second largest navy in the world. Britain, which had the largest, was worried that Germany might try to use the new navy to attack its empire.

● **In 1904**, Britain began an even larger programme of building warships. It started with the battleship, *Dreadnought*.

● **The First Moroccan Crisis** of 1905 began when France tried to force the Sultan of Morocco to sign a trade treaty. This would have given France control of the country. Germany objected. A conference was held in Spain at Algeciras in April 1906, where a compromise was reached.

● **In October 1908**, Austria announced that it was taking over the provinces of Bosnia and Herzegovina from the Ottomans. Austria had been running the area for 30 years, giving the excuse that it was protecting the Christian inhabitants from the Muslim Turks.

● **Serbia and Montenegro** objected to the takeover of Bosnia and Herzegovina. Russia backed the Serbs, while Germany supported the Austrians. In 1909, a compromise was reached and Austria bought the provinces from the Ottomans.

● **In July 1911**, the Second Moroccan Crisis began when the German warship, *Panther*, steamed into the port of Agadir. The Kaiser complained about the French treatment of Germans in Morocco. After a tense few weeks, Germany accepted a compromise.

● **On 27 August 1911,** Kaiser Wilhelm II made a famous speech saying that Germany wanted 'a place in the sun', meaning he wanted Germany to be recognized as an important power by other countries. He made it clear that Germany would not back down again in a future crisis.

● **On 29 September 1911,** Italy demanded that the Ottomans allow Italian merchants in Tripoli greater freedom. The Ottomans offered a compromise, but Italy invaded Tripoli anyway.

● **After a short war,** the Ottomans gave up all of Libya to Italy. The Balkan countries realized the Ottomans were very weak.

▶ *The German ruler, Kaiser Wilhelm II, wanted Germany to gain the power and prestige that he believed it was entitled to.*

The Balkan Wars

● **The Balkans lie between the Black**, Adriatic and Aegean seas. In 1912 it was made up of Serbia, Bulgaria, Greece, Romania and Montenegro. Both the Ottoman and Austrian empires ruled large areas of the Balkans.

● **All the smaller countries** in the Balkans had previously been part of the Ottoman Empire. They wanted to help those Christian people still living under Muslim Ottoman rule to become free as well.

● **The Austrian Empire was concerned** that various countries in the Balkans wanted to become independent. Austria opposed the expansion of the small Balkan states, especially Serbia, which was the most powerful of them all.

● **The Russian Empire exported grain** and other goods by ship through the straits at Constantinople. This was extremely profitable, thus it was vital that Russia maintained good relationships with whoever controlled these straits.

● **The Ottoman Empire was weak** and poor. The Turks wanted to control the lands they still held, while they carried out reforms of their government and economic systems.

▶ *In 1912 the small Balkan nations joined together to capture land from the Ottoman Empire.*

KEY

1 Montenegro

● **On 8 October 1912,** the tiny country of Montenegro invaded the Ottoman Empire. Within 10 days, Bulgaria, Serbia and Greece had joined the war on Montenegro's side. The Ottoman army was defeated within a few months.

● **In May 1913,** Russia, Austria, Britain and France organized a peace conference. In the Treaty of London, Bulgaria, Montenegro, Serbia and Greece were each given parts of the Ottoman Empire, which was reduced to the area around Constantinople. A new country, Albania, was created.

● **On 29 June 1913,** Bulgaria was attacked by Greece, Serbia and Romania. Bulgaria had to give up the areas it gained under the Treaty of London.

● **Austria was furious** that the small countries had grown in size and wealth so quickly. It was particularly worried about Serbia because many Serbs lived in the Habsburg Empire and may leave to join the independent kingdom of Serbia. The Austrians decided to teach Serbia a lesson.

● **After the two Balkan wars,** every country in the Balkans had a dispute with another at some time.

▶ *By 1913 the Balkan nations had defeated the Ottomans, but now argued with each other over how to divide their conquests.*

KEY

1 Montenegro   2 Albania

21

On the brink of war

● **The summer of 1914** was long, warm and peaceful. All the recent international crises had been resolved without fighting, and the small wars in the Balkans were over. The world economy was booming. Most people looked forward to a prosperous and peaceful future.

● **However, international tensions** were high. Germany wanted power and prosperity. Austria was determined to restrain Serbia's growth. Russia was suffering internal social unrest, so the Tsar wanted a foreign success. Each had decided not to back down in a future crisis.

● **France had an army** of 3.5 million men and a navy with 28 battleships and 28 cruisers. It earned about £425 million in trade and had a population of 40 million.

● **Germany could field an army** of 8.5 million men and had a navy of 40 battleships and 57 cruisers. The German Empire made about £1 billion in trade in 1913 and had a population of 65 million.

● **Russia could field an army** of 4.4 million men, with another 10 million in reserve, and a navy of 16 battleships and 14 cruisers. The Russian Empire earned £190 million in trade and had a population of 167 million.

● **The Austrian Empire had an army** of 3 million men and a navy of 16 battleships and 12 cruisers. The empire earned £198 million in trade and had a population of 49 million.

● **Britain had an army** of 711,000 and a navy of 64 battleships and 121 cruisers. It earned £1.2 billion in trade and had a population of 46 million.

● **Turkey had an army** of 360,000 men and a small navy with no battleships or cruisers. It earned £67 million in trade and had a population of 21 million.

● **Most army officers in all countries expected** that if a war did break out, it would be fought in a similar way to wars in the 19th century. Cavalry would act as scouts, artillery would shell fortified positions and infantry would fight the main battles with rifles.

● **Everybody expected that a war would be over** very quickly. It was thought that there would be one or two big battles, then the loser would offer to make peace, compromising on the original dispute.

▶ *Charge of the Light Brigade, 25 October 1854. The Crimean War (1854–1856) was fought in traditional style. If a war were to break out in 1914, most generals expected it to be fought in the same way.*

Murder in Sarajevo

- **In June 1914**, the Austrian army was due to undertake manoeuvres in the southern part of the Habsburg Empire near Sarajevo, the capital of Bosnia.

- **Archduke Franz Ferdinand**, the heir to Austrian Emperor Franz Josef, was to review the troops and supervise the action.

- **A few days before the manoeuvres** took place, it was decided that Archduke Franz Ferdinand would also visit leading citizens in Sarajevo. They wished to discuss a proposal, which would give the area self-government.

- **Three Serb extremists were planning** to murder the Archduke. They belonged to the Black Hand terrorist organization.

- **Black Hand was led** by Vojislav Tankosic, a citizen of Serbia. He received weapons, money and information from Colonel Dragutin Apis, who served on the General Staff of Serbia.

- **When Franz Ferdinand arrived** in Sarajevo, he got into a car and drove to his meeting as part of a convoy. Black Hand activists, Nedeljko Cabrinovic, Gavrilo Princip and Andri Grabez, were waiting to murder him.

◀ *Police seize Gravilo Princip after his first attempt to assassinate the Archduke.*

● **As the cars left the railway station**, Cabrinovic threw a hand grenade. He missed the cars, but about 20 civilians and an army officer were injured.

● **After the meeting**, the convoy drove back through Sarajevo. Princip pulled a gun, but was grabbed by a policeman. He freed himself and opened fire.

● **The first bullet killed the duchess**, the second injured an army officer and the third hit the Archduke in the neck. He died less than ten minutes later. Princip was arrested.

● **Although Vojislav Tankosic planned the murder** of Archduke Franz Ferdinand, he stayed safely in Serbia himself.

▶ *The Archduke and his wife prepare to climb into their car just minutes before they were both shot dead.*

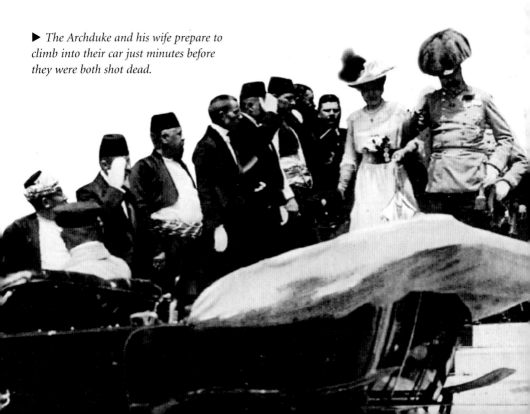

The war begins

- **After the assassination** of Archduke Franz Ferdinand, the Austrians quickly discovered that the killer, Gavrilo Princip, was a member of the Black Hand terrorist group. They knew Black Hand was supported by Serbia's army and thought Serbia had planned the murder.

- **Austrian Emperor Franz Josef** and his government decided to use the murder as a reason to crush Serbia. They began to prepare for war, but sent army commander Count Conrad von Hötzendorf on holiday to make it appear that they did not expect war.

- **Kaiser Wilhelm II of Germany** promised to support Austria, but King Victor Emmanuel III of Italy refused. He said Italy would only join Austria if Serbia attacked first.

- **Serbia contacted its ally**, Russia. Tsar Nicholas II advised Serbia to call a conference if Austria began a war. The Tsar then ordered part of the Russian army to march towards the Austrian frontier to act as a threat.

- **Russia contacted its ally**, France, to ask for support. The French government said it would only join a war if Russia were attacked, but not if Russia attacked Austria first.

- **On 23 July,** the Austrian government announced the results of their inquiry into the murder of the Archduke. They demanded that the Serb government ban anti-Austrian organizations and newspapers, sack a number of government officials, arrest Tankosic, head of the Black Hand terrorist group, and open a judicial inquiry with an Austrian judge in charge.

- **On 25 July,** Serbia agreed to all the demands, but said the inquiry should have a Serb judge. The German, Russian and French governments thought this was reasonable and believed that war had been avoided.

▶ *On 3 August 1914 the* Daily Sketch *carried reports on the mood of the British public as war began to seem more likely.*

England Prepares Against A German Invasion.

DAILY SKETCH.

No. 1,635. LONDON, MONDAY, AUGUST 3, 1914. [Registered as a Newspaper.] ONE HALFPENNY.

ENGLAND FOR WAR: Orders To The Fleet.

- **On 28 July**, Austria turned down the Serb offer and declared war. They sent a telegram to the Serb government. This was the first time that war had been declared by telegram, instead of by a meeting between the two sides.

- **At first**, Serb Prime Minister Sibe Milicic thought it was a joke, believing that a government would not declare war by telegram. Then a second telegram arrived from a frontier post to say that Austrian artillery had opened fire.

- **The war had begun** at 3 p.m. on 28 July 1914.

The Schlieffen Plan

- **As the Austrian army marched** into Serbia, the Serbs appealed to Russia for help. Tsar Nicholas II decided to send the Russian army to the Austrian frontier, then demand talks with Austria to agree a peace deal in Serbia.

- **The Russian generals told the Tsar** that if the army marched on Austria, Russia would be helpless against Germany. On 29 July 1914, the Tsar agreed to mobilize all Russia's reserves.

- **On 30 July**, Kaiser Wilhelm II ordered Germany to mobilize for war. He informed Russia that unless they demobilized, Germany would declare war.

- **Russia informed its ally**, France, of the German message. On 31 July, France began to mobilize for war.

- **Tsar Nicholas refused** to stand down the Russian army. Germany and Austria declared war on Russia on 1 August.

- **On 1 August**, Kaiser Wilhelm ordered General Helmuth von Moltke to implement the Schlieffen Plan. It detailed troop movements and how supplies would be organized.

- **The plan involved** defeating France before Russia could mobilize its reserves.

▼ *A German regiment advances in open order across a field in northern France. In the early weeks of the war there was much movement in the open.*

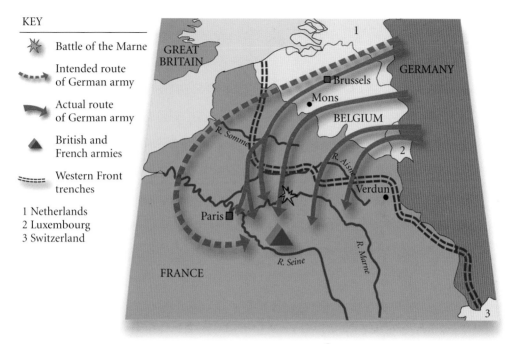

KEY

✳ Battle of the Marne

➴ Intended route of German army

➥ Actual route of German army

▲ British and French armies

▦ Western Front trenches

1 Netherlands
2 Luxembourg
3 Switzerland

▲ *The Schlieffen Plan. The Germans began the war with an attack on France that involved marching through Belgium. This plan, named the Schlieffen Plan after General von Schlieffen who invented it, went wrong, as the French and British resistance was tougher than expected.*

● **The Schlieffen Plan put small forces** on the Russian border and in fortified positions on the French border. The main German armies would then march through Belgium to capture Paris and force France to surrender. Then the German armies would be moved east to defeat Russia.

● **On 3 August**, Germany declared war on France. The German ambassador in Brussels asked the Belgian government to allow German troops to march across Belgium into France.

● **On 4 August**, Belgium refused. Germany declared war on Belgium. Britain (Belgium's ally) declared war on Germany.

'Brave Little Belgium'

● **By noon on 4 August 1914**, the main German armies were marching into Belgium. This was the same day that Britain declared war on Germany.

● **The Belgians had fortified** the town of Liége with six forts containing a network of gun positions, held by General Gérard Leman and 22,000 men.

● **The Liége forts held out** until 15 August, when German General von Emmich brought up heavy siege mortars. The new guns fired shells weighing almost one tonne and smashed the Belgian forts.

● **When German soldiers entered the Liége forts**, they found Leman senseless and badly wounded, and took him prisoner. When Leman came to, he asked Emmich, "Please put in your despatch that I was unconscious and did not surrender." Emmich did as requested.

● **The German advance into Belgium** was swift. Many Belgian reservists did not have time to get their uniforms. They began cutting telephone wires and ambushing German supply wagons while still wearing civilian clothes.

● **The Germans declared** that it was against the rules of war for civilians to attack soldiers. In reprisal they executed dozens of hostages and burned the city of Louvain.

...**FASCINATING FACT**...
British and French newspapers exaggerated the stories of German reprisals in Belgium. They printed drawings of German soldiers bayonetting women and babies.

▲ *These Belgian soldiers wear straw in their hats as camouflage so they are not seen by German riflemen.*

● **The Belgian army continued** to fight. Soon Belgium became known as 'Brave Little Belgium' for standing up to the mighty German army.

● **Meanwhile, the French had invaded** Germany at Sarrebourg and Morhange. They soon occupied most of the territory they had lost to Germany in 1871.

● **Britain began sending troops** to France on the way to help Belgium. One of the first to arrive was Lieutenant R N Vaughan of the Royal Flying Corps who landed his aircraft at Boulogne on 13 August. He was immediately arrested by the French who thought he was an Austrian spy.

Retreat from Mons

▼ *British newspapers conjured up the spirits of previous generations of British soldiers to raise morale.*

- **On 21 August**, the British Expeditionary Force arrived in the Belgian town of Mons. The force consisted of two corps, formations made up of several divisions, commanded by General Sir John French. They also had the French army on their right.

- **Kaiser Wilhelm II ordered** General von Moltke to "push aside that contemptible little army." When the British soldiers learned of this, they began calling themselves 'Old Contemptibles'.

- **On 23 August**, the Germans attacked at Mons. The British were trained in defensive warfare and rapid rifle fire, and inflicted heavy casualties.

- **The French suffered** very heavy casualties and that night they retreated. This left the British isolated, so French ordered his men to fall back towards Paris. The retreat from Mons had begun.

- **On 24 August**, a German aircraft observing the British retreat was shot down by a British artillery shell near Le Quesnoy. This was the first time an aircraft was shot down in a war.

- **A day later**, Moltke sent troops from Belgium to reinforce the troops facing Russia. This seriously weakened the German attack.

- **The British halted** at Le Cateau on 26 August and managed to drive off numerous German attacks. The delay enabled many units to escape capture.

- **On 27 August**, a force of British troops became lost and by nightfall was surrounded by Germans.

- **Just after midnight** they saw a woman carrying a lantern. She pointed towards a road that led to safety. The British soldiers said she was an angel.

- **Within days the story** of the 'Angel of Mons' was known throughout the British army. The story was printed in newspapers across the world.

Miracle on the Marne

- **On 1 September 1914**, General von Moltke ordered his advance units to swing east of Paris to cut off the French army, instead of capturing the city. It was the second change he had made to the Schlieffen Plan.

- **At noon on 2 September**, a French airman saw the columns of German troops marching away from Paris. He landed and reported to General Joseph Gallieni, commander of the garrison in Paris. Gallieni sent a message to the commander in chief, General Joseph Joffre.

- **Gallieni then sent messages** to all French units near Paris asking them to come to the city. Most responded, even if they were not under his command.

- **On 5 September**, Joffre met General Sir John French to ask the British to join the French army in attacking the Germans at the river Marne. Joffre hit the table with his fist and shouted, "Monsieur, the honour of England is at stake." French blushed and said, "I will do all that is possible."

- **Gallieni's troops were named** the 6th Army and ordered to attack. But there were not enough trains or trucks to carry the men. In desperation, Gallieni hired every taxi in Paris to take the men forward.

...FASCINATING FACT...
The German VII Corps marched over 60 km in 24 hours to close the gap and halt the British advance.

● **German General von Kluck** moved his men north to attack Paris on 7 September. This opened a gap between his men and those of German General von Bülow to the east.

● **On 8 September**, Joffre asked General Foch, commanding the French centre, what was happening. Foch replied, "My left is in retreat. My centre is yielding. My right is giving way. Situation excellent, I attack tomorrow."

● **On 9 September**, the British found no German troops in front of them. They marched quickly through the gap between Kluck and Bülow, cutting the German army in two.

● **On 14 September**, the German armies began to retreat all along the line. The Schlieffen Plan had failed. The French called these events 'The Miracle on the Marne'.

▶ *British infantry sleep in the open before digging in on the river Marne.*

The Battle of the Aisne

Russia

USA

Britain

Japan

● **After the defeat on the river Marne,** German commander in chief Helmuth von Moltke ordered his armies to retreat to the river Aisne.

● **When they reached the Aisne,** the Germans took up position on the hills north of the river. From there they could shoot accurately at any troops trying to cross the river.

● **British and French pilots scouting** the German positions found they were often shot at by soldiers of their own armies. They began painting red, white and blue stripes on the wings of their aircraft.

● **A few weeks later, the High Command** ordered the pilots to paint standard markings on their aircraft. British planes had a red circle inside a white circle inside a blue circle. French aircraft sported the same circles in reverse.

◀ *Aircraft markings. By 1915, the pilots of each nation were painting symbols on their aircraft to help identify friend from foe. The Allies chose round symbols, the Central Powers chose crosses.*

36

● **The German pilots also began** painting a black cross on their aircraft.

● **On 13 September 1914**, the British, together with the French 5th and 6th Armies, crossed the river Aisne on pontoon bridges under heavy fire and attacked the Germans. They broke the German lines and moved forwards.

● **The following day** the British and French found themselves faced by German troops in trenches and machine gun nests. Unable to advance against heavy fire, nor to inflict casualties on the Germans, the allies halted and dug their own trenches.

● **General Joffre ordered** a new attack on 18 September, but his men failed to make any advance and suffered heavy casualties. Joffre called off the attack and ordered his artillery to begin shelling the German trenches.

● **The Battle of the Aisne** marked the beginning of trench warfare on the Western Front.

● **Kaiser Wilhelm II sacked** General von Moltke as commander in chief and replaced him with General Erich von Falkenhayn.

Belgium

France

Germany

Bulgaria

The Battle of Tannenberg

● **On the Eastern Front** in 1914, the Russians fought the Austrians and the Germans. The key strategic factor was that Russian Poland extended far to the west, separating most of the Austrian Empire from German Prussia.

● **The Central Powers** – Germany and Austria – planned to remain on the defensive until France had been defeated. This was known as Plan R.

● **Russian generals had devised** a defensive Plan G and an offensive Plan A. Tsar Nicholas decided to adopt Plan A, sending two armies to invade East Prussia. At dawn on 12 August the Russian 1st Army invaded from the east while the 2nd Army invaded from the south.

▼ *Russian invasion. The Russian attack on East Prussia began well, but an outflanking move by the Germans isolated and crushed the southern Russian army at Tannenberg.*

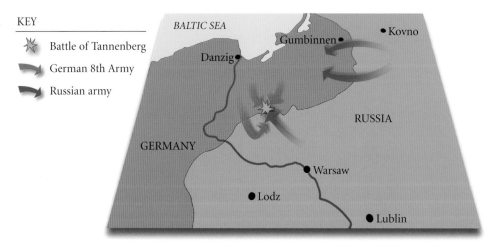

KEY

✶ Battle of Tannenberg

➤ German 8th Army

➤ Russian army

BALTIC SEA

Kovno

Gumbinnen

Danzig

RUSSIA

GERMANY

Warsaw

Lodz

Lublin

- **On 17 August**, the Russian 1st Army led by General Rennenkampf met the German 8th Army under General von Prittwitz. After three days of fighting, the Germans fell back in confusion.

- **On 20 August**, the Russian 1st Army captured Gumbinnen. Kaiser Wilhelm II sacked the defeated Prittwitz and replaced him with General von Hindenburg.

- **When he took command** in East Prussia, Hindenburg was already 67 years old and had retired four years earlier. He had not fought in a war for over 40 years.

- **Hindenburg decided to abandon** much of East Prussia to the Russian 1st Army. He moved his men south to face General Samsonov's 2nd Army. He had enough men to outnumber Samsonov.

- **On 28 August**, the Germans outflanked the Russians' left wing and attacked from the rear at Tannenberg.

- **The Russians fled south**, but were hemmed in by marshes and swamps. Of 200,000 Russians, about 30,000 were killed and 90,000 captured. Samsonov committed suicide rather than surrender.

- **After the Battle of Tannenberg**, Hindenburg moved his force northeast by rail to attack the Russian 1st Army near the Masurian Lakes. Rennenkampf retreated rather than risk defeat.

▶ *A German infantry soldier of 1915. A smooth helmet that is better suited to trench warfare has replaced the old spiked version. Puttees are worn around the legs to withstand the mud.*

From Lemberg to Lodz

- **The Russian Plan A involved** an attack on the Austrian Empire as soon as enough troops had been mobilized. The attack began on 17 August 1914.

- **The Russian 4th Army** under General Ivanov attacked near Lublin, supported by the 3rd and 8th Armies under General Brusilov. The Austrian 2nd and 3rd Armies fell back slowly. On 30 August, the Russians captured Lemberg (now Lvov).

- **On 4 September**, the Austrians launched a large-scale attack on the Russian centre. It failed, and the Austrian retreat soon became disorderly as the supply system collapsed and soldiers fled.

- **By 20 September**, the Austrians had lost 110,000 men killed or wounded and 220,000 men captured. Another 100,000 men were cut off at Przemysl. The Russians were advancing quickly through Galicia towards the vital German industrial area of Silesia.

◀ *A German Luger 9 mm automatic pistol. Officers carried pistols that were useful for close fighting, but were small enough not to interfere with their command responsibilities.*

▲ *At the Eastern Front, a unit of the Austro-Hungarian army rests as a column of German infantry march past them on their way to the Eastern Front.*

● **The German commander in the east**, Hindenburg, took two-thirds of his men from East Prussia and formed them into the 9th Army, to protect Silesia.

● **On 6 October**, the German 9th Army attacked, but the Russians threatened to cut off the advancing troops, so Hindenburg called off the attack.

● **In early November**, the Germans overheard a Russian general talking to his officers by radio. They learned that the Russians would attack Silesia on 14 November in the area around Lodz.

● **Hindenburg put the 9th Army** under General Mackensen with orders to attack first, on 11 November.

● **Mackensen's attack** went well. On 16 November the Germans broke through the Russian lines and surrounded Russian units, inflicting heavy casualties.

● **Tsar Nicholas II sacked** General Rennenkampf and appointed a new commander, General Litvinov. His first orders were for the entire Russian army to retreat to the river Bzura.

Race for the sea

- **The commander of the French armies** as the Battle of the Aisne ended was General Joffre. He was quiet, patient and believed that the Germans could be defeated by 'nibbling' – taking small advantages when he could.

- **Joffre was so old-fashioned** that he refused to use the telephone. Instead a junior officer spoke on the phone and passed on messages.

- **The British commander**, General Sir John French, was a cavalryman who believed in swift movement and decisions. He hated working with Joffre.

- **Most of the Belgian army** was trapped in and around Antwerp. On 6 October, the army began retreating towards Calais.

- **Having captured Antwerp**, the Germans hoped to capture the ports of Calais, Boulogne and Dunkirk through which Britain was sending supplies to France.

- **On 6 October**, a fresh British division arrived in France and was driven to the front in London buses. The German attack was halted.

◄ *Belgian troops shelter behind a makeshift barrier as they await advancing German troops on 20 August 1914. The Belgian troops had old-fashioned equipment and poor training.*

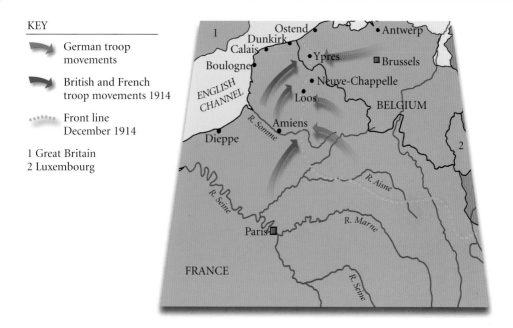

KEY

German troop movements

British and French troop movements 1914

Front line December 1914

1 Great Britain
2 Luxembourg

▲ *Once the first German attack on Paris had been defeated, the opposing forces launched a series of outflanking moves that carried the area to the north. By September a front line had been established between the English Channel and Switzerland.*

● **The Germans moved south**, reaching Lille on 11 October. They shelled the city heavily. On 13 October the city, now largely rubble, surrendered.

● **German troops from the river Aisne** were marching north hoping to outflank the French. However, the French were too fast and tried to outflank the Germans.

● **In a final attempt to outflank** the Germans, Joffre asked French to move to a certain small town – it was to play a huge part in the oncoming war and as such, its name became famous – Ypres.

● **The British arrived on 15 October**, only to find the Germans marching in from the east. A savage battle broke out around the town.

43

First Battle of Ypres

● **The town of Ypres** is in Belgium, close to the French border in the province of Flanders. In 1914, it was the centre of a road and rail network and a vital transportation centre for the British and French armies.

● **The name 'Ypres'** is actually pronounced 'weep-ers', but the British soldiers came to know it as 'wipers'.

◀ *Men of the Royal Warwickshire Regiment were transported to Ypres on London buses, commandeered by the army.*

> ...FASCINATING FACT...
> The bars in Ypres served a cheap white wine called vin blanc,
> pronounced 'van blonck' by the locals. British soldiers called it 'plonk',
> which came to mean cheap, easily obtainable alcohol.

- **On 21 October**, the Germans attacked the British around Ypres. General Erich von Falkenhayn was confident of success so he invited the Kaiser to watch the battle, and lead the victory parade.

- **As at Mons**, the German attack ran into the highly trained soldiers of the British army. Their rapid, accurate rifle fire inflicted heavy losses, but the Germans had overwhelming numbers and heavy artillery.

- **On 31 October**, the Germans broke through the British front line, then through the rear line at Gheluvelt. General Sir John French knew he had no reserves left. There was nothing to stop the Germans. He wrote later 'It was the most nerve-shattering time of my life'.

- **However, Brigadier General Fitzclarence** then remembered that 368 men of the 2nd Battalion Worcestershire Regiment were recovering from severe fighting south of Ypres. He ordered them to march to Chateau Gheluvelt.

- **The 2nd Battalion attacked** the 244th Saxon Regiment that was leading the Germans. They reached Gheluvelt and were at once assaulted by the 242nd and 245th Saxon Regiments. At sunset the German attacks ceased, by which time only 140 of the 2nd Battalion were still standing.

- **At 7 p.m. Fitzclarence sent a message** to French that read 'My line holds'.

- **The next day**, the Kaiser returned to Berlin. The First Battle of Ypres dragged on until 11 November, but the Germans did not break through.

The Christmas truce

- **By December 1914**, a dense network of trenches stretched from the English Channel to the Swiss border. The trenches were damp, cold and very dangerous places to live.

- **The weather in December** was dreadful with heavy rain and cold winds. The trenches filled with water and the earth walls collapsed in many places.

- **On 21 December**, things began to change. The weather became dry, sunny and cold. Soldiers on both sides stopped fighting while they repaired their trenches, dried their clothes and tried to make themselves more comfortable.

- **King George V of Britain sent** a Christmas card to every soldier fighting in France. His daughter, the popular Princess Mary, sent a small box of sweets to each man on active duty.

- **On the German side**, the Kaiser sent a cigar to each soldier. The German army made sure that every regiment received a Christmas tree and lanterns.

- **On Christmas Eve**, the German soldiers in the front line lit their lanterns, put up their Christmas trees and sang Christmas carols. The British joined in with the English carols that had the same tunes.

- **At dawn on Christmas Day** a sergeant in the 133rd Saxon Regiment who had worked in Birmingham before the war, waved a Christmas tree above the trench and called to the British soldiers opposite, "Happy Christmas." He then climbed out of the trench and was met by a British captain.

> ....FASCINATING FACT....
> The trenches of the opposing armies were surprisingly close, in places only 20 m apart.

Weldon, January 8, 1915

The Daily Mirror
CERTIFIED CIRCULATION LARGER THAN ANY OTHER DAILY NEWSPAPER IN THE WORLD

WHY DELAY? THE DAILY MIRROR OVERSEAS WEEKLY
Pictures and News, and is therefore the Best Weekly Newspaper for your friends
abroad. You can obtain it from your Newsagent for 3d. per copy.
Subscription rates (prepaid), post free, to Canada for six months 10/-; elsewhere abroad 19/-.
Address—Manager, "Overseas Daily Mirror," 22-29, Bouverie Street, London, E.C.

AN HISTORIC GROUP: BRITISH AND GERMAN SOLDIERS PHOTOGRAPHED TOGETHER.

▲ *A group of German and British soldiers photographed between their trenches on Christmas Day.*

● **All along the front line** similar scenes took place. By lunchtime the opposing armies were meeting in peace. Men used the time to bury the dead, swap souvenirs and in at least one place, the Germans and English played football.

● **In most areas the war began** again on Boxing Day, or soon after. In a few places along the front line, intense warfare never started up again and they became known as 'quiet sectors'. The largest of these was at the Bois de Ploegsteert, called 'Plugstreet Wood' by the British. It was still quiet in 1918.

The trenches

● **In the winter of 1914–15** the soldiers on the Western Front believed that the trenches were only temporary structures. They thought that when good spring weather arrived, the armies would return to traditional fighting tactics.

● **The trenches were based on temporary** field defences that all armies built when stationary for a few days. They were designed to shelter men from artillery shells and rifle bullets.

● **Trenches were designed** to be over 2.3 m deep, so that men could walk along them without needing to crouch.

▼ *The trenches were reinforced with timber*
supports to make them stronger.

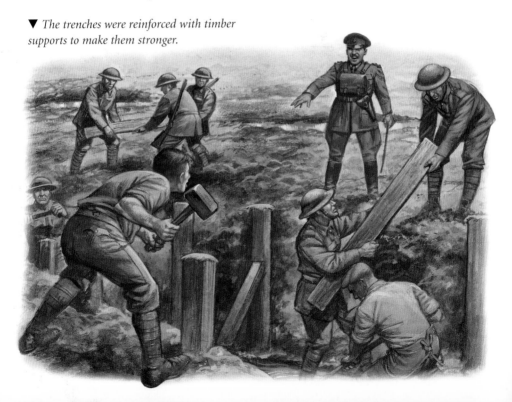

● **A firing step was built** into the front of the trench. Standing on this, a man could aim his rifle over the top towards the enemy. Sentries stood on the firing step to see if the enemy were attacking.

● **Trenches were built in zig-zag routes** so that there was no straight stretch of more than 30 m. This meant that nobody could aim a gun along the trench to kill everyone in it.

● **In 1914**, there were usually two or three lines of trenches. The front trench contained most of the men, ready to repel an enemy attack. The second and third trenches contained essential services.

● **The different lines of trenches** were linked by communication trenches that ran forwards. They were quite shallow and did not have firing steps.

● **In marshy areas or rainy weather**, the trenches often filled with water very quickly. Hand-powered pumps were installed to keep the trenches dry, but they did not work very effectively.

● **Sandbags and wooden planks** were used to give strength and shape to the trench walls. Collapsing trenches were a problem throughout winter.

● **Barbed wire was strung on metal posts** in front of the trenches to slow down attacking soldiers, so that the defenders had more time to shoot them.

▶ *Barbed wire was placed around trenches to hinder and slow down oncoming attacks.*

49

Life on the front line

● **Infantry soldiers in the trenches** had an uncomfortable life during the winter of 1914–15.

● **Each battalion stayed on the front line** for a few days, then it moved to form a reserve close to the front line. Then it would be moved to the rear so that the men could rest before going back to the front line again.

● **Battalions** changed position at night, moving along communication trenches. Units stayed in the same area for months, so they knew the trenches well.

● **Trenches were infested** with lice, fleas and other vermin. The British soldiers called these creatures 'chats'. Each day men went to the second or third trench to pick the vermin off each other. This was called 'going for a chat'.

● **Soldiers began to suffer** from a new disease called 'trench foot'. It was caused when feet were wet and cold for more than 48 hours at a time. The feet became infected with fungus. It was so painful, men could not stand.

● **In January**, February and March 1915, more than 30,000 British soldiers got trench foot. They had to be taken out of the fighting to go barefoot in warm, dry houses for two weeks to cure the condition.

> ....FASCINATING FACT....
> Boredom was a major problem. The soldiers formed choirs, drama groups and trench schools to help pass the time.

- **In April 1915**, it was found that trench foot could be prevented if boots were made waterproof by soaking them in whale oil and socks were changed three times each day. By 1916 trench foot was a rare disease.

- **Soldiers tried** to make themselves feel at home by giving familiar names to the trenches. London soldiers called trenches names such as 'Regent Street'.

- **It was often too dangerous** to retrieve bodies of men who were killed. The bodies lay rotting in the open for weeks.

▼ *A British officer inspects the feet of his men for signs of the disease, trench foot, which could cripple a man.*

The evening hate

▼ *Gas balloons carried men equipped with maps and radio sets who identified enemy targets for the artillery.*

- **Although no major attacks** were launched through the winter of 1914–15, the armies remained at war.

- **Both sides chose their best shots** to act as snipers. These men watched the enemy trenches and shot at anyone they saw moving.

- **At night, patrols of men** crept forward from the front trench. They repaired the barbed wire, spied on the enemy and sometimes slipped into the enemy trench to kill the sentries.

- **Even when no major battle** was taking place, the front line was a dangerous place. About one in every 500 men was killed or badly wounded every day.

- **Artillery placed hundreds of metres** behind the trenches would fire shells at the enemy throughout the day. They would aim at trenches, or at roads and railways behind the lines.

- **The artillery often opened fire** in the first few hours of darkness when enemy soldiers would be going on patrol, or moving from the front line to the reserves. This became known as 'the evening hate'.

- **Men began digging dugouts**, or underground rooms, which were safer than trenches against artillery fire.

- **During the day**, large balloons carrying men in baskets were flown. The men used telescopes to scout the ground behind enemy lines, then phoned messages to their artillery saying where to aim.

- **One British balloon scout** wore a top hat and purple velvet jacket. He became known as 'Burlington Bertie', from a famous song of the time.

- **Enemy balloons were shot down** with machine guns and light artillery. Whenever 'Burlington Bertie' had his balloon punctured he would step out of the basket and pretend to run in thin air, before opening his parachute.

The Battle of Neuve-Chappelle

● **In February 1915**, French commander in chief, Joseph Joffre, asked British commander, Sir John French, if he could attack in March. Joffre wanted the British to attack to divert the Germans from a larger French attack in April.

● **French chose to attack** the village of Neuve-Chappelle and Aubers Ridge. This would threaten the city of Lille.

▲ *Gurkhas, soldiers recruited from Nepal, carried a sharp kukri for close combat.*

● **The plan was to pound** the German trenches with artillery. Then the infantry would charge forwards to capture the trenches and break through. Finally the cavalry would attack German supply lines and reinforcements.

● **French hoped he could break out** of the trenches and once again return to traditional styles of fighting. The war, he hoped, would be over in a few weeks.

● **On 10 March**, 400 British field guns opened fire, smashing the German trenches and cutting the barbed wire. Nearly 50 battalions of British infantry charged forwards. Some took heavy casualties from machine guns, but most reached and captured the German trenches.

● **That night the British attacked** again. At Neuve-Chappelle the infantry broke through the German lines to reach open country. However, the messages sent back to bring up the cavalry failed to get through.

- **Similar attacks continued** for three weeks, but the British never managed to make a sustained breakthrough.

- **The troops attacking Neuve-Chappelle** included a regiment of Gurkhas. One Gurkha was the son of a nobleman and came equipped with a beautiful silver kukri, the curved knife used in close action by Gurkhas.

- **The Gurkha with the silver kukri** was part of a patrol. He slipped into a German trench and cut the throat of the sentry. Instead of returning, he then crept along the trench to kill the next sentry.

- **For weeks afterwards**, British patrols found German sentries with their throats cut. For three months the killing continued, then it stopped. Presumably the Gurkha had been killed.

▼ *British infantry attacking from their trenches went 'over the top' of the trench parapet to race forwards.*

Turkey invades Russia

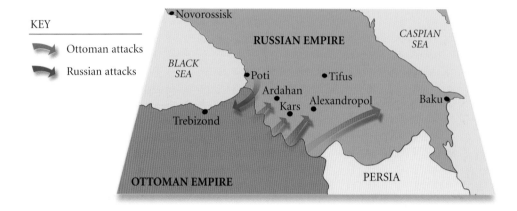

▲ *The fighting between Russia and the Ottoman Empire took place to the southeast of the Black Sea. Each side invaded the other, but heavy losses and bad weather brought an early end to active campaigning.*

● **In 1911 and 1912**, the Ottoman Empire suffered humiliating defeats by Italy and the small Balkan kingdoms. The reforming Turkish government of Enver Pasha invited Germany to send military advisers to improve the Turkish army.

● **By 1914**, the Ottomans had about 360,000 men with modern equipment who had undergone German training. There were another 750,000 men in reserve who had not yet received the new weapons and training.

● **On 29 October 1914**, the Turks allowed two German cruisers through the straits at Constantinople to attack Russian ships and towns in the Black Sea.

- **In response to the Black Sea raid**, Russia invaded Turkey near Batum. Turkey declared war on Russia, and its allies Britain and France on 5 November 1914.

- **Turkey immediately banned** all shipping from using the straits at Constantinople. The waters were sown with mines and eight batteries of heavy guns were put into strong fortifications.

- **On 7 November**, a British-Indian force of 4500 men landed at Fao on the Persian Gulf. The army seized the port of Basra, but did not move inland. It was there to protect oil exports from Persia, modern Iran.

- **In January 1915**, the Turkish 3rd Army, commanded by Enver Pasha, crossed the Caucasus Mountains to invade Russia. After savage fighting, the Turks pulled back, but were caught by blizzards in the mountains. Only 12,000 out of 140,000 men got back to Turkey alive.

- **In February**, the Turkish 4th Army sent 20,000 men to attack the Suez Canal. The attack was driven back by a force of Australian, New Zealand and Indian troops from British-occupied Egypt.

- **In March**, Russia announced that its foreign exports had been cut by 95 percent since the Turks had closed the straits at Constantinople. This blow meant Russia might soon become bankrupt.

... FASCINATING FACT ...

The Germans had also paid for and built railways in the Ottoman Empire. They also helped to modernize the economy, building new factories and advising on government laws and regulations.

Italy invades Austria

▼ *A parade through London organized by Czech nationalists living in the city. The Czechs resented their home country being ruled by Austria and supported the Italian entry into the war.*

- **When war broke out** in 1914, Italy refused to join its allies Germany and Austria. Although Italy opposed the growth of French power in the Mediterranean, it had no real interest in the Balkans.

- **The alliance did not oblige** Italy to join Austria in an offensive war, but only to join if Austria were attacked. Italy remained neutral.

- **Many people in Italy resented** the fact that the Austrian Empire ruled Italian-speaking areas. They wanted them joined to Italy. These nationalists began to think Italy should invade Austria to seize the provinces.

- **Another group in Italy** supported the democracies of Britain and France against the imperial Germany and Austria. Italy was itself a democracy.

- **The democratic position was championed** by the newspaper *Avanti!*, which was edited by the journalist Benito Mussolini. In 1922, Mussolini would become the fascist dictator of Italy.

- **In February 1915**, Italian Prime Minister Antonio Salandra asked the Austrian government if they would give the Italian-speaking lands to Italy in return for Italy declaring war on France. The Austrians refused.

- **In March**, Salandra asked the French and British if they would give Italy the disputed areas in return for Italy declaring war on Austria – assuming that Austria lost the war. The British and French agreed.

- **On 24 May**, Italy declared war on Austria.

- **On 23 June**, 25 Italian divisions invaded the Austrian Empire at the river Isonzo, which was held by 14 Austrian divisions. The attack petered out after two weeks with no real gain.

- **By the end of 1915**, Italy had lost 66,000 killed, 185,000 wounded and 22,000 captured. Its troops had advanced only 5 km into Austria.

Poison gas

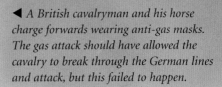

◀ *A British cavalryman and his horse charge forwards wearing anti-gas masks. The gas attack should have allowed the cavalry to break through the German lines and attack, but this failed to happen.*

● **On 22 April 1915**, the Germans tested a terrible new weapon with unexpected results. They unleashed poison gas.

● **The chlorine gas was released** from canisters poking over the parapet of the front line by men of the 3rd Saxon Pioneer Corps. It was released at 5.15 p.m. as an easterly wind wafted the deadly vapours toward the Allied lines.

● **The gas struck** the French 87th Division and the French Algerian 45th Division. It came as a greenish-white mist creeping silently and slowly over the battlefield.

● **At first the men wondered** what it was, then they began to cough and choke. Some vomited, others simply collapsed.

▶ *A pair of German engineers prepare to release poison gas from a canister through pipes leading out of the trench.*

● **Hundreds died as the whitish fog** rolled over them. The rest fled. At 5.30 p.m. the cloud reached a Canadian division. They fled before the deadly gas reached them.

● **At 5.40 p.m.** a senior British officer riding out of Ypres saw the French and Algerians running towards him in panic. He tried to question them, and managed to understand one officer who gasped, "The fog."

● **At 5.45 p.m.** a Canadian officer who had been a chemist before the war ordered his men to urinate into their handkerchiefs and hold them over their mouths. With these makeshift gas masks the Canadians manned two machine guns to await a German attack.

● **At 5.55 p.m.** the cloud of gas, by this time greatly dissipated, entered Ypres. Civilians were reduced to helplessness, but few died.

● **The gas worked by irritating** the lining of the lungs and throat, causing them to produce watery liquid. If enough gas was inhaled, the liquid gathered in the lungs and drowned the victim.

● **The Germans were unable to break through** the deserted trenches because the front line regiments had not been issued with gas masks. It was the best chance the Germans had of winning in the west, but they missed it.

Second Battle of Ypres

● **After the Battle of Neuve-Chappelle**, both sides ordered a halt to any fresh attack while the senior commanders studied what had happened.

● **The British believed** that they had found the answer to the trench deadlock. The combination of artillery, infantry and cavalry would win victory, but only if there was more artillery and a second attack to support the first.

● **All British infantry were now equipped** with metal helmets, which gave some protection against shell splinters and bullets.

● **The Germans recognized** that the British knew how to break a conventional front line of three trenches. They believed the answer was to build a second line of three trenches behind the first and put more machine guns on the front line.

● **The French thought the British** had failed because they did not show sufficient aggressive spirit. A massive attack by huge formations of men carried out without regard to initial casualties would, the French thought, break the enemy line.

◀ *The heavy machine gun now dominated the battlefield and inflicted heavy casualties.*

- **On 9 May**, the British attacked from Ypres towards the Aubers Ridge. The attack was preceded by a heavy artillery barrage.

- **The British attack at Ypres** was met by the increased number of German machine guns. Casualties proved to be very heavy, but again messages failed to get back to headquarters.

- **The supporting attack was ordered** forward by officers who were unaware that the first attack had failed. The second formations also took very heavy casualties.

- **By 25 May**, the British had lost 60,000 men, the Germans 35,000 men. General Sir John French called off the attack. Again he and his staff studied the results.

- **General Sir Horace Smith-Dorrien protested** loudly that attacking Germans who were in trenches and armed with machine guns was suicidal and would only lead to massive British casualties. He was promptly sacked by the British government.

▶ *A British soldier of 1915. He has puttees wrapped around his legs for protection against mud and a steel helmet to give protection from shell splinters.*

Landings at Gallipoli

● **In January 1915,** the British government debated what to do about the straits at Constantinople, known as the Dardanelles. Since these had been closed by Turkey, Russia had been facing economic crisis.

● **Winston Churchill,** First Lord of the Admiralty, suggested sending a force of old battleships. He knew the guns guarding the straits were old and short of ammunition, but did not know of the underwater mines.

▼ *A British medium howitzer shells Turkish positions in Gallipoli. It took several days to get these large guns into action, by which time Turkish defences were well organized.*

...FASCINATING FACT...
During an ammunition shortage in Gallipoli, Allied
troops made grenades out of jam tins.

- **On 19 March,** the British Mediterranean fleet attacked the Dardanelles. The first Turkish batteries were destroyed, but then mines sank three British battleships and damaged three more. Admiral Robeck called off the attack.

- **The troops on the British ships** intended to capture, then garrison the straits and city of Constantinople. It was now decided to use the troops to land on the Gallipoli peninsula and attack Constantinople by land.

- **General Sir Ian Hamilton refused** to land until he had more troops, which gave the German general commanding the Turkish troops, Liman von Sanders, time to prepare his defences.

- **British, Australian and New Zealand troops landed** on 25 April. There was little opposition, but Hamilton refused to allow his men to advance until scouts had been sent forward.

- **By the time the scouts returned,** a Turkish regiment had begun a furious counter attack, led by Colonel Mustapha Kemal, later to become president of Turkey.

- **By sunset on the first day,** the landings were in confusion and had advanced only one kilometre inland. Hamilton sent his reserves ashore to launch a new attack. The assault failed and by 8 May the invaders had lost 6000 killed and 14,000 wounded out of 70,000.

- **On 10 May,** Turkish torpedo boats sank three more British ships. The fleet withdrew. The troops on shore were alone.

The Battle of Gorlice-Tarnow

● **During the winter months**, Kaiser Wilhelm II and his commander in chief, Erich von Falkenhayn, had devised a new plan to win the war. They decided to crush Russia in 1915, then turn against France in 1916.

● **After the Battle of Neuve-Chappelle**, Falkenhayn believed his new double trench line could defeat any Allied attack in France. He could afford to move men, artillery and supplies to the Eastern Front.

● **During April**, the Germans built up a large force in Galicia, west of the river San, under the command of General Mackensen.

● **On 1 May**, the Germans fired 700,000 shells into the Russian forces between the towns of Gorlice and Tarnow. Then the massed German regiments poured forwards. The Russians in the front line threw down their rifles and fled.

● **In the first week** of the attack, Mackensen advanced over 120 km. Over 200,000 Russians had surrendered to the Germans.

● **In the second week**, Mackensen captured the city of Jaroslaw and crossed the river San. Two weeks later his men captured the fortress city of Przemysl.

▶ *A British .38 calibre Webley revolver. British infantry officers throughout the war carried these guns. The ring on the but (handle) was attached to a leather strap that was buckled to the man's belt.*

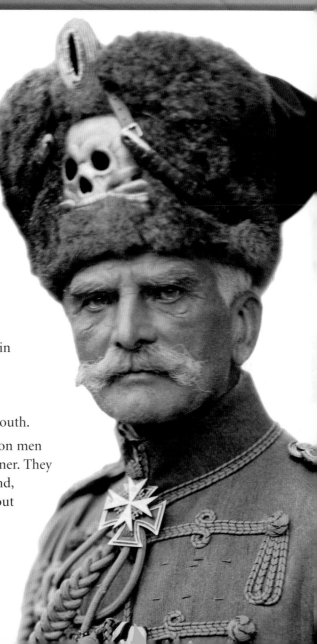

● **Meanwhile, German General von Ludendorff** attacked the northern end of the Eastern Front from East Prussia. Rather than risk being outflanked by the southern attack, the Russians retreated.

● **On 1 June**, Russian General Brusilov brought up Russian reserves to the river Dniester. He managed to halt Mackensen's headlong advance so that most of the Russian armies could escape.

● **After the battle on the river Dniester**, the Russians retreated in good shape. By September, the Germans had advanced to Vilna in the north, the Pripet Marshes in the centre and Dubno in the south.

● **The Russians had lost** 2 million men – killed, wounded or taken prisoner. They had also lost a lot of rich farmland, but they had not been knocked out of the war.

▶ *German General Mackensen wears the uniform of the Death's Head Hussars. He was one of the most talented German generals of the war.*

War in Africa

- **When the war broke out** in Europe, the Europeans living in other parts of the world were at war as well. In Africa there were numerous territories and colonies owned by the combatant nations. War flared up instantly.

- **Germany ruled Togoland** (now Togo), Cameroons (Camaroon), Southwest Africa (Namibia) and German East Africa (Tanzania).

- **Belgium ruled Congo** (now Democratic Republic of Congo).

- **France ruled French Congo** (Gabon), Algeria and French West Africa (Chad, Central African Republic, Niger, Burkina, Cote d'Ivoire, Guinea, Senegal, Mauritania, Mali and Benin).

- **Britain ruled South Africa**, Bechuanaland (Botswana), Rhodesia and Nyasaland (Zambia, Zimbabwe and Malawi), Uganda, Kenya, British Somaliland (part of Eritrea), Nigeria, Gold Coast (Ghana), Sierra Leone, Sudan and Egypt.

- **The British navy moved quickly** to cut off the German colonies from reinforcements or resupply. The Germans in the colonies were on their own.

- **Togoland was conquered** quickly by French forces for French West Africa. Southwest Africa was overrun by South African forces by July 1915. In 1915, Cameroons was conquered by French soldiers advancing from French Congo.

- **The strongest German force** was in German East Africa, with several hundred German soldiers, plus thousands of local troops.

- **The main Allied assault on German East Africa** began when the Royal Navy shelled Dar-es-Salaam in 1916. Meanwhile, British forces invaded from Kenya, South African forces from Rhodesia and a Belgian force from Congo.

- **German General Lettow-Vorbeck fell back**, ambushing his pursuers and raiding supply lines. He stayed in the Rufiji Valley until November 1918, when Germany surrendered.

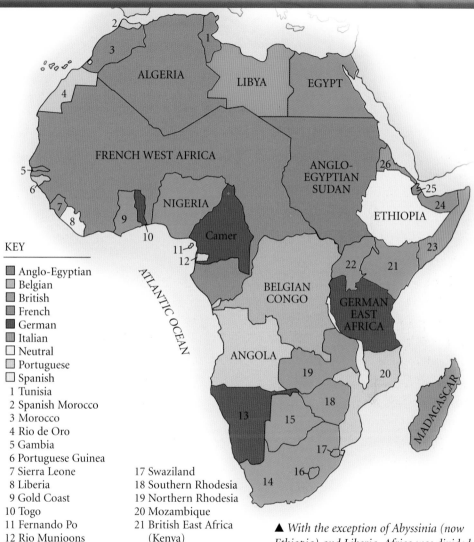

ALGERIA

LIBYA

EGYPT

FRENCH WEST AFRICA

ANGLO-EGYPTIAN SUDAN

NIGERIA

ETHIOPIA

Camer

ATLANTIC OCEAN

BELGIAN CONGO

GERMAN EAST AFRICA

ANGOLA

MADAGASCAR

KEY

- Anglo-Egyptian
- Belgian
- British
- French
- German
- Italian
- Neutral
- Portuguese
- Spanish

1 Tunisia
2 Spanish Morocco
3 Morocco
4 Rio de Oro
5 Gambia
6 Portuguese Guinea
7 Sierra Leone
8 Liberia
9 Gold Coast
10 Togo
11 Fernando Po
12 Rio Munioons
13 German South West Africa
14 Union of South Africa
15 Bechuanaland
16 Basutoland

17 Swaziland
18 Southern Rhodesia
19 Northern Rhodesia
20 Mozambique
21 British East Africa (Kenya)
22 Uganda
23 Italian Somaliland
24 British Somaliland
25 French Somaliland
26 Eritrea

▲ *With the exception of Abyssinia (now Ethiopia) and Liberia, Africa was divided up between various European countries. These colonies produced raw materials, such as metal ore, which were vital to the war industries.*

69

The build-up to Loos

● **After the Second Battle of Ypres,** many British officers complained about the lack of artillery shells. It soon became clear that the Liberal government of Herbert Asquith had not ordered enough shells from the arms factories.

● **A furious row broke out** in the British Parliament, which newspapers called the 'Shells Scandal'.

● **Asquith was forced** to form a coalition government and appointed a new Minister for Munitions, David Lloyd George.

● **On 5 August 1915,** the Germans running occupied Belgium arrested a British nurse named Edith Cavell. She admitted helping British soldiers escape capture. The Germans accused her of being a spy.

● **Cavell** was put in prison. The Germans refused to allow either Belgian lawyers or diplomats from neutral countries to see her.

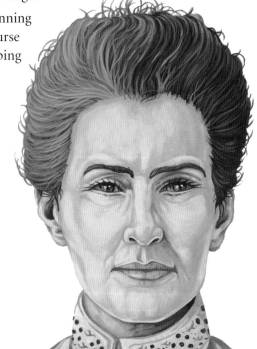

▶ *Nurse Edith Cavell, who was executed by the Germans for helping British soldiers to escape capture.*

● **On October 11**, a German court found Cavell guilty of espionage. A British chaplain was allowed to see her for 30 minutes. The next morning she was shot by the Germans.

● **Public opinion in many neutral countries** was outraged. People in the United States were particularly angry that the Germans had shot a female civilian nurse.

● **In July**, French commander Joffre promised the Russians that he would launch a major attack to divert German forces from the Eastern Front. He persuaded Britain's War Minister, Lord Kitchener, to order a British attack as well.

● **British commander in France**, Sir John French, still did not have enough artillery shells to prepare the way for a major attack. Kitchener told him to use poison gas instead.

● **When the Battle of Loos began**, the British heavy guns had only 90 shells each, the light guns just 150. French said, "We will achieve little other than to impress our allies with our sincerity."

▶ *The only defence against poison gas was to wear a mask, but these were heavy and restricted vision.*

The Battle of Loos

- **The Battle of Loos began** on 25 September, when poison gas was released by the British as a wind blew towards the German trenches. However, the wind changed direction and blew the gas back over the British lines.

- **When the British troops attacked**, the Germans were ready. The machine guns in the front line cut down thousands of men in the first few hours of the attack.

- **For the first time**, there were enough motor ambulances to evacuate the wounded back to hospitals once they had been carried off the battlefield by stretcher bearers.

- **Lieutenant Robert Graves**, later a writer, led his platoon to attack at Loos. When he reached the German trenches, only a single man was following. "Where are the men?" asked Graves. "Dead, sir," replied the soldier.

- **General Sir John French ordered his artillery** to fire every shell they had to help the infantry. On the second day, French called off the massed attacks, but continued with small-scale assaults until 8 October.

- **Of the 10,000 British soldiers who attacked** at Loos, 8200 were killed or wounded. The Germans called the battle 'The Graveyard'.

- **The French attack broke through** the German front line, but could not break the second line. Joffre claimed a great victory, but he had lost more men than the Germans.

◄ *The writer Rudyard Kipling never got over the news that his son had been killed at Loos.*

...FASCINATING FACT...

On the afternoon of the first day, Lieutenant John Kipling was killed by a German shell. His father was the famous writer Rudyard Kipling, who never really recovered from the loss.

● **The British Parliament was furious** at the high casualties at the Battle of Loos. Lord Kitchener was put in charge of recruitment. French was sacked.

● **The British appointed a new commander** in France, Scottish cavalry officer Douglas Haig. He had fought through the retreat from Mons and was liked and trusted. Haig had new ideas about how to fight the war.

▼ *German soldiers surrender to Indian troops. Small-scale raids and local attacks proved more successful than the earlier massed assaults.*

Stalemate at Gallipoli

● **At Gallipoli the Australian and New Zealand Army Corps** (Anzac) had made little progress.

● **In May**, the man who had come up with the idea, Winston Churchill, lost his job as First Lord of the Admiralty. He took command of a battalion on the front line in France.

● **General Hamilton devised** a new plan. A British force would make a new landing at Suvla Bay to outflank the Turkish defences.

● **The Anzacs would attack** the hills of Sari Bair. The troops from Suvla Bay would then attack the Turks from the rear. Within 48 hours, Hamilton believed, Sari Bair would be captured.

● **Then the British and Anzacs could march** to the straits of the Dardanelles to secure the north shore. This would allow the British battleships to steam to Constantinople and open fire. Turkey would be forced to surrender.

▲ *A British Enfield .303 MkV rifle. With a magazine holding five bullets, the .303 was the standard British rifle of the war.*

- **On 6 August**, General Sir Frederick Stopford supervised the British landings in Suvla Bay, while the Anzacs attacked Sari Bair. They reached the crest of the hill and could see the Dardanelles, but could get no further.

- **Stopford refused to follow** the plan of attacking the Turks from behind. Instead he ordered his men to concentrate on landing supplies. When Stopford ordered an attack three days later, the Turkish commander had prepared his defences.

- **On 10 August**, Mustapha Kemal led a counter attack that pushed the Anzacs off the crest of Sari Bair.

- **Hamilton ordered Stopford** to attack again in September, but the offensive was a costly failure. In October Hamilton was sacked and never again held a senior command.

- **The naval officer Roger Keyes** who served at Gallipoli, drew up guidelines for future seaborne operations, which were later used in World War II, especially at Dunkirk and on D-Day.

▶ *An Australian war memorial commemorates the heroic spirit of the Australian troops at Gallipoli and the legendary 'mateship' shown towards each other by the fighting men.*

75

Bulgaria joins the war

● **The Kingdom of Bulgaria** had been formed in 1878 from the Ottoman provinces of Bulgaria and Rumelia, but did not become completely independent until 1908.

● **In the First Balkan War of 1911**, Bulgaria gained new territory from the defeated Ottoman Empire. The following year Bulgaria lost most of the new land to Serbia and Greece in the second Balkan War.

▶ *King Ferdinand of Bulgaria was famous for his wily diplomacy and cunning strategy.*

... FASCINATING FACT ...

King Ferdinand was of German ancestry, but his people had links to Russia. Ferdinand managed to remain friendly with both empires, earning himself the name of 'Foxy Ferdinand'.

- **When World War I broke out**, Bulgaria remained neutral. However, King Ferdinand began expanding the Bulgarian army and equipping it with modern weapons. By the spring of 1915 he had 300,000 men ready for war.

- **King Ferdinand sent ambassadors** to both sides during the war. They emphasized that Bulgaria now had the largest army of all the Balkan countries and controlled the access of the river Danube to the sea.

- **The Bulgarian ambassadors also dropped hints** that Ferdinand was keen for Bulgaria to control the port of Alexandroupoli on the Aegean Sea and to regain the lands lost in the Second Balkan War.

- **The British were the first to respond** to Ferdinand. In return for Bulgaria declaring war on Turkey, they promised to give Bulgaria more lands from Turkey, and the port of Tekirdag on the Bosporus.

- **Ferdinand was impressed** by the British offer, but when the attack on Gallipoli failed, he believed that Britain could not deliver its promise.

- **Then Kaiser Wilhelm of Germany offered** Bulgaria as much of Serbia as it wanted, plus Alexandroupoli. As a sign of goodwill he sent the Bulgarian army dozens of modern German aircraft.

- **In August 1915**, King Ferdinand promised to declare war on Serbia whenever Germany asked. The Kaiser told Ferdinand to wait until a joint Austrian-German offensive on Serbia could be organized.

The defeat of Serbia

- **World War I began with a conflict** between Serbia and the Austrian Empire. However, there had been little fighting between them.

- **When German commander** in chief, Erich von Falkenhayn, learned that Kaiser Wilhelm had persuaded Bulgaria to join the Central Powers, he decided it was time to eliminate Serbia. Falkenhayn gave the task to General Mackensen.

- **On 5 October 1915**, the Germans crossed the Danube and within 48 hours had captured Belgrade.

- **Also on 5 October 1915**, the French–British force that had been heading for Gallipoli landed in the Greek port of Salonika. They began to march towards Serbia, but King Constantine, the Kaiser's brother-in-law, refused to help.

- **The Bulgarians declared war** on Serbia on 14 October. Their army crossed the border and headed for the key transport centre of Nis and the city of Skopje.

- **On 22 October**, the Allied advance from Salonika was stopped by the Bulgarians at Negotin. Nine days later the main Serb supply base of Kragujevac was captured by the Germans.

- **The Serbs retreated** southwest to Kosovo. Six hundred years earlier the Serbs had lost their independence when they lost a battle to the Turks at Kosovo.

- **On 23 November**, King Peter of Serbia ordered his men to destroy their artillery and wagons. He led them on foot into the Albanian mountains. He hoped to reach the Adriatic Sea to meet the British and French navies.

- **About a quarter of the Serb army** of 250,000 died in the snowy mountains.

- **In May 1916**, the Serb army was transported to Salonika. It was re-equipped with British weapons to prepare a march back into Serbia.

◀ *Serb machine gunners open fire as they protect the columns of the Serb army retreating into Albania.*

War in the air

- **When the war broke out**, all countries had a few aircraft that they intended to use for scouting purposes. The aircraft were made of wood, canvas and wire. They could fly at 130 km/h, but carried no weapons.

- **In November pilots began dropping** hand grenades or artillery shells on troops. Others carried shotguns and rifles with which to shoot aircraft.

- **By early 1915,** new types of two-man aircraft were being produced. The engine drove a propeller at the rear, while the gunner sat in the front with a machine gun. Some could carry a few light bombs.

- **Navigation was achieved** by looking at the ground and trying to spot a landmark. On most missions over half the pilots got lost.

- **The air crew** did not have any parachutes. Early parachutes were too big and heavy to fit in the aircraft.

- **One German pilot called** 'The Mad Major' by the British, would fly low over the trenches, then perform aerobatics before flying home.

- **On 1 April 1915,** the French pilot Roland Garros strapped a machine gun to the engine of his fast scout plane with a propeller at the front.

- **To stop the machine gun damaging** his own propeller, Garros fitted the blades with bullet-proof metal deflectors. By using the speed of his plane and carefully aiming his machine gun at the enemy, he could outmanoeuvre any German aircraft.

- **In August**, the Germans countered with the Fokker EIII monoplane. The machine gun on this plane fired in time with the propeller, so that the bullets passed between the blades, removing the need for clumsy deflectors.

- **German pilot**, Oswald Boelcke, perfected new tactics to use with the new Fokker aircraft. By October the German squadrons ruled the air.

▲ A German pilot uses the forward-firing machine gun on his Fokker Eindecker to shoot down a British gun bus. The Fokker was so deadly that British pilots called it 'the Fokker Scourge'.

The Allies think again

● **On 6 December 1915**, the senior commanders of Britain and France met at the HQ of French Field Marshal Joffre to discuss how to win the war.

● **The failures of Gallipoli and Salonika** led the governments of France and Britain to believe that the war could only be won on the Western Front. Only if Germany were defeated, could the war end in 1916.

● **The new British commander** in France, Sir Douglas Haig, had to cooperate with Joffre, but he was not under Joffre and could make his own decisions.

● **The French called up vast reserves** of men and converted much of their industry to producing weapons. Joffre was confident that a new attack would break the German army.

● **Haig also had large reserves** of men and weapons available. However, he was unconvinced by Joffre's idea of yet another infantry attack.

● **A major recruitment drive** in Britain by Lord Kitchener, boosted by outrage over the German execution of Nurse Cavell, led to large numbers of volunteers.

▶ *The Welsh politician, Lloyd George, revolutionized the British armaments industry in 1915, ensuring that the army had enough weapons and ammunition to continue the war.*

▶ *This recruitment poster for the British army showed that the famous military hero Lord Kitchener was the most successful of the war and had become an iconic image.*

- **Many of the volunteers joined up** as 'Pals' units. Groups of workmates or villages insisted on serving together.

- **Lloyd George had transformed** the munitions industry in the previous eight months. There were now more shells and guns than ever before.

- **Joffre suggested** a combined British–French attack on either side of the river Somme. Haig agreed, but he asked for time to consider the best way to make the attack.

- **Unknown to the Allies**, the Germans had their own plans – to move faster when the spring weather came in 1916.

The Kaiser's war plans

● **By the end of 1915,** Turkey and Bulgaria had joined the Central Powers – Germany and Austria. Germany was still faced by a war on two fronts.

● **The Austrians began to think** that they could not win. General von Höztendorf told his government on 4 January, "There is no question of destroying the Russian war machine."

● **German commander in chief,** Erich von Falkenhayn, and Kaiser Wilhelm decided to finish the war in the Balkans, by first crushing tiny Montenegro. The Austrians could concentrate on Russia.

● **A joint organized Austrian–Bulgarian** offensive smashed the Montenegran army in just nine days. On 17 January, Montenegro surrendered to Austria.

● **Falkenhayn studied** the Russian front. The German and Austrian armies were deep inside Russia, separated from their homeland by hundreds of kilometres of poor roads. Falkenhayn decided that a major offensive was impossible.

● **The Austrian army was ordered** to watch the Russians. After losing 2 million men in 1915, would the Russians be able to mount a major campaign?

● **To secure the Eastern Front,** the Kaiser promised the Poles, Latvians, Lithuanians, Estonians and others, independence after Russia's defeat.

● **These promises gave them a reason** to support Germany. He allowed the eastern states to set up civilian governments in areas occupied by Germany.

● **These changes allowed** the Germans to concentrate on the Western Front. The Kaiser had decided to beat France and Britain in 1916.

● **The Kaiser ordered** Falkenhayn to devise a plan to achieve victory. Falkenhayn decided to look at the history of France for an answer.

▲ *German infantry occupy a well-built front line trench to repel a British attack. Not all trenches were as well built or well maintained as this, though the German trenches were generally the best.*

Retreat from Gallipoli

● **Before the Allies could begin** to implement their plans for 1916, they had to draw to a close one of the failed operations of 1915 – Gallipoli.

● **In October 1915**, Sir Ian Hamilton was recalled to Britain. He was replaced by Sir Charles Monro. Monro spent a week studying the situation, then wrote back to London recommending instant withdrawal of all troops.

▼ *A British field gun is transported ashore in December 1915.*

...FASCINATING FACT...
On 27 November, a blizzard hit Gallipoli. Over 5000 men suffered frostbite and 300 died because of the cold.

● **Lord Kitchener was sent out** by the British government to see the situation for himself. Kitchener thought that a fortified base should be built on Cape Helles and the other positions abandoned.

● **The British government decided** to evacuate completely – the Cape Helles fortress was abandoned.

● **On 19 December,** the men at Suvla Bay and Anzac Cove were evacuated to waiting ships. The Australians invented a way of firing rifles automatically, so that it would appear that men were still present when they had in fact left.

● **On 8 January,** the final evacuation began at Cape Helles. All the men were evacuated without a single casualty. The Turks did not interfere.

● **In total, the Allies had seen** 252,000 men killed, wounded or captured at Gallipoli, out of 480,000 who took part. The Turks had lost 68,000 men killed and around 150,000 wounded.

● **The Allies also lost** a huge quantity of stores and ammunition, which the Turks gratefully gathered up. They then moved these supplies to be used against the Allies in other theatres of the war.

● **At the time,** many people thought the Gallipoli campaign had been a disaster. Later, military strategists thought that it had been a good idea that was badly implemented. Winston Churchill, who suggested the campaign, said, "We sent two-thirds of what was needed one month too late."

The Verdun Plan

- **Verdun on the river Meuse** had been fortified since the days of the Roman Empire. It was one of France's main army depots and a powerful fortress. In 1914 it had famously held out against a German attack.

- **German commander**, Erich von Falkenhayn, studied French history. He believed that the French would do almost anything to hold Verdun.

- **The area around Verdun** was a quiet sector. When a sudden flash flood washed away the earth between a German and a French trench, the men ignored their enemies while they dug new trenches.

- **The steep hills and deep gullies** of the area around Verdun were good for defence. On them the French had built a series of forts, each containing underground shelters and guns set in concrete and metal emplacements.

- **The most powerful** was Fort Douaumont. It had heavy artillery, light artillery, machine guns and kilometres of underground tunnels.

- **Falkenhayn decided to attack** Verdun, but with no intention of capturing the city or forts. He planned merely to pretend to try to capture them.

- **This would persuade the French** to pour reinforcements into Verdun. Once the French were within range, the German artillery would wipe them out.

- **Falkenhayn hoped to inflict** huge casualties on the French army, without the Germans losing many men. "We will bleed France white," he said.

- **Kaiser Wilhelm liked the plan** so much that he asked for Crown Prince Wilhelm, heir to the German throne, to be the commander. Falkenhayn arranged for experienced generals to have real control on the battlefield.

- **The French garrison at Verdun considered** that they were safe in their forts. They allowed the outer defences to fall into disrepair.

▼ *French troops man a reserve line trench at Verdun. The area has been churned up by intense artillery fire and stripped of vegetation.*

The Easter Uprising

● **Ireland had been ruled** by Britain for generations. In 1801, the Irish were given the right to elect MPs to the British Parliament in London. However, many Irish people wanted to govern themselves.

● **When World War I broke out**, thousands of Irishmen volunteered. A large proportion of the British army was made up of Irish regiments.

● **The British government was in the process** of granting Home Rule to Ireland when war broke out. It was postponed until peace was achieved.

● **In April 1916** a Sinn Fein leader, Roger Casement, was caught bringing German weapons to Ireland. He was hanged as a traitor in time of war.

● **Patrick Pearse drew up a plan** for around 1200 armed republicans to seize government buildings in Dublin. He hoped that the people of Ireland would then rise up against the British. Pearse thought the British would be too busy fighting Germany to suppress a mass rebellion.

● **On Easter Monday at 12 noon**, the Irish republicans struck. They seized five of their seven objectives with very little fighting. The British reacted by imposing martial law and blocking all roads in and out of Dublin.

...FASCINATING FACT...
A few small groups supported using terrorism and warfare to drive out the British. They lacked manpower and weapons to make a real difference.

- **On Wednesday**, British artillery began shelling the rebel strongholds. British commander, Sir John Maxwell, was ordered to put down the rising as fast as possible. He ordered infantry attacks to begin on the Thursday.

- **On Saturday**, the surviving rebels surrendered. Much of Dublin lay in ruins and around 700 civilians were killed, along with 500 rebels and 500 British.

- **Pearse and the rebel leaders** were executed a few weeks later. This act outraged many Irish who had opposed the Easter Uprising. In the election of 1918, Ireland elected a majority of MPs wanting independence from Britain.

▼ *Irish rebels defend ruined buildings in Dublin against British troops armed with machine guns.*

'They shall not pass'

● **By 21 February 1916**, the Germans had gathered 1200 artillery guns facing the French lines at Verdun. Of these, 500 were heavy guns. The guns had almost unlimited supplies of ammunition.

● **Just before dawn the German guns** opened fire. The French front line received the most intense bombardment of the war. At 4 p.m. the guns fell silent and German patrols went forward to test the defences. Enough French soldiers survived to drive them off. The guns began firing again.

▼ *A vast French cemetery at Verdun shows the sheer scale of the losses.*
Even more men were killed, but their bodies never discovered.

> ...FASCINATING FACT...
> Artillery fire from both sides was intense. Bodies were buried by
> shellfire, then new explosions blew them to the surface again.
> Thousands of dead lay in an area of a few square kilometres.

● **For two days the Germans continued** making probing attacks. On
24 February the French broke. The Germans advanced rapidly.

● **Sergeant Kunze of the Brandenburg Regiment** reached Fort Douaumont
at dawn on 25 February. He led his 45 men through an open door and found
the French garrison eating breakfast. The most powerful fortress in the world
had fallen.

● **Marshal Joffre sent** General Henri Pétain to take command at Verdun.
Pétain announced, "They shall not pass."

● **Pétain built a new road**, the Voie Sacrée, to Verdun. Along this road,
as planned by General Erich von Falkenhayn, French reinforcements arrived.

● **Meanwhile, French 75-mm guns** on the left bank of the river Meuse were
firing into the German flank. German losses began to rise.

● **Crown Prince Wilhelm ordered** thousands of men to attack the French
artillery. They captured some, but found more guns beyond them. Falkenhayn
ordered a halt to the attacks.

● **In June the Germans struck again**, on a front line of just 5 km. Using
poison gas, they breached the French lines and rifle bullets began hitting
houses in Verdun town. Then, suddenly, the German attacks stopped. Only the
artillery continued to fire.

The Brusilov Offensive

● **By early 1916**, Russian Tsar Nicholas II was permanently at army headquarters to act as commander in chief and boost his soldiers' morale. This left the Russian government in the hands of Tsarina Alexandra.

● **The Tsarina was greatly influenced** by a debauched Siberian mystic called Grigori Rasputin. They promoted their friends instead of efficient and capable men. The Russian government began to decline in effectiveness.

◀ *The uneducated peasant monk Rasputin gained enormous influence over the Russian government by influencing the Tsarina.*

> **...FASCINATING FACT...**
> The main Russian offensive started on 18 June, but halted almost at
> once when the men ran out of supplies and reserves were
> sent in the wrong direction.

- **Tsar Nicholas ordered** Marshal Alexei Brusilov to attack the Austrians to distract attention from the main attack on the German army.

- **Brusilov developed new tactics** for his attack. On 4 June, Brusilov's offensive smashed through the Austrian lines in three places. On 8 June, Austrian Archduke Josef Ferdinand had to abandon his birthday party when a Russian shell landed in the garden of the house where the party was being held.

- **For eight weeks**, the Russians advanced, but the attack came to a halt when General von Ludendorff moved German troops to support the Austrians.

- **Romania had remained neutral** when World War I began. King Ferdinand decided to see which side was going to win before committing his small kingdom. The Brusilov Offensive and optimistic reports from the Somme convinced him the Allies would win.

- **The Russians asked King Ferdinand** to attack Bulgaria. On 17 August, Romania declared war on Austria and invaded Transylvania, a Romanian-speaking province of the Austrian Empire.

- **Within six weeks the Romanian army** of 500,000 men had been crushed by a combined German–Austrian–Bulgarian offensive. The rich oil fields were in German hands.

- **Denmark, Norway and the Netherlands favoured** the Allied cause, but decided to remain neutral. They did not want to become another Romania.

Haig's new idea

● **In accordance with** the plans agreed in December, Sir Douglas Haig began preparing a major British offensive in the Somme area of northern France. He had 600,000 trained volunteers and a vast amount of artillery and shells.

● **Haig recognized** that conventional tactics had failed at Neuve-Chappelle and Loos in 1915. He and his staff questioned officers who had taken part in those battles and studied the problems of trench warfare in an effort to develop new, more successful tactics.

● **They decided** that the breaks in the German lines achieved in 1915 had been too narrow for reserves to push through – a wide front was needed.

● **Reserves had not moved** forwards fast enough to exploit the gaps in the German lines. This time the reserves would be sent forwards as soon as the first wave had reached the German trenches.

◀ *The British army of 1916 was made up of well-equipped volunteers. The uniform of a soldier consisted of a steel helmet to protect the head from shrapnel, lengths of cloth called puttees worn around the legs to protect from mud, waterproof boots and a tunic. Each soldier also carried a rifle and a bayonet. Bayonets were only used in close combat.*

● **Gas was too unpredictable** for widespread use. Instead gas shells fired from artillery would be aimed at small targets, if the weather was suitable.

● **Artillery fire** had missed many German defences. Aircraft would be sent up weeks before the attack to locate machine gun positions and bunkers so that they could be hit by artillery before the attack began.

● **A widespread breakthrough** was unlikely, so troops were given realistic objectives such as capturing particular hills or areas of German defences.

● **Cavalry would** be made ready just in case a breakthrough occurred. They were given explosive charges so they could demolish enemy railways and roads far behind the front line.

● **Previously the Germans** had guessed in advance where the attacks would take place. This time some areas that were not to be attacked would be shelled to confuse the Germans.

● **Unfortunately** for the British, the Germans had also been planning. They revised the weaknesses they saw at Loos and by the summer of 1916 had new types of defence.

▲ *A .38 calibre Colt double action revolver. A double action pistol required a stronger pull on the trigger to fire, so was less likely to go off by accident.*

97

First day on the Somme

- **British commander in France**, Sir Douglas Haig, planned his major attack in the Somme area for 15 August, when all his preparations would be made.

- **Marshal Joffre begged** him to attack earlier. Haig agreed to attack on 1 July. His junior officers were worried that the new plan would not be ready.

- **On 26 June**, a massive bombardment began. British guns pounded the German lines for five days, but many of the shells did not explode.

- **The British gunners did not realize** that the Germans had rebuilt many earth or sandbag defences in concrete. The light British shells did not damage them.

- **Most of the German soldiers** were safe in dugouts over 15 m deep beneath the Somme.

◀ French troops race forwards across the smooth, grassy fields of the Somme area. French attacks in the south proved more successful than those of the British.

- **The bombardment ceased** at 7.30 a.m. on 1 July. The Germans raced from their dugouts to man the trenches and machine guns.

- **The British began to advance** expecting most Germans to have been killed. The infantry advanced in four lines, about 100 m behind each other and with 4 m between each man.

- **The German machine guns mowed down** the first wave of British soldiers mercilessly. The Middlesex Regiment lost 622 men out of 740 in ten minutes.

- **The carnage was so horrific** that no messages got back from the first wave. According to plan, the second wave advanced and suffered similar losses.

- **By nightfall**, 20,000 British soldiers were dead and 40,000 wounded. Never before or since has the British army lost so many men in 24 hours.

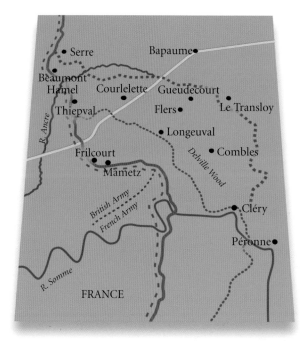

KEY

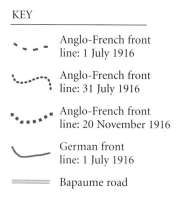

- – - · Anglo-French front line: 1 July 1916

·•··•·· Anglo-French front line: 31 July 1916

·•·■·■· Anglo-French front line: 20 November 1916

‿‿‿ German front line: 1 July 1916

═══ Bapaume road

◀ *The advances achieved on the Somme were much smaller than planned and casualties were higher than expected. The fighting ended without a decisive result.*

Death on the Somme

- **On 2 July**, British commander Sir Douglas Haig ordered the attack to continue. The reports he had received were contradictory and confused. He and his senior officers refused to believe that their plan could go so wrong.

- **By the end of 2 July**, Haig finally realized the true situation. The Ulster Division had taken the German front line. The 13 Corps captured the village of Montauban. Success was not achieved anywhere else.

- **Haig ordered for new attacks** to take place, to continue the advance of the Ulstermen and 13 Corps, and elsewhere for the useless attacks to cease.

- **On 14 July**, British General Henry Rawlinson suggested that his men should try the novel idea of attacking at night after a short, dense bombardment. Haig gave permission the next day.

- **The night attack took the Germans** by surprise. By dawn the British had broken through the German defences completely on a front line of 3 km. The infantry sent messages for the cavalry to advance.

- **A few cavalry units received** the messages and rode forward. They crossed the battered Somme battlefield, then emerged into open country and charged.

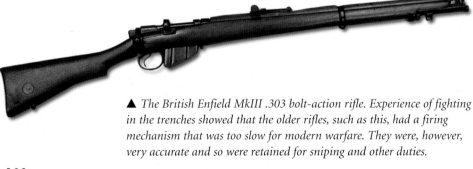

▲ *The British Enfield MkIII .303 bolt-action rifle. Experience of fighting in the trenches showed that the older rifles, such as this, had a firing mechanism that was too slow for modern warfare. They were, however, very accurate and so were retained for sniping and other duties.*

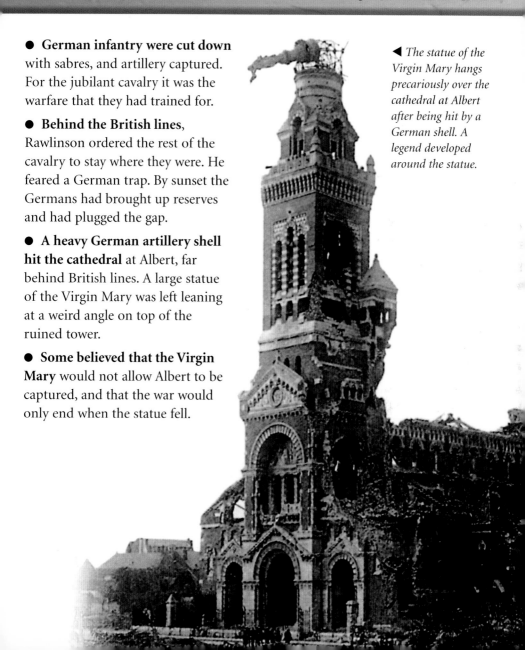

● **German infantry were cut down** with sabres, and artillery captured. For the jubilant cavalry it was the warfare that they had trained for.

● **Behind the British lines,** Rawlinson ordered the rest of the cavalry to stay where they were. He feared a German trap. By sunset the Germans had brought up reserves and had plugged the gap.

● **A heavy German artillery shell hit the cathedral** at Albert, far behind British lines. A large statue of the Virgin Mary was left leaning at a weird angle on top of the ruined tower.

● **Some believed that the Virgin Mary** would not allow Albert to be captured, and that the war would only end when the statue fell.

◄ The statue of the Virgin Mary hangs precariously over the cathedral at Albert after being hit by a German shell. A legend developed around the statue.

Enter the tanks

● **In August 1916**, General Rawlinson persuaded Sir Douglas Haig to try a new weapon that had been developed on the orders of Winston Churchill. It was called a 'land battleship', then the 'thingum-a-jig'. Finally it was named 'tank'.

● **The development of the tank** began in October 1914, when military engineer Colonel Swinton used tractors with caterpillar tracks to haul heavy equipment around the fields near Ypres.

● **It then occurred to Swinton** to build a larger tractor, then mount a gun on top of it. He could add a couple of machine guns as well.

▼ *A 'Big Willie' tank advances past a British rear trench. The large wheel at the rear was designed to help the poor steering mechanism, but failed in action and had to be replaced.*

● **In April 1915**, Swinton suggested encasing the guns and crew of the tractor in thick metal plates that would be able to stop all bullets and shrapnel. He drew up plans and sent the idea to the War Office.

● **Lord Kitchener dismissed** the idea, but Churchill was enthusiastic. He arranged for naval money to be spent developing the idea of the 'land battleship'.

● **Eventually there were two types** of tank. 'Big Willie' had two six pounder guns to destroy enemy strongpoints. 'Mother' was equipped with five machine guns.

● **When Haig ordered** Swinton to use his tanks on the Somme, Swinton was furious. He only had 50 machines, and was still having problems with the steering mechanism. Haig insisted.

● **On 15 September** the 28-tonne tanks lumbered forward at 5 km/h, impervious to all but heavy artillery.

● **By noon many had either run out of fuel**, broken down or been hit by artillery.

● **The excited tank crews were keen** to fight again, but wanted to devise special tactics. Swinton wanted to build new tanks of improved design.

▶ *Lord Kitchener was scornful of the idea of armoured fighting vehicles – tanks – but others were more enthusiastic.*

Air power's first strike

- **The Battle of the Somme** was the first time that aircraft played a significant part in the plans of senior commanders. British General Sir Douglas Haig ordered his airmen to scout behind German lines, and to shoot down any German aircraft that tried to scout behind British lines.

- **All sides were developing** specialist fighters, bombers and reconnaissance aircraft by 1916, but designs had remained fairly unaltered since 1915.

- **Reconnaissance aircraft began** to carry radios so that the observer could report back to base instantly.

- **It soon became clear** that reconnaissance planes and bombers could only operate if the fighters could keep the skies clear of enemy fighters.

- **The Germans relied** on the Fokker E series fighter, while the British produced increasingly effective 'pushers' such as the Vickers FB5 Gun Bus and the DeHavilland DH2.

- **During the Battle of the Somme** three new aircraft appeared. The British flew the Sopwith 1 1/2 Strutter, the French the Nieuport Scout, the Germans the Albatros D1. All were biplanes with synchronized guns pointing forwards.

- **German pilot Max Immelman invented** several aerobatic tricks useful in combat. The famous 'Immelman turn' allowed him to fire at an enemy, then flip over and back to fire again on the same target.

● **Another German**, Oswald Boelcke, developed tactics in which pilots could cooperate with each other in combat.

● **Boelcke insisted** that pilots flew and fought in flights of six, led by an experienced officer and all flying the same type of machine.

● **Several flights could be joined together** to form a 'flying circus'. These large formations were highly effective in controlling a given area of sky and shooting down any enemy that dared intrude.

▼ *A British two-seater scout aircraft drops a bomb on to German trenches. At first bombs were carried in the cockpit and dropped by hand, only later did proper bomb racks and aiming devices become the norm.*

Autumn slaughter at Verdun

- **The fighting at Verdun continued** throughout the summer of 1916.

- **On 11 July**, the Germans failed to take the remaining high ground in French hands overlooking Verdun. They did capture the heavily defended Fort Vaux, then ceased major attacks as they transferred men to the Somme.

- **As the intensity of fighting** at Verdun died down, General Pétain was replaced as French commander by the ambitious General Robert Nivelle.

- **Nivelle developed a plan** for retaking the ground lost to the Germans. A short artillery bombardment would be followed by infantry infiltration.

- **Infiltration involved** creeping forwards at night between German bunkers and strongpoints. These would then be attacked from all sides the next day.

◄ *A motor ambulance with the driver's seat protected by covers. Wounded men evacuated quickly stood a much better chance of survival, so these vehicles were in high demand.*

- **It was hoped** that because the French soldiers would be mixed up with the German positions, the enemy would be unable to call in artillery fire.

- **Nivelle believed that infiltration tactics** would capture the individual strongpoints and hills around Verdun. He did not intend to break through.

- **Nivelle spent three months** building up his forces and using aircraft to map out the routes to be taken by his men.

- **On 24 October**, Nivelle's attack at Verdun began. The infiltration tactics were successful. Fort Vaux was captured in a few days and Fort Douaumont on 2 November.

- **By December** Nivelle's men had recaptured much of the lost ground, ending the Battle of Verdun. The Germans lost 230,000 wounded and 100,000 killed; the French lost 300,000 wounded and 162,000 killed.

▶ *A French unit rests in a trench. Note the poorly maintained sloping sides of the trench that indicate this is in a rear area.*

Silence over the Somme

● **After the tank attack** of September, the fighting on the Somme returned to small-scale attacks and retreats.

● **During the fighting**, British regiments began reporting 'trench fever', a disease spread by lice. It quickly spread to German and French units.

● **Trench fever began** with a splitting headache, then a high temperature and pains in the legs. It lasted five days, faded for a few days, then returned.

● **Soldiers who caught** 'trench fever' were unfit for duty for three weeks to four months.

● **By the autumn**, every man coming out of the line to rest had to strip, have a hot bath and have his clothes and kit fumigated. The disease faded that winter, but was never eradicated.

● **In early October** heavy rains lashed northern France. The chalk ground became slippery and waterlogged. Men found it difficult to move quickly.

● **On 18 November**, British commander Sir Douglas Haig ordered that all attacks should cease until the following spring. The British had advanced no more than 11 km. In many places they had failed to take the objectives set for the first day.

> **· · ·FASCINATING FACT· · ·**
> Haig was depressed by the failure and by the large casualties. He considered resigning, but King George V persuaded him to stay and promoted him to Field Marshal.

▲ *Injured British and German soldiers walk away from the Somme battlefield to British first aid posts behind the front lines.*

● **The British had lost** 95,000 dead and 320,000 wounded; the Germans lost 164,000 dead and 400,000 wounded; the French lost 50,000 dead and 140,000 wounded.

● **Haig now faced** a war of attrition – he would have to grind down the German army while protecting his men from unnecessary deaths. He was unable to carry out these aims.

Lawrence of Arabia

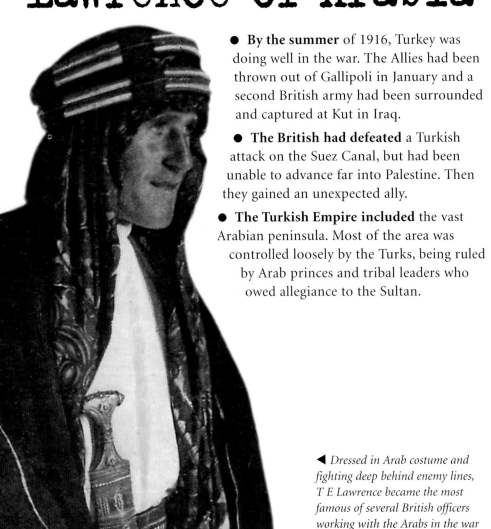

- **By the summer** of 1916, Turkey was doing well in the war. The Allies had been thrown out of Gallipoli in January and a second British army had been surrounded and captured at Kut in Iraq.

- **The British had defeated** a Turkish attack on the Suez Canal, but had been unable to advance far into Palestine. Then they gained an unexpected ally.

- **The Turkish Empire included** the vast Arabian peninsula. Most of the area was controlled loosely by the Turks, being ruled by Arab princes and tribal leaders who owed allegiance to the Sultan.

◀ *Dressed in Arab costume and fighting deep behind enemy lines, T E Lawrence became the most famous of several British officers working with the Arabs in the war against the Ottoman Empire.*

- **In June 1916**, the Hashemite princes of Hejaz rebelled against Turkish rule. The warriors of Sherif Hussein captured Mecca and Taif, but failed in an attack on Medina.

- **In October Britain sent** two officers from Egypt to try to reach Hussein and find out what was happening. Ronald Storrs and Thomas Lawrence reached Hussein and concluded that the Arab revolt would do little more than tie down a few thousand Turks.

- **Then Lawrence went on to meet** Hussein's younger brother, Amir Feisal. Feisal was a charismatic leader with several hundred Arab warriors under his control.

- **Lawrence persuaded** Feisal to abandon attacks on Medina in favour of raiding the railway line leading from Turkey to Medina.

- **The successes Feisal and Lawrence** had looting trains began to attract other Arab tribes to the uprising. By March 1917, Lawrence was dressing in Arab costume and accompanying the raiders on more daring missions.

- **In July 1917**, Lawrence persuaded Auda abu Tayi to lead the Howeitat tribe to attack the great Turkish port at Aqaba. By launching a surprise attack from the rear, the Arabs seized the port with ease.

. . . **FASCINATING FACT** . . .

Impressed by the capture of Aqaba, the British commander
Edmund Allenby, sent weapons, supplies and gold to Lawrence with
instructions to raise all the Arabs in revolt against the Turks.

War weariness

● **After the terrible losses** of 1915, and even more so after the summer of 1916, some people in most of the combatant nations became weary of the war.

● **However, the military commanders** of the major powers would not accept defeat. All armies remained intact and in high spirits.

● **Neither side was close to defeat**, though none was close to victory.

● **In Britain** the losses on the Somme led to a change of prime minister. Liberal Herbert Asquith was replaced by his fellow Liberal Lloyd George.

● **The British people were still determined** to gain victory over Germany. Despite the losses there were still plenty of recruits.

● **In France**, food prices were increasing and fuel was scarce. Trade Unions suggested that the war should be stopped given the hardships of the poor.

● **In December**, the French government responded by promoting Robert Nivelle to commander in chief with orders to win the war in 1917.

● **Russia was suffering** terrible economic problems. Food, fuel and clothes were all in short supply. In November, Tsar Nicholas asked the neutral Swedish government to suggest negotiations to the Germans. The Germans refused.

● **Emperor Franz Joseph** of Austria died in November 1916 and was replaced by Emperor Carl. The new Emperor was appalled by the state of the Empire's finances. He wanted peace, but dared not without German permission.

● **The president of the USA**, Woodrow Wilson, was willing to chair a conference to decide on a peace settlement. Both Germany and France set preconditions that the other would not accept. No conference was held.

▶ *A mobile soup wagon distributes hot food to civilians in the streets of Berlin. Fuel for cookers was in short supply, so wagons were the only way some people got hot food.*

tädt. Küchenwagen
rmes Mittagessen
ortion 35 Pfg.
eliefert vom Verein der
erliner Volksküchen von 1866

Germany's peace note

- **On 12 December 1916** the world was staggered when German Chancellor Theobald Bethmann-Hollweg announced that Germany would make peace.

- **US President Woodrow Wilson** responded by suggesting that each combatant nation should draw up a list of what they were hoping to achieve if they won the war. He would then study the lists to see if a compromise was possible.

- **France replied with a list** of idealistic concepts, plus the solid demand that the area of Alsace-Lorraine should be given to France by Germany.

- **Britain wanted Belgium** to be recognized as an independent and neutral country, as it had been before 1914. It also wanted the German navy to be reduced in size, but it was clear there was room for negotiation on this point.

- **Italy stated** that it wanted to gain the Italian-speaking provinces of the Austrian Empire, and tried to claim some islands in the Adriatic.

- **Emperor Carl of Austria stuck** to the original demands made of Serbia in 1914, adding only that he would not make peace without Germany.

- **Tsar Nicholas of Russia** said that all he wanted was a return to the situation before the war, though he also wanted Serbia to be satisfied.

- **The rulers of Bulgaria**, Romania, Serbia, Montenegro and Turkey repeated their various war aims. They all accepted that the major powers would decide whether the war would continue or not.

- **The Germans then announced** that they would not negotiate through the USA. If any country wanted to make peace, they had to deal directly with Germany or not at all.

- **Britain and France** at once refused. The war went on.

▲ *The front page of the British newspaper, the* Daily Sketch, *reports the news of Germany's peace note. The photo montage shows the Kaiser holding a bloodstained sword and urges that the offer should be turned down.*

The role of sea power

- **Throughout history**, nations with coastlines have relied to a lesser or greater extent on sea power.

- **Island nations**, such as Britain, rely on sea trade when dealing with other countries. Those with some land frontiers are not so dependent.

- **In time of war**, sea trade becomes increasingly important. The economy of a nation can be seriously damaged if its sea trade is cut off.

- **Countries build warships** to attack each other's merchant ships and to protect their own. These warships are used to control the seas.

- **Although warships** are frequently used to fight each other, these battles are secondary to the main purpose of the war navies – to control sea trade.

- **In 1805**, the British Royal Navy totally defeated the French and Spanish fleets at the Battle of Trafalgar. Thereafter no country had seriously threatened its power.

- **Countries such as France**, the USA or Italy had fleets to protect merchant ships near their own coasts, but only Britain's could rule the world's oceans.

- **The British Empire included ports** and docks worldwide. The Royal Navy used these to service its ships so that they could operate almost anywhere.

- **Then one country decided** to try to challenge the might of the Royal Navy – Germany.

...FASCINATING FACT...
The key role of ships is economic. Ships transport goods
to and from other countries to be sold for profit.

◄ *The British victory at the Battle of Trafalgar in 1805 gave Britain control of the seas for over 100 years.*

The dreadnought race

- **The introduction of steam propulsion**, steel armour and long range, breech-loading guns revolutionized warship design and naval strategy.

- **By 1890**, most navies had decided that the future lay in battleships about 10,000 tonnes in weight and able to steam at 16 knots. Main armament would be four big 10- or 12-in guns.

- **Navies continued** to have specialist ships, but these were not expected to play a major role in sea warfare.

- **In 1896**, the Germans began to produce an entirely new form of warship – the cruiser. Smaller than battleships and armed with only medium guns, cruisers were able to steam at about 22 knots and could travel long distances without needing to resupply.

- **Cruisers could** disrupt sea trade far from their home ports, sinking merchant ships easily. If an enemy battleship approached they could escape at speed.

- **The German cruisers** were intended to threaten British merchant ships around the world. Britain began building its own cruisers to face the threat.

- **In 1906** the British began building HMS *Dreadnought*. This ship made all other battleships obsolete.

- *Dreadnought* **had ten 12-in guns**, thick armour and could reach 21 knots. She could outfight and outrun any other battleship in the world.

- **When Germany's Kaiser Wilhelm** saw *Dreadnought* he ordered Admiral von Tirpitz to build four similar ships for the German navy.

- **Britain responded with seven** more ships of the *Dreadnought* class. Rivalry between the British and German navies quickly gathered pace. Britain eventually built 48 dreadnoughts, and Germany 26.

▼ HMS Dreadnought. *By 1914 the most modern warships were encased in thick armour and carried large guns mounted in armoured turrets that could turn to face different directions.*

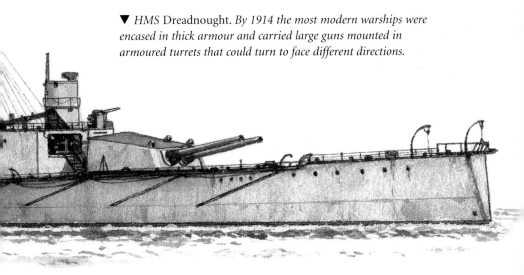

Naval war begins

- **In the summer** of 1914, neither the British nor the German naval commanders expected to fight against each other. Even if war broke out, they thought it would be fought mainly on land and be over within weeks.

- **Nevertheless, both sides were prepared** for a major conflict. The Germans had a fleet based at Tsingtao in China made up of two heavy cruisers and three light cruisers.

- **In the Caribbean** the Germans had two light cruisers. In German East Africa was another modern cruiser, and two more were in the Mediterranean.

- **The main German force** was the High Seas Fleet, based in Germany. It consisted of 15 dreadnought battleships, 32 older battleships, four battle-cruisers, nine heavy cruisers, 14 light cruisers, 60 destroyers and various specialist ships.

▼ *The main British battle fleet was known as the Grand Fleet. It was the most powerful in the world in 1914.*

- **The Royal Navy was almost twice as large** as the German navy. However, the need to protect British merchant shipping meant that it was more scattered around the globe.

- **In the last week** of July 1914, Britain's First Lord of the Admiralty guessed that war was about to break out. He mobilized the Royal Navy for war and sent the Grand Fleet to take up battle stations in the North Sea.

- **The Grand Fleet successfully escorted** the troopships carrying the British Expeditionary Force to France. Then Churchill and his senior admiral, Prince Louis of Battenberg, planned offensive moves.

- **On 28 August,** two light cruisers and some destroyers were sent to attack German shipping in the Heligoland Bight. They were supported by the Battle Cruiser Squadron under Admiral David Beatty.

- **In the Heligoland Bight,** the two cruisers met six German cruisers and fled. Beatty then sank three German ships before he lost the rest in fog.

- **On 22 September,** a German U9 submarine, commanded by Lieutenant Otto Weddigen, sighted three British cruisers off the Hook of Holland. In less than 25 minutes the Germans sank all three British ships with torpedoes.

▶ *British Admiral David Beatty was one of the most successful admirals of the war. In 1919 he was made an Earl by King George V.*

The Battle of Coronel

- **On 23 August 1914**, Japan declared war on Germany. Friendly towards Britain, Japan wanted to occupy German-owned islands in the Pacific.

- **The Japanese fleet outnumbered** the German Far East Fleet at Tsingtao. German Admiral Graf von Spee took his ships to raid widely across the Pacific.

- **The German cruiser**, *Emden*, was sent to hunt merchant ships. With his other ships, Spee shelled French bases on Tahiti and cut the transpacific telegraph cable, then headed for Chile to attack merchant shipping.

- **On 1 November**, Spee met a British fleet commanded by Sir Christopher Craddock off Coronel. Spee had two heavy cruisers and three light cruisers.

- **Craddock had two heavy** and one light cruiser plus a converted merchant ship carrying light guns, but a British battleship lay just to the south.

- **At first Craddock sighted** only one German ship, so he moved to attack. By the time he realized his mistake, the fleets were within range of each other.

- **The German ships opened fire** at a range of 11,200 m. The British replied. It soon became obvious that the German ships were more stable in the rough seas, so their gunners could aim more accurately.

- **The two British heavy cruisers** were targeted by Spee and were quickly sunk. Admiral Craddock went down with his ship.

- **The British light cruiser**, *Glasgow*, and converted merchant ship *Otranto*, turned south, hoping to lure Spee towards the waiting battleship, *Canopus*.

- **Spee did not pursue** the British ships. The first fleet action between Britain and Germany had ended with a decisive German victory.

▼ *The German cruiser* Scharnhorst *at the Battle of Coronel,* with Gneisenau, *another ship, visible in the distance.*

The Battle of the Falklands

● **By late November 1914,** the ships of German Admiral von Spee were running short of fuel. He decided to leave the Pacific for the Atlantic. As well as hoping to sink merchant ships, Spee wanted to capture the Falkland Islands.

● **Port Stanley in the Falklands** was a major coal store for the Royal Navy, but was not heavily defended. Spee wanted to refuel and use the Falklands as a base from which to attack British shipping in the South Atlantic.

● **Unknown to Spee,** the British had reacted to their defeat at the Battle of Coronel by sending out a new fleet.

● **Led by Admiral Sir Doveton Sturdee,** the British fleet comprised two battle-cruisers and three cruisers. One of the cruisers was HMS *Glasgow*, which had narrowly avoided being sunk at Coronel.

● **Sturdee arrived at Port Stanley** on 7 December. His ships were taking on coal when the German fleet of Spee unexpectedly appeared over the horizon. It consisted of two heavy cruisers and three light cruisers.

● **The British battle-cruisers,** *Inflexible* and *Invincible*, each carried eight 12-in guns. The German heavy cruisers had only eight 8-in guns.

. . . FASCINATING FACT . . .

On 14 March 1915, *Dresden* was found by British cruisers off Juan Fernandez Island. Short of fuel and ammunition, the captain scuttled (deliberately sank) his ship.

- **Realizing he was outgunned**, Spee steamed away at high speed to the southeast. Sturdee went to sea so quickly that he left crewmen on shore.

- **The battle lasted** over eight hours. Both German heavy cruisers and two of the light cruisers were sunk as they raced across the South Atlantic.

- **Only the German** light cruiser *Dresden* escaped. The cruiser was to lead an adventurous career cruising and attacking across the South Pacific.

▼ *The British warship HMS* Inflexible *picks up survivors from* Gneisenau, *another ship, after the battle.*

Long range cruisers

▼ *German cruiser* Emden *is shot to pieces by Australian cruiser* Sydney.
The German ship was later beached on the island of Cocos.

- **The first German cruiser to enter** the war was the *Goeben*, which shelled the French bases of Bône and Phillipeville less than 24 hours after war was declared. *Goeben* was accompanied by the light cruiser *Breslau*.

- **German cruisers** *Goeben* and *Breslau* arrived in Constantinople in October 1914. They officially became Turkish, but retained their German crews. They spent the war attacking Allied ships in the Mediterranean and Black Sea.

- **The cruiser *Königsberg*** was based in German East Africa. She sank British ships in the western Indian Ocean and shelled ports. She sank in July 1915.

- ***Kronzprinz Wilhelm* cruised** the Atlantic, sinking more than 20 merchant ships. In March she ran out of fuel and limped into Newport, where she was impounded by the USA.

- **The cruiser *Karlsruhe* sank** numerous merchant ships in the Caribbean. Her commander, Captain Kohler, moved to attack undefended Barbados, but his ship suddenly exploded and sank. None of the survivors could explain it.

- **The most successful cruiser** was *Emden*, nicknamed 'Swan of the East'. In August she left the German base of Tsingtao to raid Rangoon. Immediately the port was closed, disrupting British trade for over a month.

- **On 22 September**, *Emden* shelled Madras, setting fire to the vast oil stocks and destroying the docks.

- ***Emden* went** on to sink 23 merchant ships, a Russian cruiser and a French destroyer as well as blasting the docks of Penang to pieces.

- **On 9 November**, she met the Australian cruiser *Sydney* at the Cocos Islands. *Emden* ran ashore and was wrecked after a short battle.

- **After the war the cruiser** *Goeben*, renamed *Yawuz*, remained on active service with the Turkish navy until 1973.

England attacked

- **In 1914**, German and British fleets faced each other across the North Sea. The British were based at Scapa Flow in the Orkneys, the Germans at Kiel.

- **The British Grand Fleet** was made up of 28 dreadnought battleships, nine battle-cruisers, eight heavy cruisers, 26 light cruisers and 77 destroyers.

- **The German High Seas Fleet** had 16 dreadnought battleships, six battleships, five battle-cruisers, 11 light cruisers and 61 destroyers.

- **In general the German ships** were newer with more accurate guns and more effective armour than their British counterparts. However, the British commanders and captains tended to be more experienced.

- **Instead of one big battle**, the Germans intended to lure small sections of the British fleet to sea, then destroy them with a more powerful group of ships.

- **The campaign began** on 16 December 1914. A force of German battle-cruisers under Admiral Franz von Hipper steamed out of the mist to bombard Hartlepool and Scarborough. The ships shelled the docks and gun emplacements, but some shots hit the towns. Over 200 people were killed.

- **Six British destroyers** nearby came to investigate, but retreated when they realized the German ships were battle-cruisers. They radioed for help.

- **The British sent eight cruisers**, four battle-cruisers and six battleships to attack the Germans. Unknown to the British a much more powerful force of German battleships and cruisers lurked over the horizon.

- **However, the mist thickened** and a storm began. The two fleets missed each other in the bad weather and turned for their home ports.

- **The Germans believed** that their plan would have succeeded had it not been for the bad weather. They decided to try again when an opportunity arose.

▶ *A newspaper report details the damage caused by the German attack on Scarborough in December 1914.*

The Battle of Dogger Bank

● **In January 1915** the Germans tried again to lure British ships to destruction. This time they did not attack British coastal towns, but British ships.

● **On 24 January**, German Admiral von Hipper led four battle-cruisers, four light cruisers and eight destroyers to attack the British fleet at Dogger Bank.

● **British Admiral David Beatty**, with five battle-cruisers, six cruisers and four destroyers, was protecting the fishing boats.

● **Beatty ordered his ships** to open fire. The German battlecruiser *Blücher* was badly damaged, as was the British flagship HMS *Lion*.

● **Major Harvey of the Royal Marines** won a Victoria Cross for leading the fight to save HMS *Lion*. He died of his wounds.

▼ *At the Battle of the Dogger Bank, the German cruiser* Blücher *was badly damaged, causing her to capsize. She later sank in the shallow waters with a great loss of life.*

● **Admiral Beatty signalled** his ships to chase the fleeing Germans while *Lion* attacked *Blücher*. The other captains misread the signal and attacked *Blücher* instead. The *Blücher* was sunk, but the other German ships escaped.

● **The Germans lost** 954 men killed, 189 taken prisoner and 70 wounded. The British lost 15 killed and 80 wounded. The British had won the battle.

● **A hit on the German battle-cruiser** *Seydlitz* started a fire that almost spread to the main ammunition store.

● **The Germans installed firewalls** around the ammunition stores on all their ships. This was to have a major impact at the Battle of Jutland (see page 136), when Hipper and Beatty met again in battle.

▲ *The Victoria Cross is the highest award for bravery given to British servicemen and women.*

. . . FASCINATING FACT . . .
British battle-cruisers were known as 'The Big Cats' because some of them were named after wild cats.

Enter the U-boats

● **U-boats, or** *Unterseebooten,* **were German submarines** used to attack Allied merchant and naval ships. They came in various shapes and sizes, and were armed with guns, torpedoes or mines.

● **When the war broke out,** Germany had 33 U-boats in operation, with another 28 in construction. A few were 125-tonne ships able to operate only in coastal waters, but most were 200-tonne craft able to cruise the Atlantic.

● **U-boats were powered** to around 15 knots by diesel engines. As these needed air to work properly, they could only be used at the surface. U-boats used electric batteries when submerged. These lasted only a few hours and limited speed to 6 knots.

● **The rules of war allowed** enemy merchant ships to be sunk, but only after the crew had been given time to escape in boats. Neutral ships heading for an enemy port could be searched and any goods useful to the war effort could be destroyed or taken.

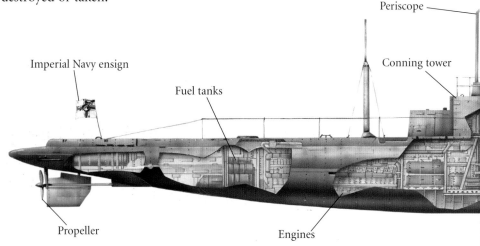

Periscope

Imperial Navy ensign

Conning tower

Fuel tanks

Propeller

Engines

● **Commanders found** the rules difficult to follow. Many merchant ships were faster than U-boats. It was more effective to sink enemy ships quickly.

● **On 4 February 1915**, Germany announced that it would sink all Allied merchant ships without warning in an area surrounding the British coast. Neutral ships were warned to make their nationality clear, or risk being sunk.

● **Kaiser Wilhelm II** was worried about possible civilian casualties. He insisted that U-boat captains should not sink passenger ships without warning.

● **Neutral nations**, especially the USA, protested fiercely to Germany. Some said they would declare war if their ships were sunk.

● **German Admiral von Pohl** ordered U-boat captains to sink ships without warning only if they were certain the target was Allied. If they were not certain they had to surface to find out, then open fire.

● **The period** that followed became known as 'restricted U-boat warfare'.

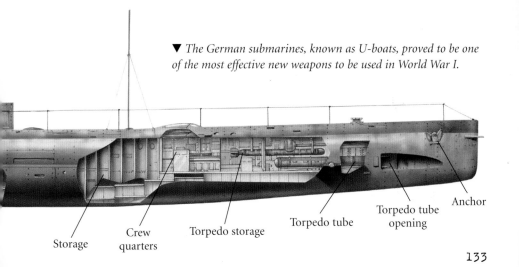

▼ *The German submarines, known as U-boats, proved to be one of the most effective new weapons to be used in World War I.*

Storage

Crew quarters

Torpedo storage

Torpedo tube

Torpedo tube opening

Anchor

Q-ships

● **The restrictions placed** on commanders of U-boats meant that they preferred to surface when attacking a merchant ship. This allowed them to ensure the ship was an enemy, and to use their gun rather than torpedoes.

● **U-boats carried many shells** for the gun, but only a few torpedoes. Captains preferred to use their gun whenever possible.

● **Captains were supposed** to give the merchant crew time to get into boats before opening fire. Some merchant captains tried to radio for help, causing the U-boat captains to open fire at once.

● **In March 1915** the British began using Q-ships. These were merchant vessels with hidden guns. Q-ships were sent to waters known to be patrolled by U-boats.

● **If a U-boat surfaced** near a Q-ship, a few men would get into a boat and row away. When the U-boat approached, the hidden guns would be revealed. Q-ships had larger guns than U-boats and usually won the fight that followed.

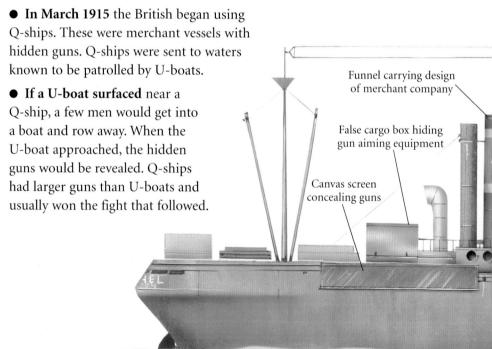

Funnel carrying design of merchant company

False cargo box hiding gun aiming equipment

Canvas screen concealing guns

- **The most successful Q-ship captain** was Gordon Campbell. He was awarded a Victoria Cross, Britain's highest medal for gallantry.

- **It was illegal** for a merchant ship to fire on a warship. The Q-ships therefore carried naval crews and naval flags, but these were only revealed just before the Q-ship opened fire.

- **Q-ships were filled** with lightweight timber so that they were unlikely to sink if holed.

- **U-boat captains soon learned** about Q-ships. They began opening fire from a distance, and used torpedoes without warning on larger ships.

- **By late in 1916** the Q-ships were no longer effective. They were withdrawn from service.

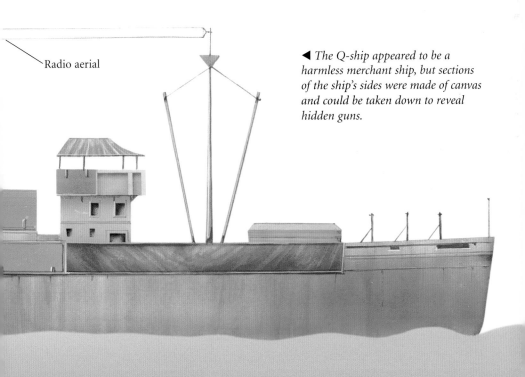

Radio aerial

◀ *The Q-ship appeared to be a harmless merchant ship, but sections of the ship's sides were made of canvas and could be taken down to reveal hidden guns.*

Lusitania

- **By May 1915,** German U-boat commanders had become wary of Q-ships. Even unarmed merchant ships could cause problems by radioing for help from fast destroyers that patrolled waters near the British Isles.

- **It had become dangerous** for U-boats to surface and warn of an attack on merchant ships close to Britain. They tended to use torpedoes.

- **The German ambassador in the USA** issued warnings about U-boat activity. He told US citizens not to travel on ships passing close to Britain.

- **On 1 May 1915,** the unarmed British liner, *Lusitania*, left New York for Liverpool. It would be legal for a U-boat to sink her, but only if warning was given so that crew and passengers could escape.

- **At 2.15 p.m.** on 7 May the *Lusitania* was hit by two torpedoes fired by U20. Captain Schwieger gave no warning, having seen British destroyers nearby.

- *Lusitania* **was steaming** at high speed and developed a serious list (leaning to one side). It was almost impossible to launch the lifeboats and she sank.

- **American public opinion was outraged** by the attack. Former President Theodore Roosevelt said the sinking was 'piracy on a vast scale'.

- **US President Woodrow Wilson protested** to the Kaiser. The Kaiser publicly ordered that passenger liners must not be sunk without warning.

- **Secretly the Germans scaled back** their U-boat warfare. They did not want the USA to join the Allies.

2—SUPPLEMENT TO THE GRAPHIC, MAY 15, 1915—1

THAT HAS STAGGERED HUMANITY: THE TORPEDOING OF THE LUSITANIA

DRAWN BY CHARLES DIXON, R.I., FROM MATERIAL SUPPLIED BY SURVIVORS

▲ *The losses on* Lusitania *were particularly heavy because lifeboats could not be launched properly due to the way the ship tilted over as it sank.*

.... FASCINATING FACT ....
Lusitania sank in only 19 minutes. In all, 1198 people died, of whom 128 were citizens of the USA.

The blockade of Germany

▼ *The British Grand Fleet at anchor in the Firth of Forth. The fleet was kept ready for instant action in case the German fleet was sighted at sea.*

● **When war began**, British First Lord of the Admiralty, Winston Churchill, ordered the Royal Navy to begin the blockade of Germany.

● **The English Channel was closed** to all ships, except those belonging to Britain or France on official war business.

● **The Shetland and Orkney islands** were patrolled by the Grand Fleet. They sank or captured any German or Austrian merchant ships they found.

● **Neutral ships were boarded** by British naval officers. If they were heading for Germany, they were searched. Goods likely to be useful to the German army or navy were seized. Such goods were called 'contraband'.

● **In March 1915**, the British navy established a search centre on the Orkneys. All merchant ships entering the North Sea were ordered to stop there, even if heading for a neutral country.

● **It was soon discovered** that the neutral countries were importing far more explosives, food, steel and other contraband goods than before the war.

● **The British began impounding** all contraband heading for neutral countries unless the ship's captain could prove it was not going to be passed onto Germany. The British government paid the market price for these goods.

● **In February 1916**, the British introduced a 'Black List of Companies' thought to be smuggling contraband to Germany. All their ships and goods entering the North Sea were confiscated without payment.

● **Many neutral countries**, including the USA, objected to the British blockade. The British refused to back down.

● **By the spring of 1916**, Germany was beginning to suffer shortages of key materials. The German navy was ordered to break the British blockade.

The High Seas Fleet goes to sea

● **Since the Battle of Dogger Bank**, Kaiser Wilhelm had refused to allow the large ships of the High Seas Fleet to go to sea. He wanted his navy intact to use as a threat during peace negotiations.

● **Sir John Jellicoe**, commander of the British Grand Fleet, also had orders not to risk his main force as this would leave Britain helpless against U-boats or invasion. It was widely said that 'Jellicoe is the only man on either side who could lose the war in an afternoon'.

● **The naval war was carried** on by U-boats attacking British merchant ships, and by destroyers and torpedo boats patrolling the North Sea close to the German coast.

- **Most of the North Sea** was in the complete control of the Royal Navy, which was therefore able to impose its blockade of Germany.

- **The Germans knew** that many neutral countries resented the British blockade, which was damaging their trade and cutting profits. However, the neutral countries would not take any real action so long as the British had unchallenged control of the seas.

- **In January 1916**, German Admiral Reinhard Scheer began sending his larger ships to sea on short patrols. These gave his men experience, but did nothing to convince neutral countries that he was able to challenge the Royal Navy.

- **The German moves** caused the British to move their battle-cruisers and their fast battleships from Scapa Flow to Rosyth.

- **The main British Grand Fleet** remained at Scapa Flow under the command of Jellicoe.

- **In April**, Scheer devised a plan to cripple the British Grand Fleet. He would send his U-boats to lurk unseen off Rosyth and Scapa Flow. Then he would take the High Seas Fleet to sea. When the British left port to attack, they would be sunk by the U-boats.

- **On 30 May 1916**, the German High Seas Fleet went to sea.

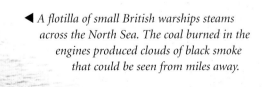

◀ *A flotilla of small British warships steams across the North Sea. The coal burned in the engines produced clouds of black smoke that could be seen from miles away.*

The Battle of Jutland begins

● **The initial plan** of German Admiral Scheer was abandoned because his U-boats were short of fuel. They were forced to return home before the weather cleared enough for the main fleet to go to sea.

● **Instead, Scheer planned** to send his battle-cruisers and cruisers, under Admiral Hipper, to threaten Allied merchant ships off Norway. This, he hoped, would lure the British battle-cruisers to sea where they could be sunk.

● **Radio signals ordering** the German battle-cruisers north were sent out for the British to intercept, while Scheer and his main battle fleet followed.

● **British Admiral Jellicoe learned** of the German signals and sent his battle-cruisers to sea under Admiral Beatty. However, Beatty also had the 5th Battle Squadron of four fast battleships, 12 cruisers and 28 destroyers.

● **Jellicoe then** took the Grand Fleet to patrol the sea to the north of Beatty.

▼ *HMS* Iron Duke, *the flagship of Admiral Jellicoe, fires its guns as it steams into action at the Battle of Jutland on 31 May 1916.*

KEY

* Battle of Jutland
* Scheer's German battle fleet
* Jellicoe's British battle fleet
* Beatty's battle-cruiser fleet
* German submarines

1 Denmark
2 Netherlands

▶ *The Battle of Jutland was fought in the North Sea. Neither the British nor German commanders realized that they faced the main battle fleet of their enemy.*

● **Beatty steamed** towards Norway, with cruisers and destroyers spread out in front to scout for the Germans.

● **Meanwhile, Hipper was heading** north with five battle-cruisers behind a screen of four cruisers and 33 destroyers.

● **At 2.15 p.m.** the British cruiser *Galatea* saw smoke to the east and set off to investigate. It proved to be from a Norwegian merchant ship. The German cruiser *Elbing* was also investigating. At 2.30 p.m. the cruisers opened fire.

● **The two cruisers radioed** to their admirals that they were in action. Beatty and Hipper ordered their ships to head towards the battling cruisers. At 3.48 p.m. the rival battle-cruisers opened fire on each other.

● **The Battle of Jutland** had begun, almost by accident.

143

The Battle of Jutland ends

- **Around 4 p.m.** British battle-cruiser *Indefatigable* and *Queen Mary* suddenly blew up. The explosions were triggered by fires in the ammunition stores.

- **When British Admiral Beatty's** four battleships came in sight, German Admiral Hipper fled south.

- **Hipper's move was to lure Beatty** towards the High Seas Fleet. At 4.33 p.m. Beatty was astonished to see the High Seas Fleet come over the horizon.

- **Beatty turned his ships** around, exchanging fire with the leading German ships. His ships were heavily outgunned, but he hoped to lure the Germans towards British Admiral Jellicoe who was now steaming south at full speed.

- **At 6.15 p.m.** the two mighty battle fleets sighted each other. The leading ships on both sides opened fire, pounding the enemy with heavy shells.

- **Unknown to the British**, many of their shells were faulty – they exploded on impact on the German armour rather than penetrating before exploding.

- **Scheer ordered his destroyers** to launch a mass of torpedoes at the British battleships. While Jellicoe manoeuvred to evade them, Scheer fled.

- **Further manoeuvring** meant that at sunset Jellicoe was between Scheer and Germany. Jellicoe hoped to begin the battle again at dawn.

- **British destroyers sighted** a damaged German battleship, *Pommern*, and mistook it for the main German fleet. Jellicoe turned in the wrong direction. By dawn on 31 May, Scheer was steaming rapidly for home.

- **John Cornwell won a VC** at Jutland, aged just 16. He stayed at his gun on HMS *Chester* even though the crew had been killed. He died of his wounds.

▲ *The letter home written by John Cornwell before he won his VC. The 16-year-old boy died in Grimsby hospital of his wounds three days after the battle.*

The U-boats return

▲ *Torpedoes being loaded into a German U-boat from a supply ship. By restocking their stores, fuel and weapons, U-boats could remain at sea for long periods of time.*

● **When the Battle of Jutland was over**, both sides studied the results. The British lost three battle-cruisers, three heavy cruisers and eight destroyers; the Germans one battleship, one battle-cruiser, four light cruisers and five destroyers.

● **The British had lost more ships**, and more important ships. Scheer realized that he had been lucky to escape with his fleet intact.

● **It was decided** that the German fleet would not go to sea again, but be retained as a threat in peace talks. The war would be continued by U-boats.

● **German supreme naval commander**, Admiral von Tirpitz, had resigned due to ill health in March 1916. He was replaced by Scheer, who also retained command of the High Seas Fleet.

● **On 24 March 1916**, a cross-channel ferry named *Sussex* was sunk without warning by a U-boat. Two US citizens were injured. Furious messages were exchanged between the American and German governments.

● **The dispute between the USA** and Germany ended in August when Germany promised to abide by the rules of war. President Wilson warned that if Germany broke its promises then the USA would join the Allies.

● **In January 1917**, the new commander of the German Army, Paul von Hindenburg, told the Kaiser that the army could not mount a war-winning offensive in that year.

● **German Chancellor Bethmann-Hollweg suggested** that Germany should concentrate on U-boat warfare.

● **In January 1917**, U-boats had been sinking an average of 320,000 tonnes of Allied shipping each month. If all restrictions on U-boat captains were lifted, it was thought the total would rise to 600,000 tonnes each month. Neutrals would probably cease trading with Britain.

● **German Chancellor Bethmann-Hollweg** thought Britain would make peace within six months. Kaiser Wilhelm agreed and the U-boats were unleashed.

British convoys

- **In January 1917**, Germany announced that it would commence 'unrestricted U-boat warfare' on 1 February. The USA immediately cut off all diplomatic relations.

- **The new style of U-boat warfare** meant that in a large area around the British Isles, the Germans could sink any ship without warning.

- **The Germans justified** this by stating that all ships bringing goods to Britain were helping to fight. It did not matter if the ship itself were neutral, nor what goods it carried. The Germans claimed it was a legitimate target.

- **In only the first month** of unrestricted U-boat warfare, sinkings almost trebled in number.

- **Within weeks it became clear** that the British would be starving by September if something were not done to stop merchant ships being sunk.

- **On 19 June**, British Admiral Jellicoe told the government that he could not guarantee food supplies unless the U-boat bases in occupied Belgium were captured.

- **The British government ordered** General Haig to launch an offensive to capture the ports. After months of bloody fighting, the attack failed.

- **In April**, seven US merchant ships were sunk after the USA declared war on Germany. US President Wilson reacted by refusing to send large numbers of troops to France unless their safety at sea could be guaranteed.

- **On 24 May**, the Royal Navy introduced convoys in the Atlantic.

- **On specified dates**, up to 50 merchant ships leaving a port in Canada or the USA would be escorted by one cruiser, six destroyers, 11 armed fishing boats and two fast motor gunboats.

▼ *A British naval airship flies above a convoy of merchant ships. From above, the crew of the airship could spot U-boats lurking beneath the surface of the sea and warn the convoy to alter course away from danger.*

Starvation looms

- **In June and July 1917**, only merchant ships not in convoy were lost to U-boat attack.

- **In June, a flotilla of American destroyers** arrived in Britain. The first convoy they escorted was attacked by U-boats, but no ships were lost.

- **The convoy system doubled** the numbers of U-boats being sunk by the Royal Navy each month to four. However, the Germans were building U-boats faster than they were being sunk – they were winning the war at sea.

- **As convoys reduced** the effectiveness of torpedoes and guns against merchant ships, the Germans made increased use of mines. Vast numbers were laid in and around British ports.

- **In August 1917**, a German motor gunboat sank the British merchant ship *Brussels* in the North Sea and captured her crew. The commander of the *Brussels* was Captain Charles Fryatt, who on an earlier voyage had fought off a surfaced U-boat by ramming it with his ship.

- **The Germans put Captain Fryatt** on trial for taking part in the war. After a one-day trial held behind locked doors, Fryatt was shot.

- **Neutral countries turned** against Germany. They were appalled that U-boats were allowed to sink without warning and that merchant ships were not allowed to fight back.

> ...FASCINATING FACT...
> A U-boat crew heard a Morse Code message: 'Surface or I will explode my depth charge'. It surfaced and was captured, but there was no depth charge. A diver had done it to see what would happen.

▼ *Naval mines were dropped from ships or submarines. When they reached the sea floor, the metal arms opened out to serve as anchors, while the mines rose on steel cables to predetermined positions.*

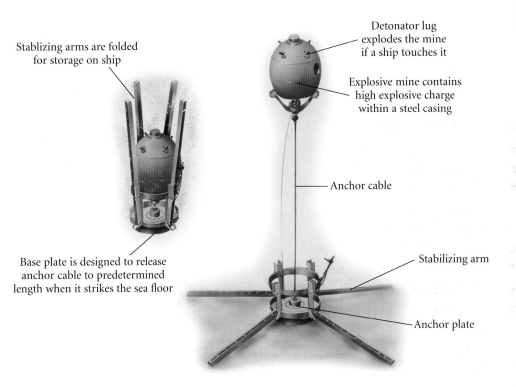

Stablizing arms are folded for storage on ship

Detonator lug explodes the mine if a ship touches it

Explosive mine contains high explosive charge within a steel casing

Anchor cable

Base plate is designed to release anchor cable to predetermined length when it strikes the sea floor

Stabilizing arm

Anchor plate

● **In October 1917** the British perfected an underwater mine. They laid hundreds in the Straits of Dover, blocking the main route to the Atlantic.

● **On 6 December** a French ship, *Mont Blanc*, loaded with ammunition, was part of a convoy assembling in Halifax, Canada. It suddenly exploded, killing 1600 people and wounding 9000 more.

War at sea ends

● **By January 1918** it was clear that the U-boats were failing to starve Britain into surrender. However, they continued to inflict losses on the merchant ships.

● **German surface warships** remained a problem. Two cruisers attacked a convoy near Norway, sinking nine merchant ships and two British destroyers. The Royal Navy was now desperate for a knockout blow.

▲ *The entrance to the harbour at Zeebrugge is blocked by old ships deliberately sunk by the British. The port was out of action for weeks.*

● **A plan was devised** by British Admiral Sir Roger Keyes to block Zeebrugge, which was extensively used by U-boats.

● **Keyes' plan involved** sinking three old cruisers filled with concrete in the harbour mouth, while two submarines packed with explosives would moor alongside the harbour wall, then be blown up. The German defences would be distracted by the landing of marines.

● **The naval raid on Zeebrugge** successfully blocked the harbour to all but the smallest craft. It was weeks before the Germans had the port working again.

● **In April 1918**, the British learned that the powerful German High Seas Fleet was once again at sea, steaming north along the Norwegian coast. The Germans just missed two large convoys, which they could have destroyed.

● **Before the British Grand Fleet** could reach the area, the German fleet had returned to Germany.

● **On 18 October**, German Admiral Scheer ordered all U-boats to return to port. On its way back, one U-boat sank the *Saint Barcham* merchant ship in the Irish Sea. It was to be the last ship torpedoed in the war.

● **On 27 October**, Scheer issued orders for the High Seas Fleet to steam up the Thames and attack London. There was an immediate mutiny. The sailors refused. The war at sea was over.

...FASCINATING FACT...
In February 1918, a liner carrying 2400 US troops was torpedoed and sunk in the Atlantic. All but 210 men were rescued.

Revolution in Russia

- **After the failed peace moves** of December 1916, the Russian government trembled. The mystic Rasputin had been murdered by a group of noblemen, but the Tsarina continued to control the government and to appoint her favourites in place of men of ability.

◀ *The* Aurora *battleship. The Russian navy was heavily infiltrated by radical politicians and posed a real threat to the government in St Petersburg from its naval base nearby. In October it was the navy that began the Communist revolution.*

- **The Grand Duke Alexander begged** Tsar Nicholas to return to the capital city Petrograd (modern St Petersburg) to dismiss the incompetents in government and take control.

- **The Chairman of the Duma,** or Council of State, Rodzyanko, wrote to the Tsar warning that if nothing was done to ease the conditions of workers in the industrial cities, there would be serious trouble.

- **Tsar Nicholas refused** to leave the command of his armies. However he sent General Khabalov with a force of 100,000 soldiers to impose martial law on the capital city.

- **On 7 March**, a few factories went on strike. Many went to the large Nevsky Prospect open square in St Petersburg, carrying banners demanding more food at cheaper prices. The next day more factories went on strike.

- **On Sunday 11 March**, vast crowds, of up to half a million, seethed through St Petersburg. Demonstrations took place in many cities at the same time.

- **When Khabalov ordered** his army to take to the streets, most refused. Some men shot their officers and went over to the side of the demonstrators. Even the most loyal Cossacks refused to leave barracks, being too frightened of the vast crowds.

- **On 15 March**, Tsar Nicholas finally visited St Petersburg. His train was surrounded by crowds of workers before it reached the city. Nicholas abdicated the throne in favour of his popular brother Michael. However, Michael refused.

- **For the first time in its history**, Russia did not have a monarch. A provisional government had to be elected and was then instructed to draw up a new constitution.

- **The first decision** of the provisional government, led by Alexander Kerensky, was to continue the war.

America declares war

- **When war broke out in 1914**, the USA remained neutral and was not directly affected by divisive European issues.

- **Many USA citizens in 1914** were immigrants from Europe. They tended to support their mother countries in the war.

- **The USA quarrelled** with Britain in the autumn of 1914 when the Royal Navy began stopping US ships from steaming to Germany.

- **It was agreed that no goods** likely to be useful to the war effort would be sent from America to Germany, but that peaceful trade could continue.

- **In February 1915**, a serious quarrel broke out with Germany. The German navy said that without notice it would sink any ships heading to Britain.

- **President Wilson told Germany** that he would declare war if any US ships were sunk. When *Lusitania* was sunk and many Americans killed, he moved to break diplomatic relations. Germany called off the campaign.

- **American public opinion** was outraged by the execution of Edith Cavell. Stories of German behaviour in occupied areas also upset Americans.

- **On 31 January 1917**, Germany once again announced unrestricted warfare on merchant ships. Wilson said he would declare war if any US ships were sunk.

- **On 1 March**, German plans to persuade Mexico to attack the USA were discovered. American public opinion turned firmly against Germany.

- **On 20 March** a U-boat sank an unarmed American merchant ship. On 6 April 1917, the USA declared war on Germany.

▶ *In front of the US Congress, President Wilson asks for a vote to declare war on Germany. The vote was carried by an overwhelming majority.*

The doughboys

◀ *An American recruitment poster of 1917 shows 'Uncle Sam', a popular cartoon figure that represented the Federal government of the USA.*

● **Just two months after the USA declared war** on Germany, General John Pershing arrived in France to take command of the American Expeditionary Forces in Europe. In fact it was an empty gesture as there were no such forces.

...FASCINATING FACT...
The Americans called their infantry 'doughboys' because the buttons on
their dress uniforms looked like doughballs. Vast numbers of
doughboys would be in Europe, but not for many months to come.

● **The USA had a population of 93 million,** larger than any belligerent
country except Russia, and produced 45 million tonnes of steel each year,
more than any country in the world.

● **However, the vast wealth,** manpower and industrial output of the USA
was being used for entirely peaceful purposes. It would take time to turn
the USA into a great military power.

● **When the USA entered** the war, the US army consisted of 190,000 men
spread in small detachments across the country and in the few overseas
possessions. They were mainly used for police or peacekeeping duties and
had no experience of modern warfare.

● **The armed forces lacked** the necessary equipment. There were few tents,
no field hospitals and virtually no cold weather clothing. American soldiers
tended to stay in base during bad weather.

● **The Americans had no heavy artillery,** nor many machine guns. The
British offered to lend the Americans the guns they needed, but Pershing
preferred to wait for his own weapons.

● **They also had no experience** of moving armies across any land except their
own, and almost no idea how to feed and supply a large force in the field.

● **It would clearly be months** before the Americans would make much
difference on the battlefields of Europe.

● **By 31 October 1917** there were 86,000 US troops in France. They were
put into a quiet sector of the front line to gain experience of real combat.

The Nivelle Offensive

- **In February 1917**, the new French commander, General Robert Nivelle, tore up the plans agreed by his predecessor with the British. He had a bold, new plan.

- **"We have the formula for victory,"** declared Nivelle. He wanted to use the infiltration tactics so successful at Verdun, but on a massive scale.

- **Nivelle planned to attack** on a 50-km front around Soisson and Rheims with 5000 guns and one million men. He said he would break through in three days.

- **Nivelle's confidence** and charismatic personality boosted French morale. But by explaining his plan to the troops, Nivelle gave away the element of surprise.

- **The British attacked** Arras on 9 April, a week before the French offensive, to divert German reserves. Canadian troops captured Vimy Ridge.

- **Nivelle's offensive began** before dawn on 16 April with a short, well-aimed bombardment of German positions. However, the Germans had resited most of their guns as they had expected the French bombardment.

- **When the French infantry advanced**, they found much of the barbed wire intact. This slowed them down so that they could not infiltrate.

- **Since the French last scouted** the area of the attack, most of the German strongpoints had been moved and new ones built.

- **The repositioned German machine guns** began firing. Casualties were high.

- **After two weeks**, the French had captured the German front line, but not reached the second line. Around 225,000 Frenchmen were killed or wounded.

▶ *British lancers ride through Arras in April 1917 on their way to the front line. Cavalry were prepared in case a breakthrough was achieved, but they were never used.*

French mutiny

▼ *British soldiers cross a wrecked canal on a narrow wooden bridge. The British army was entirely unaware of the French mutinies until weeks later.*

- **On 29 April**, a French infantry regiment paraded prior to returning to the front line. When ordered to march, the men refused. They said they would not take part in another suicidal attack ordered by General Nivelle.

- **On 4 May**, another infantry regiment refused to move. On 16 May, three more refused to obey orders to attack.

- **The disorder swept through** the French army like wildfire on 28 May. Soon, men of 54 divisions were disobeying orders. Nivelle had only two loyal divisions. He put them in the front line to defend the trenches.

- **A regiment at Soissons hijacked** a train to Paris on 30 May, determined to invade Parliament. Officials diverted it.

- **On 1 June**, a regiment at Tardenois assaulted their officers, then rioted through the town for two days.

- **At Esternay thousands of soldiers invaded** the railway station demanding trains to take them home. More rioting followed.

- **The French government concealed** what was happening. Not even British commander Sir Douglas Haig knew about the mutinies. The Germans did not attack.

- **As the mutinies and rioting** reached a peak in the first week of June, Nivelle was sacked and General Pétain became the new commander in chief.

- **Pétain listened to grievances** and promised changes to pay and conditions. He arrested men who had used violence, but peaceful demonstrations were not punished. By 20 June the mutinies had ceased.

- **The French Parliament chose** a new prime minister, George Clemenceau. Together Clemenceau and Pétain worked to restore French morale and fighting ability.

New British tactics

● **Over the winter of 1916–17**, the British under General Sir Douglas Haig devised new tactics and plans. General Sir William Robertson told King George V, "It is no longer a question of aiming at breaking through the German lines. It is now a question of attacking limited objectives with the minimum loss."

● **The British studied** French General Nivelle's infiltration tactics and decided that they would be useful for small attacks to capture specific features.

● **The tactic of attacking at night,** used the previous year on the Somme, was a success. The staff officers decided to use it on a larger scale in future.

● **Infantry officers reported** that they had most success when they attacked as soon as the artillery barrage stopped. Artillery officers suggested improving on this with what they called a 'creeping barrage'.

● **A creeping barrage meant that the artillery** aimed slightly further away with each shot fired. Infantry could therefore move forwards just behind the last exploding shell without fear of being hit.

● **Engineers suggested** tunnelling underneath the German trenches and planting large quantities of explosives. These mines could blow up a German strongpoint from underneath, as effectively as an artillery shell could be falling on top of it.

● **Infantry found** that the Germans knew where British front line trenches were. If the Germans suspected an attack, they would pound those trenches.

● **Instead of gathering** in the main trenches for an attack, the infantry crawled into holes in the ground. The German artillery missed them when it hit the trenches.

● **The Royal Flying Corps** (RFC) promised to bomb German supply dumps and transport links immediately. This would hinder the German defence.

● **The new tactics were tried out** on a small scale at Arras in April. They proved very successful and all the limited objectives were captured in just 48 hours.

▶ *A British howitzer fires on the German lines. Howitzers were guns that fired heavy shells over a short distance. They were useful in battles where the front lines did not move quickly.*

Trench raiding

- **One of the most important new tactics** devised by the British was the 'trench raid'.

- **Ever since late 1914**, patrols had launched small night attacks on enemy front trenches. These early raids were designed to kill a few Germans and find out their unit, for intelligence purposes.

- **Throughout 1915 and 1916**, regiments made larger raids. Up to 100 men would cross to the enemy trenches. After a short fight, they would return.

- **British commander Sir Douglas Haig** now ordered that all regiments should mount a large raid once a month and smaller raids whenever possible.

- **Small raids continued** to involve only a dozen or so men. They tried to creep into enemy trenches, kill a few sentries and return without being seen.

- **These raids were intended** to worry the Germans on the front line, make them nervous and stop them from relaxing at any time.

- **Larger raids might involve** up to 500 men. They were carefully planned in advance and had specific objectives, such as planting explosives to demolish a strongpoint or to demolish a section of German trench.

- **Some officers formed** special raiding units that were highly skilled at these attacks. Other officers did not approve of raiding as it could cause casualties without achieving any real gains.

- **All raids gave the British** experience of warfare and were useful for getting new recruits accustomed to fighting and the trenches.

- **Throughout the summer** of 1917 raids took place all along the British section of the front line and continued until the end of the war.

◀ *Men of the Lancashire Fusiliers prepare for a raid by fixing bayonets to their rifles, ready for hand-to-hand fighting in the German trenches.*

Messines Ridge

- **After the success** of the limited offensive at Arras in April, British commander Sir Douglas Haig decided to try the new tactics again in May.

- **General Sir Herbert Plumer** suggested that the objective of the attack should be the capture of Messines Ridge. It dominated the area around Ypres, allowing the Germans on top of the ridge to direct artillery.

- **His plan involved** engineers tunnelling 19 huge mines underneath the German trenches, packed with 500 tonnes of high explosive.

- **Plumer planned** that after the mines were blown, his infantry would move forwards behind a creeping barrage, supported by tanks. He hoped to take the ridge with minimal losses to his own men.

- **Before the attack**, Plumer insisted that no men or guns should move during daylight. They had to remain hidden under camouflage nets and move only at night. The Germans had no idea that an attack was about to take place.

▼ *British troops move towards the front line in June 1917. Units nearing the battle zone were ordered to move in loose lines so that they did not form a dense target for German artillery.*

... FASCINATING FACT ...

Plumer was renowned for careful planning and strict discipline. He hated losing men and never risked their lives needlessly. His men admired and trusted him.

- **At 3.10 a.m.** on 7 June, the mines exploded. The German front line was completely wiped out. British, Australian and New Zealand troops waiting to advance were knocked off their feet. The blast was heard as far away as Bedford, England.

- **The creeping barrage** began immediately, while the tanks lumbered forwards and the infantry began to advance.

- **By noon,** the British had captured most of Messines Ridge and were digging new trenches to defend their gains.

- **German counter attacks continued** for five days. The British held firm. Victory was complete.

Third Battle of Ypres

- **On 19 June**, British Admiral Jellicoe told the government that U-boats operating from Belgium were sinking so many British merchant ships that, unless something were done, the country would soon run out of food.

- **The government ordered** their commander in France, Sir Douglas Haig, to capture the Belgian ports from the Germans.

- **General Hubert Gough was in charge** of planning the attack. He decided to use the new tactics, but with a heavy artillery bombardment.

- **On 31 July**, the attack began after the artillery had pounded the German positions for almost two weeks.

- **At Polygon Wood**, the Scottish Black Watch regiment was led into battle by a piper in full dress uniform playing the regimental march on his bagpipes.

- **That evening it rained**, and it continued for almost a week. The heavy artillery bombardment had destroyed the drainage system of the Flanders Plain, which turned to mud.

- **On 16 August**, Gough told Haig that because of the mud, he would be unable to capture the ports. Haig ordered Gough to continue with smaller attacks.

- **September passed** without much rain, so the plain dried out. Haig put General Plumer in charge of a new attack to capture Passchendaele Ridge.

● **Plumer planned and carried out** four advances that captured most of the ridge by early November. Then heavy rains began again. The land turned to liquid mud in which survival was difficult and fighting impossible.

● **After the battle ended** it became clear that the Royal Navy was sinking more U-boats than ever before. The food supply to Britain was safe after all.

▼ *The fighting at the third Battle of Ypres, commonly known as Passchendaele, was hampered by heavy rains and the clay soil that formed thick, sticky mud.*

Knights of the air

- **By early 1917,** air warfare saw aircraft specializing in the three roles of scouting, bombing and fighting other aircraft.

- **The Germans and French publicized** their successful pilots in newspapers, books and films. The French called them 'aces', and the word spread.

- **Albert Ball was a British pilot** who shot down over 40 German aircraft and invented new tactics. He was shot down and killed in May 1917.

- **British James McCudden shot down** 54 enemy aircraft, but was killed when his engine cut out when taking off.

- **Captain G H McElroy was a British ace** and he shot down 42 Germans. He vanished on a routine patrol and no one knows what happened to him.

- **American Raoul Lufbery led a group** of Americans who volunteered for the French air force before America joined the war. The squadron was known as the Escadrille Lafayette. Lufbery was shot down when attacking a German scout in May 1917.

- **The most successful ace** was German Baron Manfred von Richthofen. Between November 1916 and his death on 21 April 1918, he shot down 80 British and French aircraft.

...FASCINATING FACT...
Canadian Billy Bishop shot down 72 German aircraft. The Canadian government did not publicize individual achievements during the war.

▲ *A British pilot in his Sopwith fighter watches a burning German Albatros pass by. At this date most pilots did not have parachutes, so combats were often fatal.*

● **Richthofen was widely known** as the 'Red Baron' because he painted his aircraft completely red. All aircraft in his squadron had red patches. His brother, Lothar, was also an ace pilot who shot down over 40 aircraft.

● **After Richthofen's death** his squadron was taken over by another ace – Hermann Goering. He later joined the Nazi Party and led the German air force in World War II.

The Battle of the Zeppelins

▲ *By flying at high altitude the Zeppelins managed to evade British defences for many months. They dropped bombs on British cities, bringing terror and destruction in their wake.*

● **Before the war** German Count Ferdinand von Zeppelin developed a type of huge airship for long-distance passenger flights. As soon as the war broke out, the airships were taken over by the German army.

● **Zeppelin's airships had a metal frame** containing large bags of hydrogen gas, which lifted the craft into the air. They were powered by engines mounted outside the craft. Crew and bombs were carried in a gondola slung underneath.

● **The Zeppelins entered combat** on 26 August 1914, when one bombed Brussels. For the next six months, Zeppelins bombed army units in France and patrolled over the North Sea.

● **On the night** of 19 January, two Zeppelins bombed the docks at King's Lynn and Great Yarmouth, England. Four people were killed. Other raids followed and much damage was inflicted.

● **Between January and June 1915**, the RFC made 79 flights to attack Zeppelins over England. No Zeppelins were shot down, but eight aircraft crashed and three pilots were killed when trying to land in the dark.

● **On 6 June**, RFC pilot Reginald Warneford managed to get above a Zeppelin returning from a raid. He dropped six bombs, one of which hit the airship and exploded. The Zeppelin crashed in flames.

● **Most Zeppelins flew too high** for British aircraft to catch and attack them. There were never more than 20 Zeppelins in operation, but they bombed Britain almost at will.

● **By the summer of 1917** new British fighters were in operation. The Sopwith Camel was able to fly as high as the Zeppelins. Armed with incendiary bullets, Sopwith pilots could shoot them down.

● **Zeppelins continued** to patrol the North Sea and mount occasional raids, but by Christmas 1917, the Zeppelin menace had been beaten.

● **From October 1917**, Germany started to send large multi-engined bomber aircraft to attack London and towns in southern England. These Gotha and Staaken aircraft inflicted some damage, but British defences were able to limit the number that got through.

The Battle of Caporetto

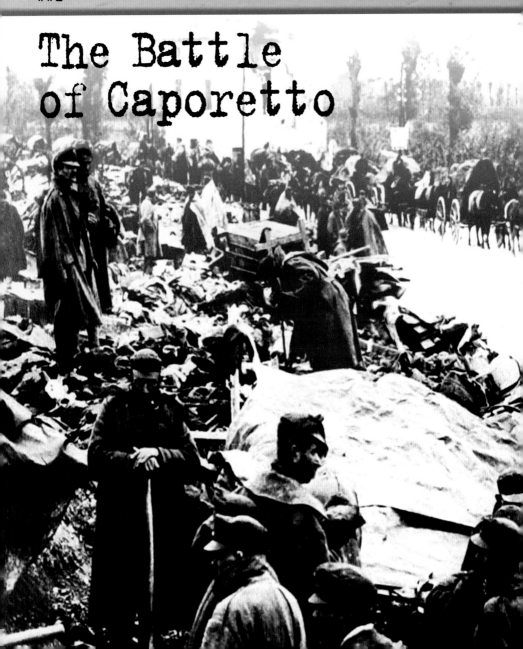

● **By the summer of 1917** the war in Italy had dragged on for two years. The Italian and Austrian armies had faced each other in the valley of the river Isonzo and in the Alps.

● **The Italians were never strong enough** to inflict serious losses on the Austrians, who had put most of their efforts into defeating the Russians. The battles fought on the river Isonzo were short and bloody, but inconclusive.

● **In September** the Italian commander, General Luigi Cadorna, ordered an end to all attacks as his forces were short of artillery shells.

● **Around the towns of Caporetto and Tolmino** there was little fighting, as the roads were used for a major offensive.

● **During August and September**, Italian-speaking Austrians fraternized with the Italians. They talked about how their families were suffering at home. It was a trick to undermine Italian morale in the quiet sector.

● **At 2 a.m. on 24 October** a massive bombardment was unleashed on the Italians around Caporetto. Vast numbers of German infantry attacked.

● **Overwhelmed**, most Italians fled, but some surrendered. By 10 a.m. the Germans had broken through the Italian lines, opening up a 24-km gap.

● **On 26 October**, Cadorna ordered his entire army to retreat. If they had stayed in the Isonzo Valley, they would have been surrounded.

● **Cadorna tried to organize** a defence on the river Tagliamento, but the Germans broke through again. The Italians retreated to the river Piave.

● **The Germans and Austrians** could not keep up with the swift Italian retreat. The Italians were able to escape and organize a defence that held.

◀ *The Italian army retreats from the Isonzo front in 1917. The Italians had fought well, but were overwhelmed by the sudden attack at Caporetto.*

Lenin's revolution

● **After the fall of Tsar Nicholas II,** the Russian Duma (parliament) elected a republican government led by the Socialist leader Alexander Kerensky.

● **Kerensky decided** that Russia would honour all agreements made by the Tsar, expecting other countries to honour their agreements with Russia.

● **As a result,** Kerensky kept Russia in the war. He promised that no offensives would be ordered and trusted that Germany would not attack Russia.

● **In September,** Kerensky had army commander General Kornilov arrested for alleged mutiny against the republic, deeply demoralizing the army.

● **Meanwhile, led by Vladimir Lenin,** an impoverished nobleman who had turned against the Tsarist regime, the Communists plotted a new revolution.

● **Communist activists joined** the committees, known as soviets, that had been elected by factory workers, peasant farmers, soldiers and others to voice their demands to the Kerensky government.

◀ *Russian soldiers carry red cloths on their bayonets as they drive through the streets to show that they have joined the Communist forces.*

● **In September**, the collapse of the food distribution system brought hunger to the cities and to the army. Strikes broke out, organized by the Communists who blamed Kerensky.

● **On 6 November**, Lenin ordered the Red Guards to seize the key public buildings in the capital, St Petersburg.

● **A shot fired** by the battleship *Aurora* signalled the final assault. Red Guards stormed the Winter Palace to arrest the provisional government.

● **Lenin agreed peace** with Germany. Russia handed over vast areas of land in return, allowing Lenin to enforce Communist rule on Russia. Now Germany could turn to the west to gain outright victory.

▼ *Communist revolutionary leader Vladimir Lenin toured the soviets of St Petersburg making a series of powerful speeches to stir up anger against the government. Behind him stands Leo Trotsky, who organized the Communist armed forces.*

The Arabs triumph

▼ *British soldiers march into the city of Kut on 3 March 1917. The rapid advance up the Mesopotamian valley secured local oil supplies for the Allies.*

- **In July 1917** an Arab force working with British liaison officer T E Lawrence captured the port of Aqaba from the Turks. This prompted many Arabs to join the uprising against Turkish rule.

- **British General Allenby was commanding** a British–Indian force in Palestine. He asked Lawrence to persuade the Arabs to coordinate their campaign with his own.

- **In October 1917,** Lawrence led the Arab armies of Sherif Hussein of Mecca to cut the Turkish supply railways near Amman in Syria.

- **On 6 November,** Allenby attacked the Turks at Beersheba. After ten days of fighting, his men reached Jaffa. The Turks fell back into Syria.

- **On 9 December,** Allenby and his army marched into Jerusalem. He became the first Christian soldier to enter the holy city since the Crusades over 700 years earlier.

- **Lawrence and Hussein's younger brother,** Amir Feisal, led the Arabs on numerous raids and attacks across the desert areas behind the Turkish lines.

- **Lawrence wore Arab clothes,** rode camels and lived among his Arab fighters.

- **Sherif Hussein established** complete control around the Muslim holy cities of Mecca and Medina. The Allies promised him that after the war was over, the Arabs would be free of Turkish rule. Hussein thought this meant they would be under his rule.

- **A British–Indian army reached Kut,** where a British army had surrendered to the Turks in 1916. Then it moved on to cut off Persia from Turkey.

- **By the spring of 1918,** Arabs who were loyal to Hussein and led by Lawrence were rampaging through the areas of the Turkish Empire inhabited by Arabs.

Marching from Salonika

- **For two years since the defeats** at Gallipoli and the crushing of Serbia, an Allied army had been camped around the Greek city of Salonika.

- **The army largely consisted** of the surviving Serb army, plus British, French and Australian troops evacuated from Gallipoli. Plans to attack Bulgaria or Austria had come to nothing due to lack of supplies and transport.

- **Greek King Constantine was married** to Sophie, sister of Kaiser Wilhelm of Germany. He did not wish to antagonize his brother-in-law, so he refused the Allies permission to move out of Salonika.

- **The Allies preferred** to keep Greece friendly, so they tried to persuade King Constantine to change his mind. By the summer of 1917, Greek public opinion had turned against Austria.

- **In June King Constantine abdicated** in favour of his son Alexander who appointed the anti-German, Eleutherios Venizelos as prime minister. On 2 July 1917, Greece declared war on Austria, Bulgaria, Turkey and Germany.

- **In December 1917**, the commander at Salonika was replaced by French General Franchet D'Esperery. D'Esperery had travelled extensively through the Balkans before the war and knew the area well. He was known as 'Desperate Frankie' by British soldiers.

- **He told his officers**, "I expect from you savage energy," and demanded a plan to attack northwards within 19 days.

- **Not until July** did D'Esperery have enough lorries and carts to transport his army and supplies over the Balkan mountains to face the armies of Austria and Bulgaria.

- **In August the forces at Salonika** were given permission by the British and French high commands to move north. Stores and supplies began pouring into Salonika onboard British ships.

- **On 15 September**, D'Esperery led his men north, heading for Bulgaria.

▼ *The Allied army marching north from Salonika was a mixed force made up of men from several different nations who spoke more than five different languages and had no agreed method of fighting.*

The Treaty of Brest-Litovsk

- **In November 1917** the Russian Communists, led by Lenin, established control over the vast Russian Empire by carrying out a daring coup in the capital, St Petersburg.

- **In December 1917**, Lenin agreed a ceasefire with Germany, and sent his deputy Leon Trotsky to Brest-Litovsk in Poland to negotiate a treaty with Germany and Austria. Trotsky was told to get peace at almost any price.

- **The Germans were keen** to annex large sections of the Russian Empire, or to see them set up as German-dominated independent nations.

- **The Austrian Empire** was on the point of economic collapse.

- **Once in Brest-Litovsk**, Trotsky came to believe that Germany and Austria were ripe for a Communist revolution, and if he could delay a peace treaty revolutions would break out.

- **In February 1918**, the Germans told Trotsky that unless he signed a treaty immediately, the war would begin again. Trotsky refused, so the Germans invaded Russia.

- **The Russian forces** did nothing to halt the German advance.

- **By 24 February**, the German armies were approaching St Petersburg in the north and were on the river Don in the south.

- **On 3 March**, the Russians signed the Treaty of Brest-Litovsk. Poland, Latvia and Lithuania were annexed from Russia to Germany. Ukraine was set up as an independent country, but was occupied by German forces.

- **Former Tsar Nicholas II** was shot by the Communists in July 1918.

▲ *A photograph of the former Tsar Nicholas II with his family taken while they were prisoners of the Communists.*

Germany turns west

- **Two days after the Treaty of Brest-Litovsk** was signed, Germany, Bulgaria and Austria signed a peace treaty with Romania. The Treaty of Buftea forced Romania to hand the province of Dobrudja to Bulgaria, but gave Bessarabia, which had belonged to Russia, to Romania.

- **As soon as the treaties** of Brest-Litovsk and Buftea were signed, the Germans began their preparations for a mighty offensive in the west. Hundreds of railway trains steamed east to carry German armies from Russia to France.

▼ *Field Marshal Paul von Hindenburg (with walking stick) and General Erich von Ludendorff (facing camera on left) meet with German officers in Brussels.*

...FASCINATING FACT...

Ludendorff believed that if Germany had not beaten Britain and France by the autumn of 1918, it would lose the war.

● **The German army was now in the hands** of two men – General Paul von Hindenburg and General Erich von Ludendorff.

● **Hindenburg was the more senior,** but Ludendorff was the logistics genius. He alone knew how to move and supply the large armies of Germany.

● **In July 1917,** Ludendorff had calculated the relative strengths in manpower, supplies and money of the various countries involved in the war.

● **Ludendorff estimated** that by spring 1919 neither France, Germany nor Austria would be able to continue fighting. Britain, he thought, would be able to continue only at sea, while Turkey would be exhausted but would not be under serious attack.

● **Only the USA,** Ludendorff thought, would be stronger in 1919 than in 1917. By then, America would have mobilized an army of over 2 million men and would be using its great wealth to manufacture huge supplies of weapons.

● **American forces would prove** to be decisive in 1919. They would win the war and impose a peace on Europe drawn up in America.

● **Ludendorff believed** that the British might continue the war alone if France were defeated, but that France would not fight on if Britain were knocked out. Ludendorff decided he had to defeat the British in order to progress. He then drew up his plans accordingly.

The Ludendorff Offensive

● **German General von Ludendorff** had drawn up plans over the winter of 1917 for defeating the British. Each meant massing the men and guns brought from Russia in a solid attacking block. In the end he chose two.

● **'St Michael' would be launched** first as an attack near St Quentin designed to split the British from the French. If that did not work, 'St George' would drive through Armentiéres and push the British into the sea.

● **Ludendorff and his staff** had devised new tactics. Each unit was divided into three waves. They had grenades, flame throwers and light machine guns.

● **These 'stormtroopers' were to race** past strongpoints and jump over trenches to reach the rear of the British lines. They would stop any reinforcements reaching the front line.

● **The second wave**, equipped with rifles and grenades, would capture the trenches. The third wave would tackle emplacements and bunkers.

● **The next day**, the Germans would repeat the manoeuvre until they had broken through. The cavalry and infantry would complete the victory.

◀ *The German Luger automatic pistol had bullets stored in the grip, allowing this model to fire more bullets before reloading than the revolvers used by the British.*

● **At 5 a.m.** on 21 March 1918 the Germans unleashed a barrage by 6000 guns on a front of 64 km. It was the heaviest and best-aimed of the entire war.

● **At 9.40 a.m.** the bombardment at the British rear areas and the German infantry swarmed forwards.

● **In the south**, the Germans did even better than planned. By evening the Germans were right through the British trenches.

● **Further north**, the British held onto the rear defences, though they had lost their forward positions. On 24 March the British retreat began.

▼ *Elite German infantry practise the new stormtrooper tactics behind the lines in the weeks before the attack.*

Ludendorff's failure

● **As the Germans surged forwards**, the senior British, French and American commanders met at Doullens. They agreed that they needed a supreme commander to coordinate the response to the German attack.

● **On 26 March**, they chose French General Philippe Pétain. He took the title General in Chief of the Allied armies in France.

● **Meanwhile, the RFC flew** hundreds of bombing attacks, but they began to run out of bombs.

● **At Hamel, an American brigade** went into battle. They had not yet had time to train in the use of their machine guns. One man had to read from the instruction booklet, while others were shooting at the Germans.

▶ *A heavy howitzer with its barrel aimed to hurl shells at a high trajectory. Shells falling steeply on to enemy defences penetrated deep into the soil before exploding. This allowed them to burst under concrete defences and shatter them.*

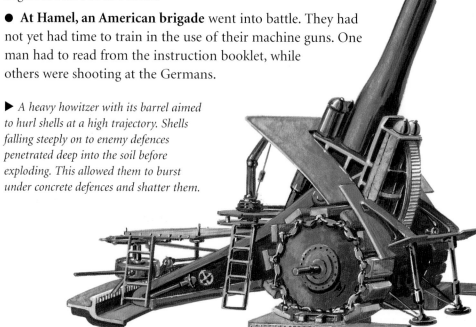

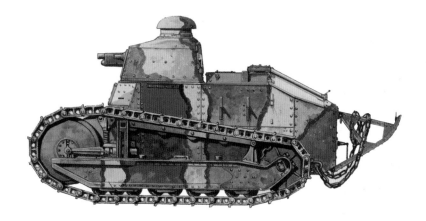

▲ *Equipped with a small gun and carrying only three men this light tank could move quickly to attack enemy infantry, but was highly vulnerable to artillery fire.*

● **On 24 March,** the Germans had built seven monstrous 15-in guns with a length of over 40 m. The shells could reach Paris.

● **The guns were positioned** around the town of Laon and fired shells at regular intervals. They killed many civilians and spread alarm through Paris.

● **On 29 March** the German attack began to lose power. There were enormous difficulties transporting supplies forwards over the shattered landscape.

● **Several German units** took to looting. One entire regiment became drunk after capturing a chateau stocked with thousands of bottles of wine.

● **On 9 April,** the Germans began their St George offensives. British commander Sir Douglas Haig issued a famous order, "With our backs to the wall and believing in the justice of our cause, each one of us must fight on to the end."

● **By 24 April** the new attack had been defeated.

America in action

- **After the mighty German attacks** had been halted by the British, the Allies believed that General Erich von Ludendorff had used up all his troops and ammunition brought from Russia. They were wrong.

- **The Blücher Offensive was aimed** at the French sector under the command of General Duchesne. The area had long been a quiet sector. Duchesne did not believe in the new tactics, nor had his men maintained their trenches.

- **Part of the line was held** by British troops from the Somme, who had been brought here to rest. Their officers asked for timber and sandbags to improve the trenches, but Duchesne refused to hand over valuable equipment.

- **On 27 May** the Germans struck. After a whirlwind bombardment, the stormtroopers poured forwards, supported by their second and third waves.

- **Duchesne refused** to believe that the Germans could break his lines, so he failed to order key bridges over the river Aisne to be blown. The Germans poured across the river Aisne and by nightfall were at the river Vesle.

- **As the Germans poured** towards Paris, French General Pétain asked US General Pershing to send his men in to hold the line.

▼ *A Smith and Wesson Model 1917 .45 calibre revolver. The heavy bullet fired by this gun was able to knock a man backwards with ease.*

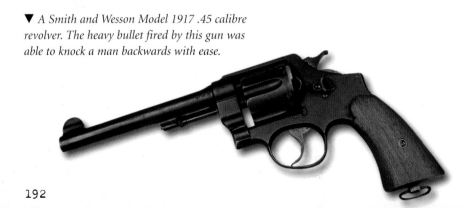

- **The first complete American division** to enter battle was the 3rd Division which marched into Château Thierry in the afternoon of 31 May. The men spent three days digging in, before the Germans arrived on 3 June.

- **The next day** the US 2nd Division entered into battle at the town of Lucyle-Bocage. As before, the German advance ended due to lack of supplies and poor discipline.

- **Ludendorff had lost** almost 25 percent of the men he had had in February. Some units began to argue about orders they did not like.

- **The Germans** began moving relatively unfit and poorly trained men up to the front. Ludendorff and Hindenburg were becoming worried.

▼ *American infantry struggle to reload their heavy machine gun during a training operation in France. To begin with, US soldiers suffered from inadequate training in modern warfare.*

The Habsburg Empire trembles

● **In 1914 the Habsburg Empire** was a complex and multi-national state united only by the fact that the whole area was ruled by the same monarch.

● **During the war**, parts of the empire generally worked together. Certainly the regiments raised in different regions supported each other on the battlefield. But as the war dragged on, problems grew.

▶ *Emperor Franz Joseph of Austria (right) was succeeded by Emperor Carl (left). The younger man proved unable to cope with the pressures of the war.*

● **During the poor harvest of 1916,** the Hungarians refused to sell corn to other areas of the empire.

● **On 21 November 1916,** Emperor Franz Joseph died after reigning for 68 years. Many people in the empire began to wonder why they should remain loyal to the Habsburg Empire. They thought they might be better off with their own national states.

● **The new emperor,** Carl, was just 29 years old. He was intelligent and cared for his people, but had not been trained to be emperor as there had been two heirs in line before him.

● **In May 1917** Carl summoned the Imperial Parliament. He promised wide-ranging social and political reforms, but said they would have to wait until after the war.

● **When Lenin's Communist** revolution grabbed power in Russia, Carl began to fear a similar revolution in his lands.

● **Some of the regiments** freed by the surrender of Russia were moved to face the Italians or the Allied forces in Salonika. Others were positioned within the empire to guard against revolution.

● **By early 1918** the Habsburg Empire was running out of money. Emperor Carl was almost bankrupt.

...FASCINATING FACT...
In Austria, Franz Joseph was emperor, in Hungary he was king and in Dalmatia he was duke. Each area also had its own local government, which cooperated with the central government.

Austria surrenders

- **During 1917,** the Czechs and Slovaks increasingly resented the fact that their wealthy industries were being taxed heavily to support the war effort. Led by Thomas Masaryk, they argued that the war was between Austria and Serbia, and had nothing to do with them.

- **In March 1918,** Masaryk persuaded the Allies to promise complete independence to a new country called Czechoslovakia after the war. Emperor Carl's idea of a federal state was no longer enough.

- **Masaryk began distributing** leaflets to Czech and Slovak regiments, urging them not to fight for the Austrians.

- **The Poles and Slavs** also set up secret organizations, but they were not as successful as Masaryk. Nevertheless, the Allies promised to support their claims to independence.

- **On 24 October 1918,** a massive Italian offensive, supported by British and French troops, took place on the river Piave front in northern Italy.

- **Italian General Armando Diaz** had 57 divisions and 7700 guns to assault the 52 divisions and 6000 guns of Austrian Archduke Joseph.

- **For several days** there was little movement. Then the town of Vittorio Veneto fell to the Italians on 30 October. Next day the town of Sacile was captured, along with bridges over the river Livenza.

▶ *A helmet perched on a rifle marks the grave of a British soldier. In the confusion of trench warfare, many men were hurriedly buried in unmarked graves – and thousands of them are still there.*

▲ The British newspaper, Daily Sketch, *celebrates the fact that Emperor Carl of Austria had announced he was breaking the alliance with Germany on 29 October 1918.*

● **On 3 November**, the Austrian army collapsed. Men threw away their guns and fled. Those that could not run fast enough, surrendered by the thousand to the Italians. In three days the Italians took 300,000 prisoners.

● **When news of the Battle of Vittorio Veneto** reached Emperor Carl, he lost his nerve. He wrote a letter that began, "Since I am filled by unchangeable love for all my nations, I will not place my person as an obstacle to their free evolution…"

● **The letter was taken** to be both an abdication of the crown and the dissolution of the empire. Austria was out of the war.

197

Bulgaria collapses

● **On 14 September 1918**, the Allied forces marching north from Salonika reached Bulgarian defences in the mountains north of the town. They pounded the defenders with artillery, then began an infantry attack.

● **On 15 September**, a 'Yugoslav' division attacked near Mount Vetrenik. The men were drawn from the southern Slav peoples who wanted freedom from the Austrian Empire.

● **On 16 September**, two Bulgarian regiments refused to attack, and discontent broke out elsewhere. Bulgarian General Lukov informed King Ferdinand that he thought the army would not fight much longer.

● **On 20 September**, Lukov ordered a general retreat. He began leading his men back to Bulgaria, abandoning the territories seized by King Ferdinand from Serbia. The Bulgarians were going home.

● **The Bulgarian Communists** led by Alexander Stamboliisky, declared that Bulgaria was a Soviet Republic on 27 September. He led 15,000 armed men towards Sofia. Bulgaria was now fighting a civil war.

● **On 29 September**, the retreating army of Lukov attacked the Communists, crushing the attempted revolution within hours.

● **The Communist leader**, Stamboliisky, fled. He abandoned Communism and became the democratically elected prime minister of Bulgaria.

> **. . .FASCINATING FACT. . .**
> When General Lukov told King Ferdinand that they were losing the war, the king shouted, "Go back to the front line and get killed."

▲ *A unit of Bulgarian infantry man the trenches near Uskub. In 1918 the Bulgarian army abandoned the front line and began marching home.*

● **On 30 September,** Lukov signed an armistice with the Allies. He agreed to hand over all heavy weapons, to allow Allied troops free movement through Bulgaria and to keep his men in barracks.

● **On 4 October,** King Ferdinand abdicated in favour of his son Boris III. Bulgaria was out of the war.

199

Turkey surrenders

● **When the overwhelming** German attacks struck the British lines in France in the spring of 1918, all reserves and supplies were sent to hold the attacks.

● **In Palestine**, British General Allenby, guided by T E Lawrence, delayed his main offensive until September. In Mesopotamia, the Allied advance halted to await supplies.

● **On 17 September**, the assault on the Turks opened with an Arab raid on the town of Deraa. Lawrence utterly destroyed the rail junction, blocking all supplies from reaching the Turkish army in Palestine.

● **On 19 September**, Allenby attacked the Turks in the Jezreel Valley. Lacking supplies and demoralized, the Turks put up little fight. By 25 September, the Australian and New Zealand cavalry were in Amman.

● **The German commander** Liman von Sanders was so surprised by the British attack that he fled in his pyjamas.

● **On 27 September**, retreating Turks massacred over one hundred Arab women and children as revenge. Lawrence began to lose control over the Arabs.

● **A cavalry charge by Australian horsemen** defeated the Turks defending Damascus on 1 October – this turned out to be the last successful cavalry charge of modern warfare.

● **After the fall of Damascus**, the Turks effectively stopped fighting. A few desultory rearguard actions in Mesopotamia and Syria took place.

● **On 30 October**, Turkish diplomats boarded the British battleship *Agamemnon* to sign an armistice.

● **The Sultan was discredited** by the defeat and overthrown by General Mustafa Kemal, who was then elected as president of the new republic of Turkey in 1923. He radically modernized the government and economy.

◄ *The entry of the Arab horsemen of Prince Feisel into Damscus, Syria, in October 1918 marked the final collapse of Turkish resistance to the Allies.*

Germany's 'Black Day'

- **On 18 July**, the French and Americans launched an attack to surround the Germans. General Ludendorff saw the trap and pulled his men back.

- **On 8 August**, a massive British–Canadian–Australian attack, led by 600 tanks, was launched on the German lines in front of Amiens.

- **At Amiens the German lines gave way**, allowing the Allies to advance 11 km by dusk. Thousands of men surrendered, many more fled to the east. Morale collapsed as six entire divisions gave up the fight.

- **When Ludendorff studied** the reports from Amiens he declared, "8 August was the Black Day of the German army." He lost hope of winning the war.

- **Ludendorff conferred** with Kaiser Wilhelm. They agreed that the war must end, but negotiations should only begin if Germany were doing well in a battle so that they could negotiate a favourable peace.

- **On 11 August**, Foch, the Allied commander in France, ordered the British to halt the attack at Amiens. German reserves were strengthening the line.

- **On 2 October**, the US 307th Regiment was surrounded by a German counter attack at Charlevaux. They held out until 7 October when an American attack reached them. Only 252 out of 700 men survived.

- **In October** a new government took over in Germany under Prince Max Scheidemann-Erzberger.

- **Prince Max sent a note** to US President Wilson asking for peace negotiations to begin.

▶ *Part of a large crowd of German soldiers captured at Amiens in August 1918. The collapse of morale proved to be catastrophic for Germany.*

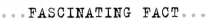

...FASCINATING FACT...
On 8 October, Sergeant Alvin York reached the flank of a German battalion. In the next hour he killed 25 Germans, captured 135 more and cleaned out 35 machine guns posts.

Armistice in November

- **On 26 October**, German generals von Ludendorff and von Hindenburg met with Prince Max. They told him that the German army could hold out until the winter weather brought an end to Allied attacks.

- **Prince Max refused** to prolong the war. He fired Ludendorff and removed Hindenburg from all but purely ceremonial roles.

- **On 6 November**, the new supreme commander, General Groener, told the Kaiser that if they did not surrender within a week the army would collapse.

- **On 7 November**, Prince Max sent a delegation to agree an armistice. He asked the Allies to suspend fighting. French General Foch refused.

- **On 9 November**, representatives of Britain, France and the USA met the German delegation in a railway train parked in the Forest of Compiégne.

- **At 1 a.m. on 11 November** Prince Max replied that the German government agreed to the armistice terms. At 5 a.m. Erzberger signed the armistice. It stated that fighting would cease everywhere at 11 a.m.

- **On 10 November**, the British marched into the Belgian town of Mons, where they had first begun to fight more than four years earlier.

- **The same day**, a British air force pilot was shot down and badly wounded. His name was William Johns, later to become the author of the Biggles books.

- **On the night of 10 November** the statue of the Virgin Mary on top of Albert Cathedral, damaged by artillery fire in 1916, fell to the ground. Ever since it had been damaged, men believed that it would signal the end of the war.

- **The last man to be killed** was Canadian Private George Price, shot by a German sniper at 10.58 a.m. on 11 November.

▼ *When news of the armistice reached London, large crowds of cheering people formed and surged towards Buckingham Palace to begin peace celebrations.*

Talks at Versailles

- **On 18 January 1919**, the Peace Conference to agree the final terms, opened in Paris, in the Palace of Versailles. Representatives of all countries attended, as did many other groups and organizations.

- **The various delegations** came to Paris with differing aims and objectives, and with very different degrees of power and influence.

- **Germany, Turkey and Bulgaria were defeated countries** with little negotiating power. Their delegations hoped to limit the penalties imposed on their countries by the victors.

- **Russia had been defeated**, but now its Allies had won the war. The Russians wanted the Treaty of Brest-Litovsk cancelled and the return of all the lands that had belonged to the Tsar.

- **France had been invaded** by Germany twice in less than 50 years. The French wanted to impose conditions on Germany that would make a third invasion impossible. France also wanted the town of Alsace and Lorraine.

- **Belgium had been almost completely occupied** by Germany, but its army had fought on and had captured areas of German colonies in Africa. The Belgians wanted to regain their pre-war border in Europe and to gain the German colonies.

- **Britain wanted Germany** to pay for the damages inflicted during the war. Britain also hoped to take control of as much of the overseas German Empire as possible.

- **Italy wanted to gain** the Italian-speaking parts of the Habsburg Empire and hoped to gain control of the Dalmatian coast and Albania as well.

● **Austria, Hungary and other parts of the old Habsburg Empire** wanted to gain their independence, but not to be penalized for the actions of the empire during the war.

● **The USA wanted a peace settlement** that would make a new war in Europe unlikely. President Wilson thought the best way to achieve this was to set up an independent state for each nationality in Europe.

▼ *A German tank is broken up ready for the metal to be sold as scrap. Once the fighting was over the weapons could be dismantled and men could return to peaceful occupations.*

A new Europe

- **In June, the Treaty of Versailles** ending World War I was signed in the Palace of Versailles. Few countries got what they wanted – the victors got most.

- **Other treaties were signed** between smaller countries, known as the Versailles Settlement. The map of Europe was completely redrawn.

- **France gained** the towns of Alsace and Lorraine from Germany, while Belgium and Denmark also gained small border areas. Italy gained the Italian-speaking parts of the Habsburg Empire.

- **Serbia was merged** with the Slav-speaking areas of the old Habsburg Empire to form the new Yugoslavia. The Habsburg Empire was divided up into Austria, Hungary and Czechoslovakia. Romania gained Transylvania.

- **Poland was created** by joining the Polish-speaking areas of the former Russian, Habsburg and German empires.

- **Russia was given** back the Ukraine, but was forced to accept the independence of Finland, Estonia, Latvia and Lithuania.

- **Bulgaria lost small slices of territory** to Greece, Yugoslavia and Romania. Turkey retained only the lands that make up modern Turkey.

- **Several areas of Europe** voted on which country they wished to join.

- **German colonies overseas were divided** up between Britain, Australia, Japan and France.

- **The Arabs were freed** from Turkish rule, but did not become fully independent. Iraq (Mesopotamia), Palestine and Jordan were put under British mandate. Syria and Lebanon went to a French mandate.

KEY

1 Norway	10 Hungary
2 Sweden	11 Czechoslovakia
3 Denmark	12 Lithuania
4 Netherlands	13 Latvia
5 Belgium	14 Estonia
6 Luxembourg	15 Albania
7 Saarland	16 Greece
8 Switzerland	17 Bulgaria
9 Austria	18 Portugal

▲ *The Versailles Conference sought to satisfy the ambition of the smaller nations of Europe to achieve self-government, while respecting historic divisions and frontiers. The new face of Europe was destined to survive less than 20 years.*

The League of Nations

- **The cost of World War I** was horrific for all involved. There was a widespread desire to avoid any future war. Nobody wanted to face such a terrible conflict again.

- **All countries had lost large** numbers of soldiers killed in battle, or dying of their wounds. Over eight million soldiers died.

- **US President Wilson suggested** that the countries of the world should join together to form a League of Nations that could ensure future peace.

- **The League of Nations** would be open to any country that wished to join. The members would pledge to work in friendship to solve any disputes.

- **If any country attacked** a member of the League, then all members of the League would mobilize their armed forces to impose a peaceful solution.

- **It was decided** that the League of Nations should be based in Switzerland. Large, luxurious offices and debating chambers were built in which the diplomats could meet.

- **A wave of optimism** swept the world that the Great War that had just ended was 'the war to end all wars'. It was hoped that the League of Nations would allow sensible people from each country to ensure world peace.

- **However, the League** had no method of enforcing any decisions it took. If a country chose to ignore the League, nothing could be done about it.

- **Some countries chose not to join** the League of Nations, even the USA.

- **For a while** the League of Nations worked well. However, new disputes arose that divided its members. Within 20 years it would be obsolete.

Military casualties

Germany	1,800,000
Russia	1,700,000
France	1,380,000
Austria	1,290,000
Britain	743,000
Italy	615,000
Romania	335,000
Turkey	325,000
Others	434,000

▲ *The numbers of military personnel killed during World War I was enormous. Although Germany lost more men than any other country, this represents 2.8 percent of its population, while France lost 3.5 percent and Russia almost 10 percent.*

Storing up trouble

● **US President Wilson wanted** the new borders to mark out areas where people of different nationalities lived. However, many areas had mixed populations that would not allow this. The Treaty of Versailles drew frontiers that left many people living in the 'wrong' country.

● **The borders of Poland** caused a particular problem. The Polish-speaking areas were large, but had no access to the sea that would allow trade with the rest of the world. Poland was therefore given the port of Danzig (Gdansk), which had a population 98 percent German.

● **Article 231 of the Treaty of Versailles stated** that the war had been caused by German aggression. The Germans believed that they had been responding to Russia's attack on Austria and deeply resented the clause.

● **Those countries deemed** to have attacked their neighbours were made to pay for damage caused (reparations). The bill for Germany was £24 billion – about £22,000 billion today. Bulgaria and Turkey were expected to pay less.

● **Germany was forbidden** from having an army of more than 100,000 men or more than six battleships. It was not allowed to have any submarines nor to have an air force of any type.

● **Many areas of eastern Europe** would suffer from unrest as people of different nationalities argued about rights in different areas.

> ... **FASCINATING FACT** ...
> The war was followed by a severe economic depression, caused partly by damage incurred during the war and partly by the reparations and other economic clauses of the Treaty of Versailles.

▶ *A cartoon from 1919 predicts that war will return by 1940 – it proved to be an accurate prophecy.*

PEACE AND FUTURE CANNON FODDER

The Tiger: "Curious! I seem to hear a child weeping!"

● **The Germans greatly resented** being blamed for the war, being forced to pay such vast reparations and losing so much territory.

● **In the 1920s and 1930s** the anomalies of the Treaty of Versailles were exploited by politicians eager to gain power.

● **In 1939 Nazi Germany**, led by Adolf Hitler, invaded Poland to regain Danzig and nearby areas. World War II had begun.

Mr. Melvin Millon
2–1571 Coronation Dr
London ON   N6G 5N9

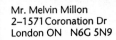

WORLD WAR II

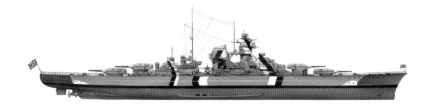

Rise of the Nazis

● **After its defeat** in World War I (1914–1918), Germany was demoralized. Money became worthless, unemployment was high, businesses were ruined.

● **Germany's new democratic government** became unpopular. Adolf Hitler and his National Socialist Party (Nazis) saw an opportunity to win support.

● **Hitler joined** the German Workers Party in 1919. In 1920 it was renamed the National Socialist Party and Hitler became its leader in 1921.

● **Born on 20 April 1889** in Austria, then part of the Austria-Hungary Empire, Adolf Hitler had fought in the German army in the 1914–18 war.

● **Hitler did not accept** Germany's defeat. He wrote a book called *Mein Kampf* (My Struggle) while in prison in 1923 for trying to overthrow the government. It contained anti-Communist, anti-Jewish and racist ideas.

▼ *Hitler is honoured with the Nazi salute, often accompanied with 'Heil Hitler'.*

- **The Nazis used violence** to intimidate opponents. Their own private army, the Brownshirts, beat up protestors, such as Communists and democrats.

- **In 1932,** the Nazis won 230 seats in an election for the German Parliament or *Reichstag*. On 30 January 1933 Hitler became Chancellor (head of the government).

- **The *Reichstag*** building burned down on the night of 27 February 1933. The Nazis blamed Communists, and used the fire as an excuse to ban more opposition.

- **In August 1934,** Hitler was pronounced leader, or *Fuhrer*, of Nazi Germany.

- **Germans hoped that Hitler** would restore prosperity as the Nazis built roads, factories and weapons. However, Hitler also intended to reform society. He began to limit personal freedom and to persecute the Jews.

▶ *Hitler emerged from World War I with a vision of Germany reborn and a new German Empire.*

Nations re-arm

- **After World War I**, people hoped there would never be another 'great war'. There were calls for disarmament – no more guns, battleships or warplanes.

- **The USA** became isolationist. People in America did not want any more war and thought Europe should settle its own problems.

- **In 1935**, Britain and Germany signed a naval treaty allowing Nazi Germany to modernize its fleet, though with fewer ships than Britain. Navies began building new battleships.

- **There had been little development** in warplanes since World War I until the 1930s when new, faster designs began to appear in the USA and Europe.

- **Hitler wanted to tear up the Treaty of Versailles** (the 1914–18 peace treaty). He demanded an end to reparations (compensation paid by Germany to countries it had invaded) and the return of territory taken from Germany after World War I.

- **Germany was not supposed** to have an air force, but German pilots learned to fly at glider clubs. They then joined Hitler's new *Luftwaffe* (air force).

- **In 1936**, Hitler sent German soldiers to reoccupy the Rhineland, an area on Germany's western border occupied by the Allies from 1918 until 1930. It had been demilitarized under the Treaty of Versailles.

- **Japan, Italy, USA, Britain and France** also began to rearm. There was an international peacekeeping body, the League of Nations, but it was powerless to stop the great powers from rearming.

- **War preparations** began. In July 1936, the British government ordered the mass production of gas masks in case of poison gas attacks.

...FASCINATING FACT...

In 1936–39, German volunteers fought in the Spanish Civil War.
German pilots tested the new Me 109 fighter and other
warplanes in Spain.

▶ *Women assembly
workers helped the arms
drive, as factories in
Britain increased
production of Spitfires,
Hurricanes and other
new warplanes.*

Czech crisis

● **In 1937 Hitler wanted a new *Reich* or empire**, with all German speakers in Europe living inside the enlarged borders of Germany.

● **In March 1938**, Hitler entered Austria, declaring it a province of Germany. Many Austrians cheered, but Jews faced persecution.

● **In Czechoslovakia**, 3.5 million German speakers lived in an area known as the Sudetenland.

● **In April**, Britain and France discussed what to do if Hitler threatened the Czechs. He wanted the Sudetenland, saying that German speakers there were being ill-treated.

● **In May**, Czechs under 60 years old were called up for defence training. The Czech government feared war and tried to negotiate with Hitler.

● **In August**, Britain promised to help the Czechs if they were attacked. Prime Minister Neville Chamberlain hoped this would stop Hitler.

● **On 30 September**, European leaders met in Munich, Germany. Hitler (Germany), Daladier (France), Chamberlain (Britain) and Mussolini (Italy) were present, but there was no Czech leader.

● **The Munich agreement** conceded the Sudetenland to Hitler. Chamberlain came home, promising 'peace for our time'.

▶ *In 1938, Germany took over the Sudetenland, signalling the end for the Czechs. Hitler surveys his new territory with high-ranking military escort.*

220

KEY

◼ Allies	7 East Prussia	15 Albania
◼ Axis Forces	8 Netherlands	16 Greece
1 Norway	9 Belgium	17 Bulgaria
2 Denmark	10 Luxembourg	18 Republic of
3 Sweden	11 Czechoslovakia	Ireland
4 Estonia	12 Switzerland	
5 Latvia	13 Austria	
6 Lithuania	14 Hungary	

▲ *The frontiers of pre-war Europe had been drawn by the peacemakers at Versailles, after World War I (1914–18). Political unrest of 1938–39 began in Austria and Czechoslovakia, then Poland. Britain and France were allies of Poland, but did little to stop Hitler taking Czechoslovakia.*

● **German troops** entered the Sudetenland, and on 5 October Konrad Heinlein, the Sudeten leader, welcomed Hitler.

● **On the same day**, Czech President Benes resigned. The Czechs were doomed.

Japanese Imperialism

● **Japan had ambitions** to create an empire in Asia, to provide raw materials for its industries and markets for its goods.

● **In the 1920s,** Japan signed international disarmament treaties, but Japanese army leaders blamed their government for giving in to the demands of the USA, Britain and France.

● **Some Japanese generals** disapproved of parliamentary government and did their best to get rid of the democratic politicians that they disliked.

▼ *A terrified baby cries amid the rubble of Shanghai, August 1937, after the Japanese air raids.*

● **A new emperor**, Hirohito, came to the throne in 1926. The Japanese revered the emperor as a god, although Hirohito's main interest was marine biology.

● **In 1931**, Japan attacked the region of Manchuria in northeast Asia and set up a puppet government under a Manchurian prince. Japan was preparing for war with China.

● **When the League of Nations** criticized Japan for its aggression in Manchuria, Japan pulled out of the League in 1933.

● **In November 1936**, Japan signed a pact with Germany to fight worldwide Communism.

● **In July 1937**, Japan invaded China. In August 1937, the Chinese city of Shanghai was bombed by Japanese aircraft. Around 7000 British civilians were evacuated. By the end of 1938, Japan controlled most of eastern China.

● **In December**, Japanese forces opened fire on British and US ships in the river Yangtze, claiming they had mistaken them for Chinese vessels.

● **By 1938**, Japan's navy was strong enough to challenge the Americans and British in the Pacific. It included battleships and aircraft carriers.

▶ *Hirohito, emperor of Japan. Shy and inoffensive in person, the emperor was. effectively controlled by warmongers in his government.*

Mussolini

▶ *Mussolini, Italy's Fascist leader, dreamt of a new Roman Empire. The name 'Fascism' comes from the Latin word 'fasces', which were bundles of rods carried before magistrates in ancient Rome.*

● **Benito Mussolini (1883–1945)** was leader of Italy's Fascist Party, which he founded in 1919. He fought in World War I and later edited a newspaper.

● **He seized power in Italy** in 1922 after 24,000 of his 'Blackshirt' followers marched on Rome. The king made Mussolini the new prime minister.

● **Mussolini was known as 'Il Duce'** or 'The Leader' – he dreamed of a new Roman Empire. He also promised to make Italy a modern state. His government built the first motorways in Europe.

● **After Hitler became Germany's leader** in 1933, Mussolini sought friendship with the Nazis, but hoped another European war could be avoided.

● **In 1935, Mussolini sent** Italian troops to invade Abyssinia (Ethiopia), which had repulsed Italian troops in the 1890s. The Abyssinians were ill-equipped, and by May 1936, Mussolini claimed victory.

● **In May 1938**, Mussolini signed a 'friendship treaty' with Britain, saying Italy did not want a war in Europe. He later went to the Munich talks (see page 13).

● **But in May 1939**, Mussolini joined Hitler in the 'Pact of Steel', a political and military alliance between Germany and Italy – the start of the Axis alliance.

● **In 1939**, Italy attacked Albania, forcing King Zog to flee. Mussolini wanted his army, navy and air force to control the Mediterranean.

● **Mussolini kept out of World War II** until June 1940. Hoping that the fighting would soon be over, he then declared war on France and Britain.

...FASCINATING FACT...
In 1934, Italy's soccer players gave the Fascist salute before the World Cup final – which Italy won 2–1, beating Czechoslovakia.

Spain's Civil War

- **In 1931**, Spain became a republic. The new government had many opponents, including the Roman Catholic Church and Catalan and Basque nationalists who wanted self-government.

- **The government lost control** as peasants seized land and workers went on strike. In July 1936, General Francisco Franco led a revolt to save Spain from Communism.

- **Franco's revolt** started a civil war between Republicans and Communists on one side and Nationalists and Fascists of the Falange Espanola on the other.

- **Nazi Germany and Fascist Italy** sent help to Franco, including aircraft and pilots of the German Condor Legion, and 50,000 soldiers.

▲ *Franco, a national hero after army service in Spain's North African colonies, led the Nationalists to victory, and ruled as dictator of Spain until his death in 1975.*

- **The Communist Soviet Union** helped the Republicans with over 5000 Russian troops. The Soviet Union took the Republic's gold for safekeeping, but kept it.

- **An International Brigade** of over 50,000 foreign volunteers fought alongside the Republicans. One was the English writer George Orwell (who later wrote *Animal Farm* and *1984*).

- **The bombing** of the Basque city of Guernica in April 1937 caused international outrage. Picasso's painting of the horrors is called *Guernica*.

● **Both sides committed** atrocities. Catholic priests were executed by Republicans. International Brigade commander Lazar Stern was shot on Stalin's orders when he went back to Russia.

● **The Republicans** held most territory, but Franco's army had more tanks, guns and planes. Barcelona and Madrid were captured by Franco's troops in January and March 1939.

● **In April 1939**, the war ended. Franco became dictator. He was friendly to Nazi Germany, but Spain did not fight in World War II.

▼ *Republican soldiers prepare to toss grenades. Fighting in Spain was bitter and bloody. Neither side showed much mercy to the other, or to civilians.*

War clouds gather

- **In November 1938**, Jews in Germany were attacked on *Kristallnacht* (Crystal Night). Jewish-owned shops were looted, while police looked on.

- **In January 1939**, the German government mobilized women under 25 years old for civilian service.

- **German factories** were producing 600 planes a month. In February 1939, the British government announced plans to distribute air raid shelters to civilians.

- **Hitler threatened** Poland. He demanded Danzig, officially a free city, belonging to neither Poland nor Germany. The Poles refused.

- **In March 1939**, Britain's Prime Minister Neville Chamberlain promised to defend Poland, should Germany attack the Poles.

- **In April 1939**, Britain announced it was conscripting for military service all young men under 21 years of age.

- **On 23 August**, Hitler and Stalin signed a surprise non-aggression pact. Hitler knew he could attack Poland, without fear of Soviet interference.

◀ *A Czech woman tearfully gives the Nazi salute. After their country was taken by the Nazis in 1938, Czechs knew they had lost their freedom.*

▲ In Britain, newspaper headlines warned that war was imminent. Sir Neville Henderson was British Ambassador in Berlin, Ribbentrop the German Foreign Minister.

- **Two days later**, Britain declared that there would be war if Poland were attacked. Britain and France would fight.

- **The Poles tried** to call the Germans' bluff. They had a large army, but its equipment was old. Polish cavalry was matched against German tanks.

- **In Britain**, Winston Churchill had long warned of the danger posed by Hitler and had called for increased military readiness. He was about to be proved right. The British government planned civil defence.

Air raid precautions

● **Trenches were dug** in parks for people to shelter in during air raids. This was one of the first signs that Britain feared war was coming.

● **Sandbags were piled up** around building entrances and windows. The sand shielded people from the effects of blasts and shrapnel (bits of metal from an exploding bomb).

● **To cope with expected** heavy casualties, London Transport made plans to convert 400 buses into ambulances within five hours as soon as war began.

● **Air raid sirens** were set up in cities, often on roof tops. There were two kinds – one hand-worked siren, one electrical. The sirens' wail warned people that enemy planes would soon be overhead.

● **Sirens made two signals** – one to tell people that an air raid was expected, the other giving the all clear when the raiders had flown away.

● **To protect people** from poison gas attacks, 38 million gas masks were given out. There were also cot-masks for babies.

● **Leaflets were circulated** detailing what to do in an air raid. One tip was to put sticky tape over windows to reduce the risk of being hurt by flying glass.

● **Public air raid shelters** were built. The biggest were deep tunnels 425 m long and big enough to hold 9000 people. Smaller DIY shelters were given to poor families, and sold at a small charge to wealthier families.

● **The outdoor Anderson shelter** was made of corrugated metal and was erected in the garden. It was big enough for several people.

● **The indoor Morrison** shelter looked like an upturned steel table with wire mesh sides. People could sleep inside it. It was strong enough to protect them even if the ceiling fell on top of them.

▼ *Inside an Anderson shelter, with (inset) an outside view showing the roof covered with soil and grass. Around 2.5 million of the steel DIY home safety kits were issued before September 1939.*

Evacuation

▼ *Off to the country. Young evacuees leave London with bags, gas masks (in the cardboard boxes) and identity labels.*

● **The sufferings of civilians** in the Spanish Civil War showed that aerial bombing could destroy a town in less than one hour.

● **Military planners** thought that in any new war, the main threat would come from the air, from vast fleets of enemy bombing planes.

● **New bombers**, such as the German Heinkel III and British Wellington, came into service. They were as fast as the enemy fighters of that time.

● **Governments feared** that mass bombing would cause panic in cities. Never before had civilians been exposed to this kind of attack.

● **So in 1937**, the British government started to draw up plans to evacuate mothers and children from the towns to the country, where evacuees were to live with host families.

● **In January 1938**, it was announced that all children in Britain were to be issued with gas masks.

● **Evacuation began** in the summer of 1939. On 30 August, 1.5 million British children were on the move. Each child had a name tag and a bag with clothes, books, comics and sandwiches for the train.

● **Some schools** moved their staff and pupils away from London to country houses. Some children thought it was fun, like going on holiday.

● **About 10,000 German–Jewish children** were brought to England under the *Kindertransport* (child-moving) scheme during 1938 and 1939.

...FASCINATING FACT...
Statues, paintings and other historic treasures were moved to safe places – some were even hidden in caves.

Poland invaded

- **Just before 6 a.m. on 1 September 1939**, German troops began crossing into Poland. Air attacks had begun an hour before.

- **Poland was easy to invade** because it had a very long land frontier with Germany and the ground was flat – ideal for tanks and trucks.

- **In late summer**, the ground was dry and firm. This was important because in 1939 Poland had few good roads.

- **German radio broadcasts**, disguised as Polish messages, spread confusion among the Polish forces.

- **The German airforce** or *Luftwaffe* was too powerful for the Poles, though Polish pilots put up a brave fight in old-fashioned aircraft.

- **The Polish army** had few defensive positions. Polish generals relied on counter attacks, including cavalry, to stop the German advance.

- **Polish forces** were forced to retreat, but many soldiers were trapped on the wrong side of the river Vistula as the Germans rolled forwards at high speed.

- **By 12 September**, German armies were running low on fuel, but Polish resistance was reduced to isolated pockets of troops.

- **On 17 September**, Poland's fate was sealed when Soviet armies invaded from the east. The next day, the Polish government fled into exile.

- **Poland's capital, Warsaw**, held out until 28 September. Resistance forces fought on through the winter, and more than 80,000 Poles escaped abroad. Many came to Britain, to continue the fight.

▶ *Nazi atrocities began soon after Poland was invaded. On 5 September 1939, Jews in this Polish village were forced to dig their own graves before being executed in reprisals for the killing of four German soldiers.*

Britain and France at war

● **On 3 September 1939**, Britain and France declared war on Germany. They were sworn, as allies, to help Poland.

● **However, Britain and France** did little to help the Poles. Their forces were not ready to attack Germany. None of their planes could even reach Poland without refuelling.

● **Britain and France** had to mobilize for war. The French took 16 days to get their heavy guns out of storage. By then the Germans had won the battle for Poland.

● **The British and French waited** to see what Hitler would do next. Generals made plans to attack Germany – through Norway, Belgium, or Greece – but none of these plans could be carried out.

◄ *Scanning the skies, a 'spotter' uses binoculars to look for enemy planes approaching London.*

● **The French army** was Europe's biggest, with over 5 million men. Britain had a much smaller army, but it had Europe's biggest navy.

● **Many believed the German army**, or *Wehrmacht*, was not ready for war because the Germans had no heavy tanks, unlike France.

● **However, Germany had** more than 1000 bombers – twice as many as Britain's air force and four times more than France.

● **The Royal Air Force** (RAF) re-equipped with modern aircraft but by September 1939, it still had many old planes.

● **Britain relied on the Royal Navy** to protect its trade routes around the British Empire and to blockade German ports, cutting off fuel and war supplies.

● **Germany had concentrated** on building submarines, called U-boats. In September 1939, the German submarine *U-29* sank the British aircraft carrier HMS *Courageous*.

▶ *To defend London, barbed wire was put up, especially around important buildings, such as Big Ben.*

'The Phoney War'

LET'S GO-

WINGS FOR VICTORY

▲ A famous wartime poster of a young RAF pilot was designed to boost morale.

● **In the first month of war**, Britain expected terror-bombing. Hospitals were cleared for thousands of casualties, but few German planes appeared.

● **People waited for a German attack** on the Western Front of France and Belgium, as in 1914, but nothing happened. People called it 'The Phoney War' – the war that did not happen.

● **One sign of war** was the blackout. Every home had to have tightly closed blinds and curtains at night to prevent light showing and attracting enemy bombers.

● **Propaganda reminded people** that there was a war on. Ministry of Information posters urged Britons to save pennies, dig trenches, work harder, and not spread rumours.

- **The British** sent an army to France. The British Expeditionary Force had 158,000 men, who were mostly experienced troops. The order was to await a German attack.

- **There were casualties** at sea. The liner *Athenia* was sunk by a U-boat on 3 September – the day war began. More than 100 people died.

- **The RAF** dropped leaflets calling on Germans to surrender.

- **After his victory** in Poland, Hitler made vague offerings of a peace conference, but these were rejected by Britain and France.

- **The USA remained neutral**, saying it would not ship weapons to any of the countries at war. Sweden and Norway were also neutral.

▶ *British soldiers in training, wearing anti-gas clothing.*

...FASCINATING FACT...
In Britain, road deaths doubled in the winter of 1939. Streetlights were turned off – cars and buses had headlamps covered with cardboard.

First shots at sea

- **German ships and planes** began laying magnetic mines in November 1939 and 60 Allied ships were sunk in two months.

- **U-boats went on patrol** into the Atlantic and North Sea. Their mission was to attack British and French shipping.

- **British battleship** *Royal Oak* was sunk by the *U-47* on 14 October 1939. The attack took place at the Royal Navy base of Scapa Flow, in the Orkneys north of Scotland.

- **The German navy's** fast ships raided Allied convoys. On 5 November 1939, the merchant ship *Jervis Bay* fought the German battleship *Admiral Scheer*, but was sunk.

- **The British set out** to hunt German raiders, such as *Graf Spee* and *Scheer*, known to be lurking in the Atlantic Ocean.

- **On 13 December 1939**, the Royal Navy cornered the *Graf Spee* off the coast of Uruguay, in South America. Three cruisers, *Exeter, Ajax* and *Achilles*, opened fire on the larger German battleship.

- **The Battle of the river Plate** left *Exeter* badly damaged, but *Graf Spee* was also hit by gunfire and damaged.

- **Captain Langsdorff**, commanding *Graf Spee*, entered Montevideo harbour for repairs. Uruguay was neutral and by law, no warship could stay there longer than 24 hours.

- **After 72 hours**, *Graf Spee* was ready to leave. Langsdorff believed a large force of British ships was waiting outside Montevideo. Fearing a humiliating defeat, he ordered *Graf Spee* to be scuttled (deliberately sunk).

- **Only three British ships**, *Ajax, Achilles* and *Cumberland*, were waiting outside. The British celebrated a naval victory.

▼ Graf Spee *in flames in Montevideo. The world had waited to see what the German ship would do. Now the press reported that it was a blazing, crippled wreck.*

Rationing

▶ *In Britain, ration books became part of everyone's daily life, along with an identity card.*

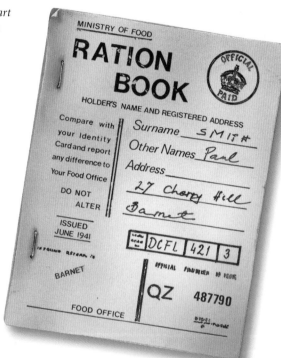

MINISTRY OF FOOD

RATION BOOK

OFFICIAL PAID

HOLDER'S NAME AND REGISTERED ADDRESS

Compare with your Identity Card and report any difference to Your Food Office

DO NOT ALTER

ISSUED JUNE 1941

BARNET

FOOD OFFICE

Surname ____ SMITH
Other Names ____ Paul
Address ____
27 Cherry Hill
Barnet

DCFL 421 3

QZ 487790

- **Rationing was a way** to make sure that food and clothing were available to everyone in wartime. The British government controlled the sale of food, including meat, eggs and sugar.

- **In November 1939**, the British Ministry of Food announced that butter and bacon would be rationed, from January 1940.

- **Food rationing began** in Britain on 8 January 1940. Imported foods such as bananas became very hard to find in shops, and chocolate and ice cream became rare treats.

- **People were given ration books** containing coupons that they handed over to the shopkeeper when making a purchase.

- **The ration in 1940** allowed each person 170 g of butter each week. Meat was rationed from March 1940.

- **Hotel guests** had to hand their ration books to the hotel owner or manager during their stay.

- **The Ministry of Food** set up 1300 regional food offices to run the national rationing scheme.

- **Food became daily news**, and the BBC 'Radio Doctor', Charles Hill, broadcast advice on healthy eating.

- **People living in the country** ate better on the whole than people in towns. Rabbit, game and fish were not rationed and fresh vegetables were easier to get.

- **Hoarding food** was discouraged, but still went on. There was also a 'black market' trade in illegal food. In March 1940, a London woman was fined £75 for having 140 weeks' ration of sugar.

▼ *Queuing for food on a cold winter's day in 1940. Women did most wartime shopping and cooking, and most of the waiting outside shops that often had little on sale.*

Denmark and Norway

▶ *A German cycle battalion spearheads the invasion of Norway in May 1940.*

- **Fighting in northern Europe** began in November 1939 when the USSR attacked Finland. By March 1940, the Finns were forced to give up.

- **Norway, Sweden and Denmark** wished to stay neutral. However, on 10 February 1940, British ships entered Norwegian waters to rescue Allied prisoners, mostly sailors, from the German ship *Altmark*.

- **On 8 April 1940**, British ships began laying mines off Norway. Britain aimed to stop German ships carrying metal ore from Sweden to Germany.

- **On 9 April**, German troops overran Denmark, without much resistance. The Germans also attacked Norway, sending naval ships to land troops.

  - **Britain and France seized** the key port of Narvik in northern Norway. However, British troops were not equipped for Arctic warfare and lacked air support.

  - **The Norwegians fought gallantly**, and shore guns sank the German cruiser *Blucher* off Oslo.

    - **Ten German destroyers** were sunk in a fierce naval battle at Narvik. Allied forces took Narvik by 28 May, but by then the Germans controlled all of southern Norway.

    - **By June 1940**, British and French troops were forced to withdraw, leaving Norway to be occupied by the Nazis.

    - **King Haakon of Norway** escaped to Britain. A Norwegian Nazi sympathizer, Vidkun Quisling, set up a pro-German government.

    - **Greenland, Iceland and the Faroe Islands** (Danish territories) remained free. They became valuable bases for the Allies.

Blitzkrieg in the west

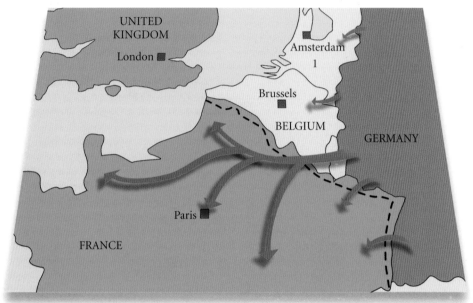

▲ *Map of the German advance in 1940. The combined land and air onslaught relied on speed to knock out Belgium and the Netherlands, and to drive deep into France to bring a swift end to the war in the west.*

● **Hitler feared a French attack** on Germany, but by the spring of 1940 he planned to strike first with *Blitzkrieg* (lightning war) attacks, like the onslaught on Poland.

...FASCINATING FACT...

Rumours spread across Belgium and the Netherlands of thousands of German paratroops landing from the skies. In fact, most of the 'paratroops' were dummies, dropped to cause confusion.

- **The French were confident** that their Maginot Line of forts built in the 1930s, would keep the Germans out.

- **Belgium was the weak link** in France's defences. It was neutral, but Hitler had already overrun neutral Norway and Denmark.

- **On 10 May 1940**, Germany invaded Belgium and the Netherlands. Hitler said he was protecting their neutrality, in case Britain and France attacked.

- **The French planned to** stop any German advance, but German Panzers (armoured divisions) were too fast, racing across Belgium and into Holland.

- **The *Luftwaffe* attacked airfields**, roads, railways and bridges. The massive Eban Emael fortress in Belgium was captured by German paratroops.

- **The Dutch port of Rotterdam** fell after heavy bombing raids by the *Luftwaffe*. The Dutch government felt that their war was lost.

- **Queen Wilhemina of the Netherlands** handed over the Dutch merchant fleet and the diamond riches of Amsterdam to Britain. On 13 May, she and her family were evacuated to Britain.

- **On 14 May**, Dutch troops stopped fighting. Belgium fought on until 28 May. By then, German armies were in France. The French and British armies retreated.

The fall of France

- **The French commander**, General Gamelin, was taken by surprise by the speed of German attacks.

- **The French air force** was outclassed and outnumbered by the *Luftwaffe's* bombers and fighters.

- **Belgium's surrender** left a gap in the defences of France. German tanks raced towards the French Channel ports.

- **Boulogne fell on 22 May** and by 27 May, Calais was in German hands. Refugees and retreating Allied troops jammed the roads.

- **General Lord Gort**, in command of the British Expeditionary Force, ordered a retreat towards the port of Dunkirk.

- **On 26 May**, a rescue operation was begun, to bring home as many British troops as possible from Dunkirk.

- **The German army** halted within a mile or so of Dunkirk, which was fiercely defended by French and British troops.

- **France crumbled**, though Prime Minister Reynaud asked the USA for help and vowed to fight on from French colonies if necessary.

- **On 14 June**, German troops entered Paris. Two days later, a new French government led by Marshal Petain asked Hitler for an armistice.

- **France surrendered** on 22 June 1940. The ceasefire was signed in the same railway coach used for the 1918 armistice. A jubilant Hitler sat in the same seat used in 1918 by French victor Marshal Foch.

▼ *Hitler enjoys the sights of Paris in June 1940, after the French surrender. This photo of him in front of the Eiffel Tower had immense propaganda value, and represented humiliation for France.*

Dunkirk

- **As German tanks** burst through Belgium towards the French Channel ports, the French and British fell back, abandoning much of their equipment.

- **Thousands of British and French troops** became trapped on the coast at Dunkirk. German tanks pulled up, leaving the *Luftwaffe* to finish off the trapped Allies.

- **British Admiral Bertram Ramsay** was asked to rescue as many troops as possible. Within days, he organized a fleet of small craft and warships.

- **Operation Dynamo** began on 26 May. A small armada of ships sailed to France, including destroyers, pleasure steamers, fishing boats, yachts, even a Thames fire-boat. Many were crewed by civilians.

- **The French 1st Army**, cut off near the town of Lille, surrendered on 31 May. Its three-day stand won precious time for other Allied troops to escape.

- **On the beaches**, thousands of exhausted Allied troops were bombed and machine-gunned. Lines of men waited to board the rescue ships.

- **Of almost 900 rescue ships** that crossed to and from Dunkirk, 200 vessels were sunk by German attacks.

- **By 3 June**, more than 338,000 men had been picked up from the beaches and brought back to England.

- **Operation Dynamo was a defeat**, but 'the miracle of Dunkirk' saved most of Britain's best soldiers, needed to defend Britain against invasion.

> ...FASCINATING FACT...
> One British soldier arrived in Dunkirk riding a German motorbike. He had taken it after shooting its rider, a German soldier carrying messages.

▲ Winding lines of exhausted
soldiers wait for rescue on the beach
at Dunkirk. Experienced troops
maintained superb discipline, even
when being attacked by German
planes flying low over the beaches.

Britain alone

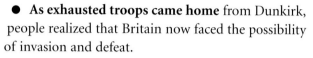

- **As exhausted troops came home** from Dunkirk, people realized that Britain now faced the possibility of invasion and defeat.

- **Britain had a new prime minister** – Winston Churchill. Chamberlain had resigned on 10 May. Churchill now led a 'war government', a coalition of politicians from the Conservative, Labour and Liberal parties.

- **An Emergency Powers Act** gave the government powers to confine foreigners or others suspected of links with the enemy. Those detained included Sir Oswald Mosley, leader of Britain's small Fascist party.

- **A few British politicians** argued that Britain should seek a peace deal with Germany, as Hitler had what he wanted.

- **But Churchill's aim** was 'Victory – victory at all costs'. Yet with France defeated, Britain had no ally in Europe.

- **From 11 June**, Italy was at war with Britain, too. Mussolini sent Italian planes to bomb the island of Malta, a key British naval base in the Mediterranean.

◀ *Sir Oswald Mosley and his 'Blackshirts' had supported Hitler's policies before the war. Mosley, once a vocal politician, was now silenced by wartime imprisonment.*

- **Britain would now have to fight** in the Mediterranean and North Africa, where Italy had powerful armed forces, and also defend itself against Germany.

- **On 16 June,** Churchill suggested that Britain and France unite as one to fight Hitler. By then it was too late. France was on the verge of collapse.

- **Australia and Britain's other Commonwealth allies** sent soldiers, pilots and ships to Britain's aid. There were plans to move the royal family and the government to Canada, should the Germans invade Britain.

- **During June 1940,** the German airforce began heavy attacks on British ships in the English Channel. *Luftwaffe* commander Hermann Goering hoped to draw the RAF into battle and so reduce its strength in pilots and planes.

▼ *Britain listens to the gloomy war news on the BBC. The 'wireless' was the main source of war news each evening, though censored by the government.*

Britain's new leader

- **When World War II began**, Churchill was 65 years old. He had not held a government job since 1929.

- **Born in 1874,** he was a soldier and war correspondent before entering politics as a Member of Parliament in 1900.

- **Before World War I**, Churchill was Home Secretary and in charge of the navy. He resigned in 1915 after the failure of the Gallipoli campaign.

- **Churchill was Chancellor of the Exchequer** until 1929, when he lost the job following a change of government and it was thought his career was over.

- **In the 1930s**, he was still an MP, and a fierce critic of disarmament. He believed Germany was preparing for war. People called him a warmonger.

- **He was one of the few** to back Edward VIII in the abdication crisis of 1936. When Edward gave up the throne, his brother became George VI.

- **On 4 September 1939**, Churchill returned to the government as First Lord of the Admiralty.

- **The defeat of British** troops in Norway led to a furious debate in Parliament on 8 May 1940. Churchill became Prime Minister and Minister of Defence.

- **An inspiring speech-maker**, Churchill said he had little to offer except 'blood, sweat and tears'. Britain was in great danger.

- **He hoped that if Britain** could hang on, America would enter the war. He was half-American (his mother was the daughter of a New York millionaire).

▶ *Churchill, in RAF uniform, displaying his infamous 'V' for Victory sign. His hope in 1940 was that the USA would soon join the war to tilt the balance.*

Invasion fears

- **Britain had become a refuge** for Europe's resistance fighters. French patriot General Charles de Gaulle escaped to England to lead the Free French Forces – a group fighting against Axis forces after France's surrender.

- **Hitler thought about** offering Britain a peace deal. He said that the war would be over in six weeks.

- **Churchill's** response was characteristic. He believed Britain should continue, whatever the cost.

▲ *A sub-machine gun. Many of Britain's volunteer defenders had far less effective weapons.*

- **On 18 June**, Churchill told Parliament that, "…the Battle of France is over. I expect that the Battle of Britain is about to begin."

- **Invasion preparations** included miles of barbed wire along beaches and concrete pillboxes for machine guns. Road signs were removed, so that German invasion troops would not be able to find the way to London.

- **Church bells** were to be rung at the first sign of invaders. People watched for German parachutists dropping from the air to seize radar stations, airfields and main roads.

- **Men, young and old**, joined the Local Defence Volunteers, later renamed the Home Guard. They had all kinds of weapons, from shotguns to medieval spears, and were nicknamed 'Dad's Army'.

● **The German invasion plan**, code-named Operation Sealion, relied on gaining control of the skies over the channel, to keep the British navy away while German invasion barges landed troops in England.

● **Hitler hoped** that Churchill would be removed from power and a new government would make peace. The war would then be over.

● **On 30 July**, Hitler ordered Goering to send his aircraft into battle to finish the war. Target date for the invasion of Britain was 15 September 1940.

▼ *Local Defence Volunteers drill with sticks, instead of rifles. More than one million men signed up for home defence, but few received weapons at first.*

257

The Battle of Britain

● **Hermann Goering was confident** that the Battle of Britain would be short and his *Luftwaffe* bombers would destroy the RAF in a few weeks. Attacks began on RAF bases.

● **Though outnumbered**, the RAF had re-equipped its fighter squadrons with modern Spitfires and Hurricanes.

● **Britain also had** radar. A chain of top-secret radar stations along the south coast gave the RAF vital early warning of approaching *Luftwaffe* formations.

● **The German bombers** were escorted by fighters. RAF fighters flew from their bases to attack the raiders. Many of the pilots were young, under 21 years old.

● **The aerial combats** were known as 'dogfights'. Some planes limped back to base riddled with bullet holes. Lucky pilots baled out using their parachutes. German pilots that landed in England became prisoners of war.

● **The RAF had 1434 fighter pilots** when the Battle of Britain began. They included Britons, New Zealanders, Canadians, South Africans, Poles and Czechs.

◄ *Hermann Goering, a World War I fighter pilot, had such faith in the German air force that he persuaded Hitler that the* Luftwaffe *could defeat Britain on its own.*

- **Pilot losses** were 120 a week, replacements only half that number, and by September the RAF was short of combat pilots. During July–October 1940, the *Luftwaffe* lost 1294 aircraft, the Royal Air Force lost 788.

- **On 15 August 1940**, almost 1800 *Luftwaffe* planes attacked. The Germans lost 76 planes, but the British claimed they'd shot down at least 182. Both sides exaggerated their victories.

- **On 7 September 1940**, German bombers switched their attacks from RAF airfields to London. This was in retaliation for a British air raid on Berlin.

- **In October 1940**, Hitler abandoned his plan to invade Britain.

▶ *An aerial 'dogfight'. RAF Spitfires attack German Heinkel bombers, with Messerschmitt Bf 109 fighter escorts. For a few minutes the air is crowded with twisting, diving planes, machine guns chattering.*

Spitfires v Me 109s

● **The Germans showed off** their new Messerschmitt 109 fighter in May 1935. It was the fastest warplane in the world at that time.

● **The Me 109 first saw action** in 1937, flown by German Condor Legion pilots during the Spanish Civil War.

● **By 1939**, the *Luftwaffe* had more than 1000 Me 109 fighters in service. By the end of the war around 35,000 had been built.

● **The Me 109** escorted bombers. Over southern England in the summer of 1940, they fought Spitfires and Hurricanes in the Battle of Britain.

▼ *RAF fighter pilots relax next to their Spitfires while waiting for the signal to 'scramble' (take off) and battle with enemy aircraft.*

▲ *The Me 109 was capable of over 600 km/h and was armed with two machine guns and three 20-mm cannons.*

● **The Supermarine Spitfire** fighter was designed by R J Mitchell. It was powered by a Rolls Royce Merlin engine.

● **The first Spitfire flew** in March 1936 and the first combat Spitfires joined RAF 19 Squadron in July 1938.

● **The Spitfire and Hurricane carried** eight machine guns in the wings, fired by the pilot using a button-control.

● **By August 1940**, the RAF had 19 squadrons of Spitfires. The slower but reliable Hurricane was more numerous in the Battle of Britain.

● **Battle of Britain** Spitfires had a top speed of about 580 km/h, roughly the same as a German Me 109. Later models were faster and flew higher.

....FASCINATING FACT....
A Me 209, a special version of the Me 109 (but not really much like it), set a world speed record of 755 km/h in April 1939. The Germans used this for propaganda purposes.

The 'few'

- **Winston Churchill praised** the RAF pilots who won the Battle of Britain as 'the few'. Many fighter pilots were school or university leavers.

- **Most pilots** flew solo after 10 or 12 hours 'dual' flying. After a few weeks, some were flying fighters on their first combat patrols.

- **RAF Squadron commanders** were experienced pilots, but in 1940 they had to rethink their tactics against German pilots who had mastered new combat skills in Spain and Poland.

- **Fighter planes** were cramped, with just room in the cockpit for one man in a flying jacket, boots and a helmet with an oxygen mask and radio. With the canopy closed, some pilots felt shut in.

- **Armour plate and toughened glass** gave the pilot some protection, but a plane could break up in seconds if hit by a long burst of machine gun fire.

- **Fighter pilots used radio** to talk to one another and to ground control, where the movements of friendly and hostile planes were marked on large maps as the air battles developed.

- **Top-scoring pilots** became known as 'aces'. One of the RAF's first aces was New Zealander 'Cobber' Kain (1918–40). He shot down 17 Germans by June 1940, when he was killed while performing aerobatics.

- **The top-scoring RAF pilot in World War II** was 'Johnnie' Johnson, with 38 enemy planes destroyed. He was still flying fighters in 1945.

- **Another ace** was A G 'Sailor' Malan from South Africa. He fought through the Battle of Britain and survived the war, with a total of 35 kills.

- **Douglas Bader lost both legs** in a pre-war flying accident, but returned to the RAF with tin legs. He led a fighter wing during the Battle of Britain, until he was shot down and taken prisoner.

▼ *The cockpit of a Spitfire fighter. The pilot sat on his parachute, holding the control column, with the dials on the panel before him. He looked for enemy aircraft through the glass canopy.*

KEY

1 Altimeter
2 Machine-gun firing button
3 Speed indicator
4 Joystick or control column
5 Pilot's seat

Blitz on Britain

● **In 1940**, German planes began bombing raids on British cities. This battle over Britain became known as the Blitz, from the German word *Blitzkrieg* meaning 'lightning war'.

● **From mid June 1940**, daily German air raids on Britain began. People got used to seeing the white trails left by aero engines in the summer sky, as British and German planes fought one another.

● **In July 1940**, German planes attacked southern ports and shipping.

● **On 24 August 1940**, RAF bombers dropped bombs on the German capital, Berlin. The Nazis had boasted that Berlin could never be bombed, and Hitler threatened to devastate London in revenge.

● **On 7 September 1940**, swarms of German bombers flew in across east London, following the river Thames. The Blitz had begun. Woolwich Arsenal and the docks were early targets.

▼ *The Germans sent waves of bombers and fighters from bases in occupied Europe to attack London and other cities. Here London's docks burn with Tower Bridge (right) unscathed.*

▶ *Ministry of Information posters urged Britons to keep blackout curtains in place all night. The blackout was designed to make it difficult for German navigators in bombers to locate targets.*

● **Air Raid Precautions** (ARP) wardens checked that no houses were showing lights in the blackout.

● **After each raid**, wardens reported damage and unexploded bombs. Women volunteers drove ambulances.

● **Many people were 'bombed out'** or made homeless. Rest centres and canteens were run by the Women's Voluntary Service (WVS). They served refreshments to victims and rescuers.

● **Firefighters fought fierce fires** in London's warehouses, which were packed with sugar, paint, oil and timber.

WAIT FOR DAYLIGHT

the last hours of the **BLACKOUT** *are as important as the first*

● **On 14 November 1940**, the *Luftwaffe* changed tactics again – it attacked Coventry by night, with no warning.

Cities under fire

● **The Germans hoped** that heavy casualties would destroy Britain's will to fight. So in the winter of 1940–41, they bombed towns and cities across Britain. They targeted ports, industrial centres and railway towns.

● **Coventry was bombed** on the night of 14 November 1940. An 11-hour attack damaged three-quarters of the city centre and destroyed the cathedral.

● **Other British cities**, such as Sheffield, Manchester, Glasgow, Swansea, Hull and Belfast were attacked. Clydeside was blitzed by 388 planes in May 1941.

● **Many of the bombs** were incendiaries – small bombs that started fires on landing. In the one-night blitz on Coventry, 30,000 were dropped.

● **The most versatile German bomber** was the Junkers Ju 88, which had a top speed of 460 km/h and could carry 900 kg of bombs.

● **To find their targets**, German bomber crews followed radio navigation beams like an invisible searchlight. The device used two radio-signal beams and the point where beams crossed, marked the target.

● **World War II bombs** were not guided, like today's missiles, though they did have stabilizing fins. They were dropped in clusters known as 'sticks'.

● **Most bombs were packed** with chemical HE (high explosive) and exploded on impact. A direct hit from a bomb could demolish a house. Land mines parachuted to the ground, exploding after they had landed.

● **By Sept 1941**, the Fire Guard watched for incendiaries, and a National Fire Service ran local firefighting services. In December 1941, London suffered its worst fire-bomb raids of the war.

▶ *Coventry Cathedral, the morning after the air raid of 14–15 November 1940. The heart of the medieval cathedral was gutted by German bombs.*

···FASCINATING FACT···
People could sometimes hear bombs falling. The bomb you didn't
hear, they joked grimly, was the bomb that would kill you!

Blackout and balloons

- **The blackout** was enforced by police and ARP wardens. They told people to put their lights out. Dark material was used to cover windows.

- **Outside, it was so dark at night** without street lighting, especially with smoke from burning buildings, that many pedestrians carried torches. Bus drivers were guided by white paint on the kerb.

- **Observation posts were manned** by the Royal Observer Corps. There were over 1400 posts in 1941, manned by men and women. They watched and listened for enemy planes.

- **Barrage balloons** were hydrogen gas-filled balloons on the end of long wire cables. Each balloon was 206 m long. Balloons above factories, airfields and city streets stopped German planes flying low enough to pick out a target.

- **Sometimes a German bomber** hit the balloon cable, and crashed. One balloon crew at Dover shot down a German plane with their rifles.

- **To confuse the *Luftwaffe* pilots**, decoy targets were laid out, using lights to look like streets or airfield runways, and putting up dummy buildings.

- **Searchlights shone powerful beams** of light into the night sky to target enemy planes for guns and fighter planes.

- **Anti-aircraft (AA or 'ack-ack') guns** blasted shells into the air at bombers. There were two main types of heavy AA gun used in Britain – the 4.5-in gun threw a shell weighing over 20 kg to a height of 13 km. The 3.7-in gun fired a smaller shell but faster.

- **Shrapnel shells** fired from AA guns scattered flying metal and produced 'cotton-wool' puffs of smoke in the air.

- **Gunfire forced bombers** to fly high, making it difficult for bomb-aimers to drop bombs accurately.

◀ *Barrage balloons rose on their cables in their hundreds above key targets, such as airfields and armament factories.*

Night-fighters

● **When World War II began**, the RAF did not have specialist night-fighters. The Defiant, a two-man fighter with a power-operated four-gun turret, was too slow for daytime fighting in 1940–41, but more successful at night.

● **At first, RAF pilots** flying at night only had their eyes to guide them – they looked for the glowing exhausts of the engines of enemy bombers.

● **One unsuccessful idea** was to use two planes – one with a searchlight to find the enemy, the other with guns to shoot it down.

● **Twin-engined Beaufighters** and Mosquitos, and the German Me 110, proved much better night-fighters than Hurricanes and Spitfires.

● **The Beaufighter's first victory** was using the new A1 Mark IV radar on 19 November 1940 – a pilot shot down a German Ju 88 bomber over Oxford.

● **Interception became more successful** when a new ground communication interception (GCI) system came into operation in January 1941 – this guided the pilot close to his target.

● **Most night-fighters** had two-man crews – one man to handle the radar and navigation, the other to pilot the plane and fire the guns.

● **The RAF's most famous night-fighter pilot** was John Cunningham. The press nicknamed him 'Cats' eyes' because cats have excellent night vision.

● **At night, German bombers relied** on their radio direction-finding apparatus to guide them to target cities. The British sent out fake signals to confuse the bombers' navigators so that they followed fake beams.

● **By January 1941**, British defences were bringing down one German bomber in 100 – a success rate three times better than when the Blitz began.

▶ *Anti-aircraft gunners on the ground kept up a bombardment while night-fighter pilots hunted enemy bombers through the skies over Britain.*

Factory front line

◀ *The government used advertising to urge women to join the wartime workforce.*

● **The war was as much a battle** between factories as between armies, navies and air forces. The government kept telling people to work harder.

● **A key minister in Britain's wartime government** was Lord Beaverbrook, in charge of aircraft production. Another was Ernest Bevin, who was Minister of Labour, in charge of factories and mines.

● **Many factories switched** to war production. Some furniture factories, for instance, began building aircraft. Electrical appliance workers were retrained to assemble bombsights, radar sets and control systems for planes.

● **Car production** practically stopped. Many private cars were locked up until the war was over because petrol was rationed. Factories turned to making tanks, armoured cars and army trucks.

- **Factory workers worked** as long as 70 hours a week in spite of sleepless nights, snatching a nap, when they could.

- **Cheerful music on the radio** was supposed to keep up factory production. Canteens provided meals for workers and often entertainment, too. Many factories were humming day and night.

- **Posters urged people** to work harder. One compared unpatriotic Britons with zealous Germans, and pointed out that German workers did not take tea breaks and never went home early.

- **From December 1941**, the British government could order people to 'essential war work'. Women aged 20–30 had to register as available.

- **People not at work were** asked not to use buses and trains after 4 p.m., so tired workers could get home.

- **The Germans targeted** key factory cities. In May 1941, Liverpool was bombed for seven nights. In December 1941, German planes pounded Sheffield, which had weapons factories and steelworks.

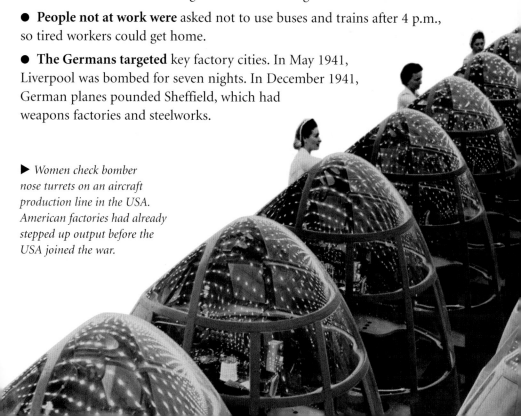

▶ *Women check bomber nose turrets on an aircraft production line in the USA. American factories had already stepped up output before the USA joined the war.*

Women go to war

● **Before the war**, many women had stayed at home after they were married. In fact, some employers refused to keep married women in their jobs.

● **In wartime**, women took over jobs previously done by men. Women of all ages went to work.

● **Films, newspapers and magazines** showed women factory workers in trousers and headscarves. Many worked 12-hour shifts.

● **After work, many women** had children to care for, and a home to keep going. Some had to cope with losing their home and their families during the Blitz.

● **Some single girls** were sent to do war work away from home. For many, it was the first time they had ever lived away from their families.

● **Women were trained** as aircraft fitters, car mechanics and assembly workers. They worked in munitions (explosives) factories, which was often dangerous.

● **In London, women** took their children into Tube stations to seek shelter. Women workers on the Underground and other rail lines had taken over 100,000 jobs.

● **Many British women** joined the uniformed ATS, WAAF and WRNS. In 1941, these became units of the armed forces, under the same rules as men.

● **Some women in Britain learnt to fire rifles** and other weapons, in case the Germans invaded. Women were often caught up in air raids on Navy and RAF bases, but only in Russia did women fight in combat.

● **Women factory workers** were paid less than men doing the same job. This was seen as unfair, but little was done about it while the war lasted.

▶ *Women and children bed down in London's Piccadilly Tube station. Underground platforms became more crowded at night than during the working rush hour.*

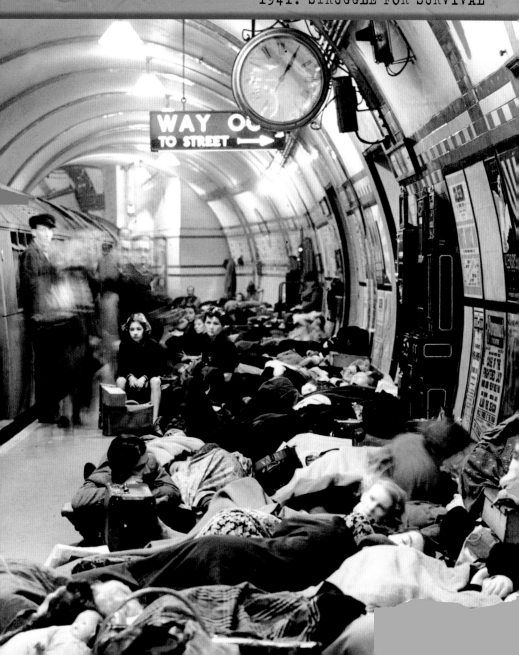

WAY OUT
TO STREET →

Greece and Yugoslavia

● **Hitler needed oil** to fuel Germany's war. He wanted to gain control of Romania's oil fields, to stop the Russians getting hold of them first.

● **Romania had replaced King Carol** with his young son, Michael, but power was held by General Antonescu, who was pro-Nazi.

● **Hitler's interest in** Romania annoyed Mussolini, who regarded the Balkans as Italy's area of influence. In October 1940, Mussolini attacked Greece.

● **Around 155,000 Italian troops** invaded Greece from Albania, but within one month they had been driven out by the Greeks.

▼ *German troops moved into Greece on 6 April 1941. These infantry soldiers are crossing the border in fairly lesiurely fashion.*

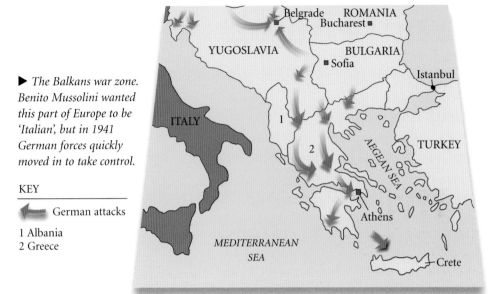

▶ *The Balkans war zone. Benito Mussolini wanted this part of Europe to be 'Italian', but in 1941 German forces quickly moved in to take control.*

KEY

German attacks

1 Albania
2 Greece

- **British troops landed** in Greece. Hitler persuaded Romania, Hungary and Bulgaria to back an attack on Greece and its neighbour Yugoslavia.

- **In March 1941**, the British navy defeated the Italians at Cape Matapan in the Mediterranean. On 6 April, German troops invaded Greece and Yugoslavia.

- **The Yugoslav capital, Belgrade**, was captured on 12 April 1941 and five days later Yugoslavia surrendered.

- **On 27 April**, Greece gave in. The next target was the Greek island of Crete.

- **Around 30,000 British and Commonwealth soldiers** were taken prisoner in Crete when the Germans attacked the island in May 1941. The British navy suffered heavy losses from German air attacks.

- **With Greece and Yugoslavia occupied**, Germany controlled southern Europe. Britain held on to the eastern Mediterranean, from Egypt, and guarded the Suez Canal and the sea route to India.

Sink the Bismarck

● **The German navy** was not strong enough to defeat British battleships in a full-scale battle at sea. Instead, its big ships attacked merchant convoys.

● **German ships** operated from French ports after 1940 and could catch Allied convoys in the mid-Atlantic, where they were usually without naval escorts.

● **The German raiders** included fast battleships such as *Admiral Scheer* and *Scharnhorst*, and the new and larger *Bismarck*.

● ***Bismarck* was the pride** of the German navy. A massive ship carrying eight 15-in (350 mm) guns, it was claimed to be unsinkable.

▼ Bismarck *was the sister-ship of* Tirpitz *(see page 170), and one-to-one more than a match for most British warships. In the end,* Bismarck *was outnumbered.*

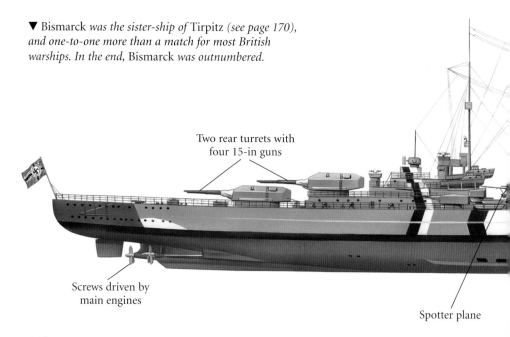

Two rear turrets with four 15-in guns

Screws driven by main engines

Spotter plane

● **In May 1941**, the *Bismarck* sailed from Germany, escorted by the cruiser *Prinz Eugen*. They were spotted off the coast of Greenland and on 24 May, the British battleship *Hood* led an attack on them.

● *Hood* **blew up** and sank when hit by shells from the *Bismarck*. Only three crew members survived. *Bismarck* was damaged and she headed for France.

● **On 26 May**, *Bismarck* was sighted by a Catalina flying boat west of Land's End. Swordfish torpedo planes from the aircraft carrier *Ark Royal* attacked.

● **On 27 May**, the crippled *Bismarck* was sunk by gunfire and torpedoes from the battleships *King George V* and *Rodney*, and the cruiser *Dorsetshire*.

● *Bismarck* **had taken** between eight and 12 torpedo hits before the ship sank, 640 km west of the French port of Brest.

● **The chase to sink the** *Bismarck* lasted five days and covered over 2000 km, the hunt involving over 19 warships.

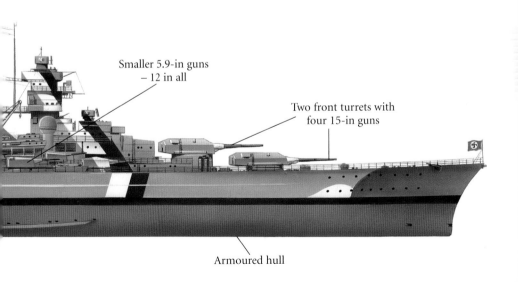

Smaller 5.9-in guns
– 12 in all

Two front turrets with
four 15-in guns

Armoured hull

The fires of London

- **London was a prime German target** for air raids in 1940–41. Incendiary bombs dropped caused huge fires and destroyed large areas of the city.

- **Many Londoners** took turns to 'fire-watch'. Incendiaries were small at only 12 cm long, but they were packed with chemicals that could start a fierce fire.

- **Posters warned people** to beware of 'Firebomb Fritz' – an advertising campaign teaching people how to deal with small fires before they spread.

- **The best way to put out an incendiary bomb** was to shovel sand on it. Throwing water spread the flames.

- **London's firemen fought heroically** to contain huge fires in the East End and City of London. Some were killed by falling buildings or suffocated by fumes.

- **Air Raid Precautions** (ARP) wardens often worked for two or even three nights in a row, only sleeping for an hour or two. One in six was a woman.

- **From 1941**, ARP was renamed Civil Defence. Each bomb was reported as an 'incident' by an ARP warden to a control centre, which alerted the fire brigade and reported damage to gas and water pipes.

- **The control centre** sent ambulances and rescue squads. First aid workers removed the injured, who were given immediate treatment or taken to hospital.

- **Heavy rescue teams** worked with ladders, shovels and bare hands to shift bricks and rubble, to free the injured and bring out dead bodies.

- **The House of Commons** was badly damaged. Churchill stood amongst the smouldering ruins where he had made his first defiant speeches of the war.

▶ *St Paul's Cathedral was wreathed in smoke and flames, but somehow Wren's great church survived the Blitz. Buildings around the cathedral were flattened or reduced to hollow ruins.*

Desert battles

● **Italian troops from Libya**, an Italian colony in North Africa, attacked Egypt in September 1940. British and Commonwealth troops including South Africans, Australians and Indians drove them back.

● **In the desert**, soldiers on both sides had to fight in fierce heat and put up with sandstorms, dust and flies. Water and fuel supplies were vital.

▼ *British troops dig in, ready to fight the Afrika Korps. Much of the desert fighting was done by infantry, armed with rifles and light machine guns, such as the Bren (below).*

● **Trucks and planes** often broke down when their engines became clogged with sand. Tanks and 'half-tracks' were better than trucks at moving across desert, but British tanks were inferior to German tanks.

● **Many soldiers wore shorts** to keep cool, and the Australians' bush-hats helped keep off the sun, but it was cold at night. Long-range patrol units travelled far across the desert in trucks on sabotage and reconnaissance missions. They often wore a mixture of Army and Arab clothes.

● **The key port of Tobruk** in Libya was captured in January 1941 by British and Australian troops, commanded by General Wavell.

● **In February 1941**, German troops of the Afrika Korps began arriving to help the Italians. Hitler did not think much of Mussolini's army and could not tolerate a British victory in the desert.

● **The German commander** was General Erwin Rommel. In March 1941, he launched an attack on the British 8th Army.

● **Tobruk was besieged** by German and Italian troops for eight months, until relieved by Commonwealth forces.

● **Rommel skilfully used tanks** and aircraft, moving at speed across the desert. He was a tough commander and by the end of 1941, the Afrika Korps was a serious threat to Egypt, and the Suez Canal.

...FASCINATING FACT...
Allied airmen and soldiers carried a message in Arabic asking desert peoples to help them, in case they got lost.

Empire at war

- **Britain was not entirely alone** as from 1939, the British Empire was also at war. The largest empire in the world, it included self-governing dominions, such as Australia, as well as colonies.

- **Australia, Canada, New Zealand and South Africa** all declared war on Germany in 1939. They sent soldiers, sailors and airmen to Britain's aid.

- **Canadian troops began arriving** in Britain in December 1939. Canadian pilots and ships were soon in action, too.

- **Commonwealth pilots fought with distinction** in the Battle of Britain, and as bomber pilots when raids against Germany were stepped up in 1941.

- **The Australian 6th Division** of 20,000 soldiers left for the Middle East in January 1940. Two more divisions followed. The 8th Division was sent to help defend Malaya in February 1941.

- **Commonwealth troops**, many of them Australians, took part in the rearguard fighting in Crete and North Africa in 1941.

- **Until 1941**, New Zealand's warships sailed as a division of the Royal Navy, but that year the Royal New Zealand Navy became an independent force.

- **Indian troops** were also in action. The Indian Army was very large and an important part of Britain's military strength. India was a British colony, but Indian nationalists hoped the war would win India independence.

- **Ireland was officially neutral**, but many Irishmen also joined the British armed forces.

- **Troops from many parts of the Empire** – from the Caribbean, Africa, Asia and the Pacific – were based in Britain during the war. People welcomed them as friends and allies.

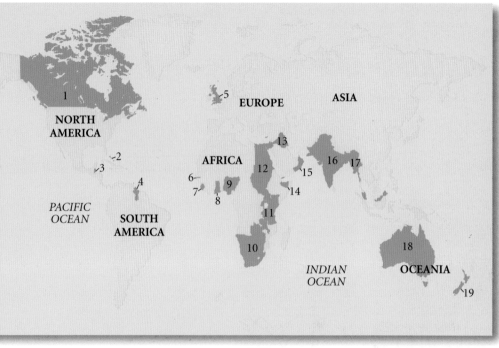

▲ *Britain's Empire, both self-governing nations and colonies, sent troops, ships, planes and supplies to help the war effort. Aid came from big countries, such as Australia, Canada, Nigeria and India, and from small countries, such as the islands of the West Indies and Pacific.*

KEY

⬜ British Empire
1 Canada
2 West Indies
3 British Honduras
4 British Guiana
5 United Kingdom
6 Gambia
7 Sierra Leone
8 Gold Coast
9 Nigeria
10 South Africa
11 Rhodesia, Kenya, Tanganyika
12 Anglo-Egyptian Sudan
13 Palestine, Trans-Jordan, Iraq
14 British Somaliland
15 Trucial States
16 India
17 Burma
18 Australia
19 New Zealand

Hitler attacks Russia

- **Hitler dreamed of a Europe** dominated by Nazi Germany. The Third Reich (German Empire) would reach the European (eastern) part of the USSR.

- **Hitler was fanatically** anti-Communist. Even after he signed a pact of non-aggression with the Soviet leader, Joseph Stalin, he still planned to destroy Stalin's Communist empire.

- **Hitler also feared** Stalin might seize the vital oilfields in Romania, on which Germany depended.

- **The invasion of the USSR** was planned for May 1941, but Hitler first sent his troops to attack Greece and Yugoslavia (see page 68), so it had to be postponed.

- **The German invasion of the USSR** began on 22 June 1941 without warning.

◀ *A German infantryman throws a stick grenade. Grenades (small bombs) were used a lot in close-range and street fighting.*

● **The Germans had massed a huge army** of 3 million men, 3000 tanks, 7000 big guns and 2500 planes. They poured east from Poland and other occupied countries, driving the Russians back.

● **Soviet forces** were bigger, but their equipment was not as good as that of the Germans – except their tanks.

● **Three German army groups** began the invasion of the USSR in the summer. Their commanders, Leeb, Runstedt and Bock, had all led armies to victory in France in 1940.

● **The Russians fought** fiercely to defend their homeland. As they retreated, they burned houses and fields of crops to leave nothing for the Germans.

● **There were** many atrocities. The Germans killed Russian civilians as well as soldiers. Both sides often shot prisoners. The Nazis treated Russians as inferior people.

▼ *A German Panzer III tank climbs out of a river as it advances into Russia.*

Atlantic lifeline

- **Britain depended on the sea** for food and war supplies. Merchant ships crossing the Atlantic were in danger from armed U-boat attacks.

- **Mines were also** a threat. In 1941, the Germans began using acoustic mines, which exploded when triggered by the sound of a ship's engines above.

- **Ships equipped to clear mines** were called minesweepers. They towed sweeps on the end of wires, to cut through the cables holding the mines in place. When the mine surfaced, the sailors blew it up on the surface.

- **By 1941**, U-boats were operating from bases on the French coast. Cruising far out into the Atlantic, they were sinking more than 100 ships a month.

- **Merchant ships** sailed together for protection in convoys on the 5000-km voyage from North America to Britain. The drawback was that a convoy steamed at the speed of its slowest member. Many cargo ships were slower than a U-boat travelling on the surface.

- **After the USA lent 50 elderly destroyers** to Britain, convoys had more escorts. Escort warships attacked submarines with depth charges, which exploded underwater.

- **From 1941–42**, long-range planes, such as the US *Liberator* and British *Sunderland*, flew far out to sea hunting U-boats. They attacked submarines on the surface with bombs and guns.

- **In August 1941**, President Roosevelt met Winston Churchill onboard a British warship. They made an agreement, the Atlantic Charter. It showed that America was ready to help Britain, even though not yet at war.

- **In September 1941**, the first convoy sailed from Britain to Russia, carrying war supplies from the USA and Britain to help Soviet armies fight off the German invasion.

▼ *An Atlantic convoy of cargo ships, photographed from a patrol plane. Danger lurked
beneath the waves where U-boats waited, ready to attack.*

U-boats

● **German submarines** or U-boats (*Unterseeboot*) were of several types. One of the most widely used was called the Type VII U-boat. It was quite small at 67 m long and displacing 770 tonnes on the surface.

● **It could travel** at 17 knots (30 km/h) on the surface, using the power of its diesel engines and at 7.5 knots (14 km/h) underwater, when it relied on power from chemical storage batteries.

● **The Type VII submarine** was armed with one deck gun, anti-aircraft guns and five torpedo tubes, four firing forwards and one firing backwards.

● **The submarine could carry** a total of 14 torpedoes, which it fired at ships, and the same number of mines, which it could release to float in the water.

● **The crew of 44 men** had to live in cramped, stuffy conditions inside the submarine. U-boat commanders had orders, but could also follow their own instincts, about where to lurk to wait for Allied ships.

● **Special tanker-subs refuelled** the U-boats. Each could carry up to 39 torpedoes and fuel oil. By December 1941, there were over 230 U-boats prowling the Atlantic.

▼ *A U-boat had torpedo tubes at the front and rear, and one deck gun for use when surfaced.*

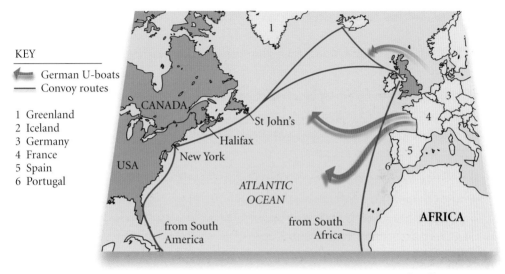

KEY

German U-boats
Convoy routes

1 Greenland
2 Iceland
3 Germany
4 France
5 Spain
6 Portugal

CANADA

St John's

Halifax

New York

USA

ATLANTIC
OCEAN

from South
America

from South
Africa

AFRICA

▲ *German U-boats operated in groups from bases in western Europe. They ranged as far as the coasts of Canada and the USA, from which most convoys set out for Britain. Allied air patrols could at first cover only part of the route, leaving a mid-ocean gap, the submarines' favourite killing-ground.*

● **The Germans were constantly improving** their U-boats. New types were faster, able to dive deeper and stay at sea longer.

● **In 1940–41**, U-boats were fitted with the schnorkel, a pre-war Dutch invention. An extending tube for sucking in air, it allowed a submarine to use its diesel engines to recharge its batteries while still submerged.

● **Allied ships hunted submarines** using a sound-detector known as sonar. This sent out a stream of sound signals that bounced off the sub's metal hull and echoed back to a receiver.

● **Once the warship** located a U-boat, it attacked with depth charges – explosive charges that sank into the water to a pre-set depth before exploding.

Pearl Harbor

- **In 1941,** the Japanese were still fighting in China. Japan was also keeping a watchful eye on what was happening in Europe.

- **The Japanese hoped** to take advantage of Hitler's victories, by seizing French Indo-China, British Malaysia and the Dutch East Indies.

- **Alarmed by Japanese aggression** in Indo-China, the US government cut off oil supplies to Japan in 1941. The Japanese protested, but were told they must withdraw from territory that they had occupied.

- **The Japanese decided to strike,** to cripple US power in the Pacific. Admiral Yamamoto's plan was to send the Japanese navy's aircraft carriers to attack the US Pacific fleet in its base at Pearl Harbor, Hawaii.

- **The Japanese strike force** steamed to within range of Hawaii on 7 December 1941. Many Americans in Pearl Harbor were off-duty that morning.

- **The Japanese carriers** launched 360 planes in two waves. The planes flew in across the island, taking the US defences totally by surprise. There was no declaration of war.

- **At Pearl Harbor,** eight US battleships were hit by bombs and torpedoes, and three were destroyed. More than 180 planes on US airfields were wrecked. However, the Pacific Fleet's three aircraft carriers were at sea and escaped.

- **US casualties** were more than 2300. President Roosevelt called 7 December 'a day that will live in infamy'. Americans were incensed by Japan's treachery.

- **On 8 December,** the US Congress declared that America was at war with Japan. The battle of Pearl Harbor was a day that would never be forgotten.

▶ *US battleships lie stricken by bombs and torpedoes after the Japanese attacks on Pearl Harbor.*

...FASCINATING FACT...
Lieutenant Annie Fox was a nurse at Hickam Field base, Hawaii in December 1941. For her courage during the Japanese attack, she was one of the first women to be awarded the Purple Heart medal.

The US are coming

- **Immediately after Pearl Harbor**, Germany announced that it was at war with the USA and would help Japan – Hitler despised America.

- **Churchill was encouraged** by America joining the war. He believed that America's financial and industrial support would tip the balance.

- **US troops began arriving in Britain** in January 1942. Luxury liners, including the huge Cunard ships, *Queen Mary* and *Queen Elizabeth*, were converted into troopships.

- **The Americans also began flying** their latest warplanes, including the Flying Fortress B-17 bombers, to bases in Britain. They took over airfields in East Anglia, to prepare for a bombing offensive against Germany.

- **Most people in Britain** had never met an American before. What they knew about America came from Hollywood films. US troops were told 'don't show off, don't eat too much, and don't criticize the King and Queen'.

- **The British knew little of US race laws**, so they were surprised that black Americans did not serve in the same units as white soldiers.

- **British and American commanders** set up a Combined Chiefs of Staff to coordinate their military planning. At first, the British were surprised by the American informality of calling everyone by their first names.

- **Churchill and Roosevelt** already had a friendly relationship. Churchill persuaded the US president that the war in Europe must be won first, then the war in the Pacific.

- **The US army began to train** thousands of new recruits. The US army grew fast, from 190,000 soldiers in 1939 to over eight million by 1945.

▶ *US troops loaded with equipment arrive in Britain. Many of the young soldiers crossing the Atlantic had been in the army only a few weeks and had not yet been near a battle.*

...FASCINATING FACT...
American soldiers were given a leaflet telling them what to expect and how to behave in Britain.

The Philippines

- **On 8 December 1941**, the day after Pearl Harbor (see page 84), Japanese planes attacked the Philippines. On 10 December, Japanese troops invaded, landing on Luzon Island.

  - **The Philippine Islands** were a vital US base in the Asia-Pacific region. They had airfields, such as Clark Field, on the islands.

    - **However, the armed forces there were weak**, and by 24 December the Japanese had reached the capital, Manila.

      - **Manila was captured** without a fight in January 1942. US forces pulled out to spare the city from Japanese bombing.

      - **US and Filipino troops**, led by General Douglas MacArthur, took up defensive positions on the Bataan Peninsula and on Corregidor Island.

        - **The US army suffered** its first casualties and on 11 March, MacArthur was ordered to leave for Australia. He vowed that he would return.

◀ *Japanese troops celebrate their victory at Bataan in April 1942. Japanese officers wave their swords, in medieval samurai fashion.*

KEY

 Japanese land/
  sea attacks
1 Formosa
2 Philippine Islands
3 French Indo-China
4 Malaya
5 Dutch East Indies
6 New Guinea
7 Australia

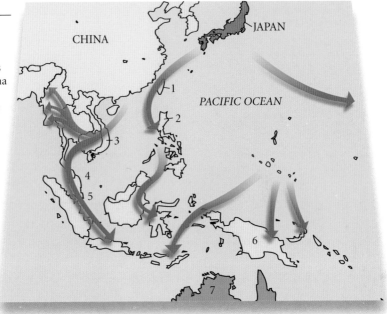

▲ *British, French and Dutch colonies in Southeast Asia were overrun by the Japanese, as were the US-controlled Philippines. The Japanese hoped to seize land, raw materials and fuel supplies, and stir up anti-colonial feeling among local peoples.*

● **The defenders of Bataan** held out against the Japanese until 9 April. Then the survivors surrendered and were taken prisoner.

● **US forces fought on** under Lieutenant General Wainwright. Some Americans and Filipinos retreated into the mountains to carry on a guerrilla campaign.

● **Corregidor Island** fell to the Japanese on 6 May and within three days they controlled the Philippines.

● **The collapse of the Philippines** left the way open for further Japanese attacks in the Pacific.

Malaya and Singapore

▲ *British troops surrender to the Japanese. In Britain,*
the fall of Singapore was seen as a national disaster.

- **On 20 January 1942,** Japanese troops crossed into Burma, forcing British troops to retreat. The rapid Japanese advance in Southeast Asia caught the British and Americans by surprise.

- **British forces in Asia** were weak. Top-grade military equipment was needed in Britain. The air force in India and Malaya had few modern planes to fight off the Japanese.

- **On 8 December 1941,** the day after Pearl Harbor, Japanese soldiers and aircraft attacked Malaya from Thailand.

- **The same day** Japanese aircraft sank two large British warships, the *Prince of Wales* and *Repulse*. The ships were supposed to defend Malaya and Singapore. They had big guns, but no air cover against bombers.

- **British and Commonwealth troops** in Malaya retreated south to Singapore, where they were surrounded by the end of January 1942.

- **The fighting intensified,** and on 15 February the British commander, General Percival, surrendered Singapore to the Japanese unconditionally.

- **Thousands of Allied troops** were taken prisoner, along with many civilians who had been unable to flee. Many later died in captivity because of ill-treatment by their captors.

- **The fall of Singapore,** thought to be an impregnable fortress of the British Empire, was Britain's worst defeat since the fall of France in 1940.

- **The Japanese were poised** to move south through the Dutch East Indies towards New Guinea. From there, it was only a short hop to Australia.

- **India also seemed** in danger. In April 1942, Japanese planes attacked Ceylon (modern Sri Lanka) and sank the British aircraft carrier *Hermes*.

Dig for victory

- **The Dig for Victory** campaign was part of the Home Front. It was designed to boost food production and reduce the amount of imported foods.

- **People in Britain, USA, Canada and Australia** were urged by their governments to Dig for Victory and plant Victory gardens.

- **Books and newspaper articles** showed people how to prepare soil, plant seeds and grow vegetables. This was Britain's first healthy eating campaign.

- **People grew vegetables** on top of air raid shelters in the back garden, in school grounds and in public parks.

- **Children's books** also contained gardening tips, telling readers how to dig, rake, hoe, sow seeds and water the young plants.

- **The BBC in London** ran a 'Radio Allotment', broadcasting news every week to the nation about how the potatoes, carrots and onions were getting along.

- **In Britain**, servicemen and women on leave were urged to 'Lend a Hand on the Land', giving up an hour or two to help with the harvest.

- **Many women in Britain** joined the Women's Land Army. They went to work on farms – doing everything from mucking out the pigs to driving tractors.

- **Meat was scarce**, so recipes showed how to make meat pies without meat. Potatoes and carrots were plentiful and recipes gave new ways of cooking vegetables, such as 'Potato Pete's Recipe Book'.

...FASCINATING FACT...
Magazines tried to make farm work look glamorous, by showing pictures of land girls in sun hats carrying sheaves of wheat.

► *A poster encouraging women in Britain to become land girls. The work was made to look and sound idyllic.*

The propaganda war

● **Germany's propaganda chief**, Joseph Goebbels, was a master of manipulation and misinformation, but he also knew the importance of modern media, such as radio and film.

● **Newsreels showed German cinema audiences** pictures of victories in which the German soldier appeared to be a 'superman'. Nazi rallies were stage-managed as epic events.

● **Both sides used the press and radio** to show their side in the best light. A defeat became a 'tactical retreat' or at worst 'a glorious escape from disaster'.

● **Newspapers and radio** were censored – bad news was hidden from the public, good news printed in big, bold headlines.

● **British propaganda often relied on humour**, especially in cartoons and posters. Hitler was made to look ridiculous – a little man with a funny moustache.

● **The Ministry of Information** was in charge of British wartime propaganda. At times it was criticized for talking down to people.

▶ *Goebbels masterminded the Nazi propaganda effort. He often used potent images, such as children, to promote his vision of Nazi superiority.*

▶ *A poster for one famous wartime film, about the Royal Navy and based partly on the real-life war of Lord Louis Mountbatten's ship HMS Kelly.*

● **Feature films** were also used as propaganda. The Hollywood film *Mrs Miniver* was about a British family in the Blitz, yet did not show the dust and dirt of a real air raid.

● **Patriotic war films** such as *In Which We Serve* helped raise morale by showing British servicemen being brave even when facing disaster – the film featured a warship being sunk.

● **Two propaganda slogans** were 'Walls have ears' – telling people to be wary of spies lurking everywhere and 'Coughs and sneezes spread diseases' – telling people to use a handkerchief – a day off sick meant a day's war work lost.

...**FASCINATING FACT**...

As part of the 'waste not, want not' propaganda campaign, pencil sharpeners were removed from government offices in Britain, so that civil servants did not waste pencils.

Commando raids

- **Wartime special forces** included Commandos, Rangers and the Special Air Service (SAS). These were volunteer soldiers trained for difficult and often dangerous missions.

- **The first British Commando unit** was formed in 1940. Commandos went through extra-tough training, which mainly took place in Scotland.

- **There were French, Dutch, Norwegian and Czech Commandos**, and the US Rangers trained in a similar way.

- **Commandos** had to be very fit. The soldiers were taught to find food and shelter in the countryside, to climb cliffs and swim rivers.

- **Commandos used all kinds of weapons**, from knives to rocket-launchers. They often used non-standard weapons, chosen because they fired more quickly or were light to carry.

- **Camouflage clothing** and blackened faces helped hide Commandos when they were creeping up on an unsuspecting enemy at night.

- **In March 1941**, the first British combined operations raid landed Commandos on the German-held Lofoten Islands, off the coast of Norway.

- **In 1942**, the first US Rangers unit of 2000 men was formed and trained in Britain for Commando-style operations.

- **In March 1942**, Commandos raided St Nazaire, France. They damaged the submarine base, sinking an old British destroyer to block the dry dock.

> ...FASCINATING FACT...
> The British Special Air Service, formed in 1943,
> had the motto 'Who dares, wins'.

Camouflage on
helmet

Pack with
rations, explosives,
special tools

Unit insignia

Ammunition
pouches

Sub-machine gun

▶ *A Commando in full kit,
ready for combat. When
landed in enemy territory,
Commandos faced extra
danger, for Hitler ordered all
Commando prisoners to be
shot. Some were, although
most German army officers
ignored Hitler's order.*

305

Malta under fire

● **Malta was an important British base** in the Mediterranean, midway between Italy and North Africa.

● **The British navy** used Valetta harbour for repairs and refuelling, and there was also an airfield.

● **The Germans and Italians** tried to starve Malta into submission, by attacking convoys bringing fuel, food and supplies to the island.

● **In March 1942**, a much-needed convoy fought its way into Malta. Two cargo ships sank within sight of the island. The other two reached harbour but were sunk while being unloaded.

● **The island's air defences** were at first weak. In 1940, three ageing Gladiator biplanes, known as *Faith*, *Hope* and *Charity*, fought off much faster German and Italian planes.

● **Royal Navy and US Navy** aircraft carriers were used to ferry new planes, including Spitfires, within range of Malta so that pilots could fly them in to aid the island's defence.

● **Sea Hurricanes**, naval versions of the Hurricane fighter, were flown from aircraft carriers to fight off waves of German and Italian bombers.

◀ *The Gloster Gladiator first flew in 1934. The planes that defended Malta so valiantly were naval Sea Gladiators –* Charity *and* Hope *were lost in action,* Faith *survived the 1940–41 air battles.*

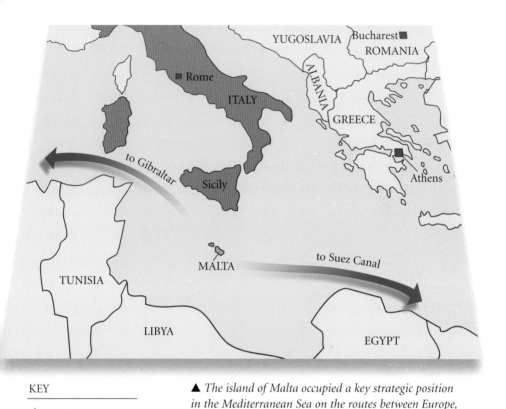

KEY

![arrow] Strategic route

▲ *The island of Malta occupied a key strategic position in the Mediterranean Sea on the routes between Europe, Africa and the Middle East.*

● **The Mediterranean** was a dangerous sea for big ships. The Royal Navy's most famous aircraft carrier, *Ark Royal*, was sunk in November 1941.

● **In August 1942**, another carrier, *Eagle*, was sunk while escorting a convoy. The big ship sank within ten minutes of being attacked by enemy planes.

● **Malta was heavily bombed,** but its people did not give in. In recognition of their courage, the island was awarded the George Cross, Britain's highest civilian decoration.

Air power at sea

● **The battleship was less effective** in World War II than the aircraft carrier. Air power at sea was often the decisive factor.

● **The United States** lost 11 carriers from 1941–45, more than half to air attacks. Britain lost 10, seven being sunk by submarines.

● **Japan suffered the heaviest carrier losses** with 21 Japanese carriers sunk in the fierce naval-air battles of the Pacific war.

● **Germany did not have any carriers** and its largest battleships, *Bismarck* and *Tirpitz*, spent most of the war in harbour until destroyed by the Allies.

● **Allied battleships fought in the Atlantic**, Mediterranean and Pacific. They could bombard enemy shore positions with their huge guns.

▼ *A US Navy F6F Hellcat fighter crash-lands in flames on the deck of the carrier USS* Enterprise. *An officer struggles to rescue the pilot.*

▶ *A B-25 bomber gets airborne from USS* Hornet, *on its way to bomb Tokyo in the Doolittle Raid of April 1942.*

● **Smaller ships**, such as destroyers, frigates and corvettes, escorted convoys and protected larger warships from submarines.

● **Aircraft carriers in the Atlantic** and Mediterranean escorted convoys. In the Pacific, carriers fought air battles – as at Pearl Harbor (see page 84), the Coral Sea (see page 102) and Leyte Gulf (see page 176).

● **Carriers had** three main kinds of aircraft – fighters, torpedo planes and dive bombers. The Royal Navy's Fleet Air Arm operated from British carriers.

● **In April 1942**, the US carrier *Hornet* launched 16 B-25 bombers to bomb Tokyo – the first Allied raid on Japan. The planes landed in China. In total, 12 men did not return. Three were captured and executed by the Japanese.

...FASCINATING FACT...
In July 1942, Allied convoy PQ 17, heading through Arctic waters to Russia, was attacked so fiercely by German planes and naval units that only four of 33 ships reached the Russian port of Archangel.

Coral Sea victory

- **By April 1942**, US forces had taken charge of the Pacific war, with help from Britain and Australia. Britain was responsible for the Indian Ocean.

- **The Japanese planned to take the Solomon Islands** and New Guinea, from where their bombers could raid Australia. Another target was the US stronghold of Midway Island in the north.

- **The US Navy** barred the way. Admiral Nimitz had two US carriers ready for action, *Yorktown* and *Lexington*.

- **On 3 May**, Japanese forces captured the island of Tulagi in the Solomons, while a strong naval force with two carriers steamed south.

- **On 4 May**, there was a skirmish between naval aircraft and on 8 May the serious fighting began. In the air battle of the Coral Sea, neither fleet was in sight of the other.

- **The Japanese and Americans** each had around 120 planes and the same numbers of cruisers and destroyers.

- ***Lexington***, nicknamed the 'Lady Lex' by sailors, was hit by torpedoes and bombs, and sank.

▶ *The sinking of a Japanese Navy destroyer, seen through the periscope of the US submarine that delivered the death blows.*

▲ *US submariners relax with their torpedoes. They lived in claustrophobic conditions.*

● *Yorktown* **was also hit**, but only by a single bomb. The Japanese carrier, *Zuikaku*, was badly damaged by US attacks.

● **Both sides withdrew**, but the Americans came off slightly better. The Japanese move towards New Guinea had been halted. They had lost 1000 men and 80 planes.

● *Yorktown* was soon repaired. Both Japanese carriers were out of action for the fight at Midway.

Midway

- **Despite the setback** at the Coral Sea, the Japanese pressed on with the next stage of their plan – part of which involved the capture of Midway Island.

- **Almost the whole Japanese Navy** was at sea – 8 carriers, 11 battleships, 22 cruisers, 65 destroyers and 21 submarines.

- **The Americans had only 76 ships** in the Pacific, a third of which were too far away to help. Only three US carriers were ready for combat, one being the hastily patched-up *Yorktown*, and no battleships.

- **The Japanese split their fleet**, to attack the Aleutian Islands and to escort battleships and slow troop transports. They stuck to their rigid plan, instead of adapting to changing circumstances.

- **Unknown to them**, the US fleet had 233 planes on three carriers north of Midway when the Japanese attacked.

- **Although 35 of 41 US Navy** torpedo-bombers had been shot down, 37 American dive-bombers swooped on the Japanese carriers, *Akagi*, *Kaga* and *Soryu*. The Japanese planes were on deck being refuelled and rearmed.

- **All three Japanese ships** were hit and had to be abandoned, leaving only one carrier, *Hiryu*. Its aircraft attacked *Yorktown*, which later sank.

- **US planes caught *Hiryu*** and sank her. In one day, Japan had lost four aircraft carriers and over 300 planes. The US admiral, Raymond Spruance, had won a major victory.

> ... FASCINATING FACT ...
> Japan's fleet at Midway included the *Yamato*, the world's largest
> battleship, 70,000 tonnes with nine massive guns.

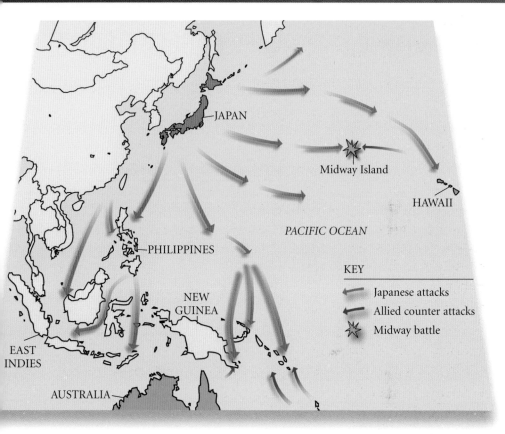

JAPAN

Midway Island

HAWAII

PACIFIC OCEAN

PHILIPPINES

KEY

NEW
GUINEA

Japanese attacks

Allied counter attacks

Midway battle

EAST
INDIES

AUSTRALIA

▲ *Midway Island was a key target in the Japanese Pacific campaign. Both sides needed island bases for ships, planes, fuel and supplies as they fought across vast expanses of ocean.*

● **At Midway**, the Japanese navy lost 200 of its best pilots. Lacking air cover, Japanese forces had to rely on land-based aircraft for their attacks on the Solomons and New Guinea. The Japanese abandoned the attack on Midway. They continued with their invasion of the Aleutians, although these islands were of less importance.

Bombing Germany

- **In the first years** of the war, the RAF did not have any really big bombers. It used twin-engined Hampdens, Blenheims and Wellingtons to raid Germany, but suffered heavy losses.

- **By 1942**, the RAF had received new four-engined Stirling, Halifax and Lancaster bombers. They could fly further and carry more bombs.

- **On 30–31 May 1942**, the RAF launched its first 'thousand bomber' raid on the German city of Hamburg. Half the bombers were Wellingtons.

- **Sir Arthur Harris**, chief of Bomber Command, believed that 'area bombing' of German cities could wreck German war production and win the war.

- **Bombing became more accurate** in 1943. RAF planes were fitted with the new H2S radar and Oboe radio-beam system to guide them to their targets.

- **RAF bombers dropped strips** of metal foil, known as 'window', to confuse German radar defences.

- **The RAF plan** was to bomb Germany at night, to reduce losses from German anti-aircraft fire, known as 'flak', and German fighters.

- **The USAAF planned to bomb** by day, flying high and relying on their bombers' machine guns to fight off German fighters. Their main bombers were the B-17 Flying Fortress and B-24 Liberator.

- **Bombers flying over occupied Europe** usually flew without fighter escort. Allied fighters, such as the Spitfire, could not carry enough fuel to fly to Germany and back.

- **The first long-range Allied fighter plane** was the American-built P 51D Mustang, which began escorting bombers in 1943.

▲ *US B-17s release clusters of bombs as the Allied air offensive over occupied Europe intensifies in 1942.*

Stalingrad

- **During the summer of 1942**, the fighting in the Soviet Union grew even fiercer. On 1 July, the Germans captured Sebastopol, in the Crimea.

- **By August**, two German armies, the 4th and 6th Panzers, were poised to attack the industrial city of Stalingrad on the river Volga. German General Paulus led the 6th Army with more than 330,000 troops.

- *Luftwaffe* **bombers** began the attacks, their bombs setting fire to Stalingrad's many wooden houses.

- **The Soviet army defended the city**, using the river as a barrier and supplying troops on the far side of it by boat.

- **By September**, German troops were in the outskirts of Stalingrad, fighting street by street. Winter now began to close in.

- **The Germans began to run short** of food, fuel and ammunition. Planes could not keep them supplied. The winter fighting was house-to-house and grew even more desperate.

- **Soviet relieving armies**, led by Zhukov, Vasilevsky and Voronov, closed in around the German 6th Army in a two-pronged pincer movement.

- **This left 250,000 Germans** cut off at Stalingrad. Hitler refused to allow Paulus to break out of the city to join German units to the west. The Nazi leader told the 6th Army to fight to the death – they were doomed.

- **The fighting went on** until 31 January 1943, when Paulus finally surrendered. 91,000 German soldiers were taken prisoner – all that were left alive. Very few of the prisoners got home. Most died in Soviet prison camps.

- **Stalingrad was a great Russian victory** and a turning point in the war. The cost in lives was terrible. German losses were over 400,000, plus 450,000 Romanians, Hungarians and Italians. The Soviets lost 750,000.

▼ *Warmly clothed Russian infantry charge forwards during the battle for Stalingrad. The Russians had moved vital arms factories far to the east, beyond the reach of German air attacks, to re-equip their forces for the fight against the Nazi invaders.*

El Alamein

● **In North Africa**, the British were building up their forces to defeat German General Erwin Rommel. By 1942, they had more tanks and twice the number of planes.

● **Rommel was hard** to beat. He had been driven back towards the end of 1941, but had counter attacked in the spring of 1942.

● **The German and Italian forces** were suffering from shortages of fuel and ammunition. The British were losing tanks in ineffective attacks on Rommel's defences and began to retreat eastwards.

● **In July 1942** British General Auchinleck stopped Rommel at the first battle of El Alamein. Despite his victory, he was then sacked, and Churchill appointed a new commander, General Montgomery.

▼ *German prisoners are escorted into captivity by a British soldier.*

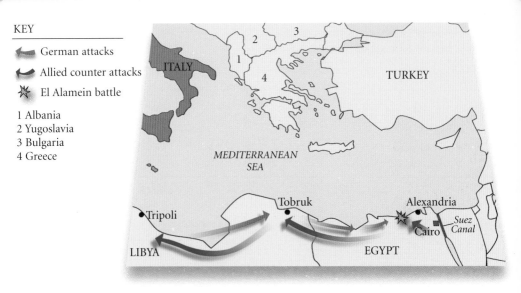

KEY

German attacks

Allied counter attacks

El Alamein battle

1 Albania
2 Yugoslavia
3 Bulgaria
4 Greece

▲ *The fighting in North Africa ebbed and flowed across the desert, as the British fought to hold onto Egypt and the vital Suez Canal.*

● **Montgomery had** 1230 against 210 enemy tanks and 1500 against 350 enemy planes. He also had a three to one advantage in soldiers.

● **The British used 270** of their new US Sherman tanks, which had bigger guns and thicker armour than older tanks, such as the Stuart and Grant.

● **On 23–24 October 1942,** the British 8th Army attacked, after a thunderous artillery barrage.

● **The infantry and tanks** advanced, and within days Montgomery was able to report a victory at the second battle of El Alamein.

● **The victory at El Alamein** caused great rejoicing in Britain. It made Montgomery a hero overnight.

● **Rommel began to withdraw** westward. But there were now more Allied troops in Morocco and Algeria. German and Italian armies were trapped.

Jungle war

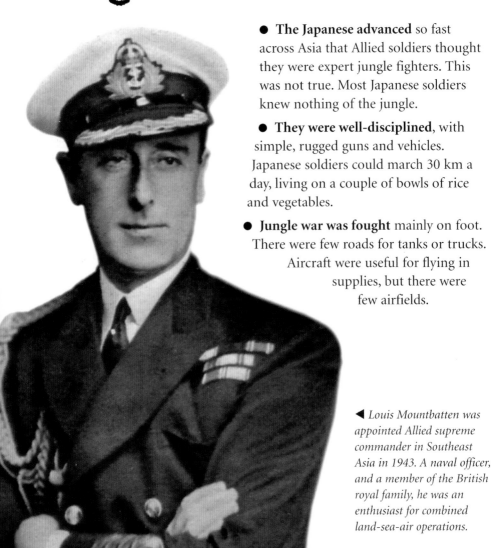

- **The Japanese advanced** so fast across Asia that Allied soldiers thought they were expert jungle fighters. This was not true. Most Japanese soldiers knew nothing of the jungle.

- **They were well-disciplined**, with simple, rugged guns and vehicles. Japanese soldiers could march 30 km a day, living on a couple of bowls of rice and vegetables.

- **Jungle war was fought** mainly on foot. There were few roads for tanks or trucks. Aircraft were useful for flying in supplies, but there were few airfields.

◄ *Louis Mountbatten was appointed Allied supreme commander in Southeast Asia in 1943. A naval officer, and a member of the British royal family, he was an enthusiast for combined land-sea-air operations.*

● **Local people in Burma** were usually willing to help the Allies, although the Japanese tried to win them over to their side.

● **The Allies wanted to hold Burma** because the Burma Road was the only land route into China, where Chinese military leader Chiang Kai-shek was fighting the Japanese with support from US General Joseph Stilwell.

● **British officer Orde Wingate** suggested sending groups of raiders into enemy territory for weeks at a time. These raiders were known as Chindits and they lived rough in the jungle.

● **Doctors handed out pills** to protect soldiers from malaria, a disease spread by mosquitoes. Troops were supposed to sleep under nets, for protection from mosquitoes.

● **In March 1942**, two Chinese armies crossed into Burma to attack the Japanese and relieve pressure on the British, but they were soon defeated and in retreat.

● **Indian and British troops** at first did little better and were forced back westwards to the town of Imphal, on the Indian border. Japan had complete control of Burma.

...FASCINATING FACT...
In the jungles of Burma, Allied and Japanese soldiers copied local people's skills. They learned how to make camps in the forest and how to hunt and trap wild animals to eat.

Wartime entertainment

- **Wartime entertainment at home** came from radio, known as the 'wireless' in Britain. The first TV service by the BBC closed down when war began.

- **Cinemas, theatres and museums stayed open** throughout the Blitz.

- **Many film stars**, such as James Stewart and Clark Gable, were in the armed forces. US and British studios turned out thrillers, Westerns, cartoons, comedies, romances – and war films.

- **Popular war films** included *The Way to the Stars*, about the RAF, and *Went the Day Well?*, about an English village taken over by German invaders.

- **Variety shows and concerts** were held in works canteens. ENSA, the British forces' entertainment unit, sent out travelling shows. ENSA, people joked, stood for 'Every Night Something Awful'.

- **In Britain**, League soccer was at first cancelled, but soon restarted. As so many players were in the forces, teams often featured guest players.

- **On BBC radio**, *Music While You Work* played bouncy tunes to get weary workers singing – and working faster.

- **Popular British radio shows** included Tommy Handley's *ITMA* (It's That Man Again) and the more serious *Brains Trust*.

> **...FASCINATING FACT...**
> Sherlock Holmes, played by actor Basil Rathbone, was updated
> from the 1890s to the 1940s in a Hollywood film series to combat
> Nazi spies and saboteurs.

▲ *Before the war, cinemas had shown films about the likely horrors. This 1938 feature had a grim message – 'heed the warning', a message reinforced by the soldiers, patriotic flags and searchlight (far right) outside the cinema. Most wartime films helped keep up morale, with cheerful messages.*

● **Comedian Bob Hope was just one of the entertainers** doing shows for the troops. Film star Betty Grable and singer Vera Lynn, the Forces Sweetheart, toured the war zones.

Women in uniform

- **In 1939,** Britain had 43,000 women in the services and by 1942 there were 400,000. Women served on military bases all around the world.

- **Women in the services** did many jobs – cooks, clerks, electricians, drivers, code experts, radio operators, ferry pilots, searchlight operators and intelligence.

- **Only in the Soviet Union** did women fight alongside and against men. More than half the 800,000 women in the Soviet army served as machine-gunners, tank drivers, snipers, combat pilots and first aiders.

- **In Britain,** the three main women's services were the Women's Royal Naval Service (WRNS or Wrens), Women's Auxiliary Air Force (WAAFs) and Auxiliary Territorial Service (ATS).

- **Women served in the navy** as Wrens (Britain) or Waves (US), but very few ever went onboard a ship. Most worked at land bases.

- **In 1943,** the US Women's Flying Detachment (WFD) merged with the Women's Auxiliary Ferrying Squadron to form the WASPs (Women Airforce Service Pilots). Over 1000 women qualified as WASP ferry pilots.

- **Women pilots in Britain and North America** ferried new aircraft from factories to air force bases. They flew all types of planes from fighters to four-engined bombers.

- **Air raid defences relied** on many women, to spot and track incoming enemy planes and to operate searchlights, and balloon and anti-aircraft guns.

- **The Nazis did not put women** into uniform. They thought women should stay at home. One exception was Hanna Reitsch, who flight-tested warplanes.

▶ *WAAF plotters direct RAF pilots on their missions, using a tabletop map board to show all of the aircraft movements.*

...FASCINATING FACT...

Britain's most famous woman pilot was Amy Johnson. In 1930 she flew solo from Britain to Australia. A ferry pilot with the Air Transport Auxiliary (ATA), she was killed in 1941 when her plane crashed.

Soldiers' weapons

- **An infantry soldier had a rifle** or a carbine. A carbine had a gas-powered firing mechanism, rather than a mechanical lever for loading a new bullet into the firing chamber.

- **Officers usually carried revolvers**, which were only effective at close range.

- **Most rifles also had a bayonet**, a short stabbing knife fitted to the end of the rifle barrel.

- **The US M-1 carbine** weighed 2.5 kg, about half the weight of the standard British Lee-Enfield rifle.

- **The range of a rifle** was between 500 and 1800 m. Some rifles fired one shot and then had to be reloaded by working the lever action to eject the spent cartridge.

▼ *A Lee-Enfield .303 rifle with ammunition belt and bayonet.*

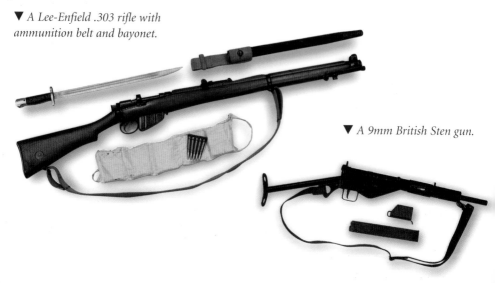

▼ *A 9mm British Sten gun.*

● **Semi-automatic guns**, such as the US Browning, fired a short burst of bullets when the soldier squeezed the trigger. The soldier loaded his gun with a magazine holding between 15 and 30 bullets or rounds.

● **Machine guns fired a stream of bullets** at high speed. There were sub-machine guns like the Thompson or 'Tommy gun' and the Sten. Heavy machine guns rested on metal legs to keep them steady while firing.

● **Infantry soldiers carried hand grenades** and tubelike anti-tank weapons, such as the US bazooka and German *Panzerfaust*.

● **Mortars were tubes that lobbed shells** up in the air. Big artillery guns, such as howitzers, were towed on wheels, and needed a crew of five or six men to load and fire them.

● **World War II soldiers did not wear body armour**, but each army had its own style of 'tin hat'. The US army helmet weighed 450 g.

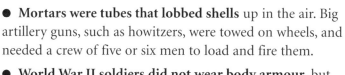

▶ *A US gunner aims his twin Browning machine guns.*

Secret war

● **The Allies were helped** by knowing the secret codes used by German and Japanese military. They also used spies and double agents.

● **In November 1939**, a package of secret papers turned up outside the British Embassy in Norway. Inside were details of German rockets, bombs, homing torpedoes and radar.

● **Most German spies working in Britain** were soon detected. Some were caught and executed. Others changed sides and became double agents working for the Allies.

● **The Germans used Enigma machines** to code all their military communications.

● **The Allies got hold of an Enigma machine** and discovered how it worked. The Germans believed Enigma was unbreakable – Hitler was told it would take 42,000 years to decode all the combinations!

▲ *A German Enigma machine. German coded signals used one machine to encode a message and a second machine to decode it.*

... FASCINATING FACT...
Not all top-secret suggestions were worth pursuing. One suggestion was to drop poisonous snakes on Berlin, another was to drop poisoned cabbage leaves across Germany to kill cows.

▲ *Code-breakers at Hut 6, Bletchley Park, 'Station X', in England. By January 1940, the British had cracked the Enigma code.*

● **From intelligence HQ at Bletchley Park**, England, code-breakers listened to German radio 'traffic', and passed on the information to the military.

● **At Bletchley Park was Alan Turing**, one of the brains behind the computer. Computers were developed to speed up code-breaking.

● **Information from German code-messages** was known as Ultra – Churchill told the Americans about it and in return they shared the secrets, known as Magic, from the Japanese code machine, Purple.

● **The Allies later agreed** that all information would be referred to as Magic. The Germans went on using Ultra, thinking that only the Japanese codes had been broken.

Life under occupation

● **Countries in Europe** under Nazi rule were known as occupied. Only half of France was occupied by the Nazis. The southern half, known as Vichy, had a puppet French regime that was pro-Nazi.

● **In occupied Europe**, the Nazis controlled all the media. It was a crime to listen to the BBC or Voice of America radio, which broadcast war news and messages to people from friends or relatives.

● **People were not allowed** to travel freely. They might be stopped on the street by police, demanding to see their identity papers.

● **The Nazis persecuted Jews** all over Europe. Jewish schools and shops were closed, and synagogues were destroyed.

▲ *The Star of David, worn by all Jews in Nazi-occupied Europe. Millions of Jews were arrested, forced to work as slaves, starved and murdered.*

● **Jewish families were ordered** by the Nazis to wear yellow stars on their clothing to show they were Jewish. Some Jewish communities were shut inside ghettos. This happened in Warsaw, Poland's capital (see page 128).

. . . FASCINATING FACT . . .
Only one part of the British Isles came under Nazi occupation – the Channel Islands, which were invaded by German troops in 1940 and remained occupied until 1945.

- **Thousands of Jews were taken in trains** to concentration camps where they worked as slaves. Many became sick due to starvation and ill-treatment, and died.

- **In occupied countries people lived** in fear of the 'knock on the door', which meant a visit from the police or the Gestapo, the Nazi security police. People who helped the Resistance (see page 124) were arrested and executed.

- **Families in occupied countries** knew they might be blown up by bombs that were dropped by Allied planes. Even so, they still helped the pilots who were shot down.

- **Collaborators were people** who chose to help the Nazis. Some acted as spies, informing on their neighbours. Some betrayed people in hiding, including Jewish families.

▶ *Heinrich Himmler, head of the SS, or Schutzstaffel (Protection Squadron), was in charge of concentration camps and internal security across occupied Europe. The Nazis devised* die Endlösung, *the final solution, to what they called the 'Jewish problem' – the extermination of as many European Jews as they could capture – and Himmler was a key figure in this programme of mass murder.*

Resistance

- **Resistance fighters in occupied countries** formed an underground army. They were organized into local groups, with help from the Allies.

- **Resistance groups set up escape routes** to help Allied airmen who were shot down over France or the Netherlands, to escape from Nazi territory. The fliers were hidden in people's homes, and given clothes and false papers to help them escape.

- **The French Resistance or Maquis** became skilled at sabotage, blowing up factories and railways. The Maquis also fought German soldiers.

- **Resistance gunmen tried to kill** Nazi officials. Czech Resistance fighters, known as partisans, assassinated a top Nazi, Reinhard Heydrich, who had carried out atrocities in Czechoslovakia.

- **The Allies helped resistance groups** by sending guns, radios and explosives, which were dropped by parachute from planes.

- **Specially trained Allied agents** were dropped by parachute too, to help organize resistance. They went to France, Norway, Greece, Yugoslavia and other countries.

◀ *General Charles de Gaulle led the Free French Forces from exile in London. He had a prickly relationship with the British government, which tended to keep secrets from him.*

- **Agents were also flown in** by light aircraft able to land in fields, where local resistance fighters marked out a landing area.

- **Agents trained in Britain** by the Special Operations Executive (SOE) were all volunteers, usually fluent in the language of the country they were sent into.

- **Any soldier in uniform**, if captured, was supposed to be treated as a prisoner of war (see page 142). However, a secret agent, with no uniform, could be tortured and then shot as a spy.

- **Several brave women were Allied agents** in France, including Violette Szabo, Nancy Wake, Odette Sansom and Noor un Nisa Inayat Khan.

▼ *'Underground army' fighters of the Polish Resistance line up for final orders before an attack on German occupying forces. The men are wearing white capes, for camouflage in the winter snow.*

Guadalcanal

▼ *US Marines dash up the beach from a landing craft during the Guadalcanal landings.*

● **In July 1942,** Allied reconnaissance planes reported that the Japanese had occupied the island of Guadalcanal in the Solomon Islands, and were building an airstrip.

● **Although wooded and mountainous,** the island was a useful base for either side in the Pacific war. The US decided to push the Japanese off Guadalcanal.

● **Around 19,000 US troops,** most of them Marines, were landed from a naval task force. The Japanese withdrew into the hills, then counter attacked.

● **Five Japanese cruisers** opened fire on the US fleet, sinking four ships in a night battle.

● **By October 1942,** there were around 45,000 fighting men on the island, which was only 145 km long. The two sides were evenly matched, but the Americans had more warplanes.

● **US Marines seized** Henderson Field airfield. American planes attacked Japanese soldiers, who suffered heavy casualties as they charged US defences.

● **The USS *Hornet*,** an aircraft carrier, was sunk, but the Japanese lost the battleship *Hiei* – the first battleship they lost in the war. Another was so badly damaged that it was scuttled (deliberately sunk).

● **By January 1943,** the US had more than 50,000 men on Guadalcanal. The Japanese were unable to land many reinforcements and their weary troops were starving and ill.

● **In February,** the Japanese evacuated the island, having lost 600 aircraft and more than 25,000 men, 9000 of them to disease.

● **The US victory at Guadalcanal** meant that the Japanese were clinging onto one base in the Solomons, the largest island, Bougainville Island.

Rising in Warsaw

▼ *German soldiers round up Jewish women and children from the Warsaw ghetto,*
the scene of one of the most poignant wartime tragedies.

- **The Nazis** treated occupied Poland savagely. They moved eight million Poles from the western part of the country, to clear the land for German settlers.

- **Many of Poland's three million Jews** were herded into ghettos, then taken to death-camps such as Treblinka and Auschwitz in overcrowded railway trains. Men, women and children were killed in the gas chambers.

- **Many Jews lived in the Polish capital** city of Warsaw. Since October 1940, all the Jews in Warsaw had been forced to live in the walled ghetto.

- **The Germans** let the Jews starve and grow ill. Many people died, even though some food and medicine was smuggled in from outside.

- **In 1942**, the Germans began rounding up Jews for the death-camps. By the end of the year, there were fewer than 50,000 Jews left in the ghetto.

- **Fears that they would all** be exterminated or removed made some Jews determined to make a last defiant stand against the Nazis.

- **In January 1943**, armed with rifles and a few light weapons smuggled in by the Polish Resistance, the Jews of Warsaw turned on the Germans.

- **General Jurgen Stroop of the SS** was ordered to crush the uprising. In fierce fighting, German troops blasted their way into the ghetto.

- **The ghetto fighters fought** for as long as they had ammunition. The battle ended in April 1943, but only about 100 Jews escaped.

...FASCINATING FACT...
A few Jewish children were smuggled out of the Warsaw ghetto.
Parents pretended babies had died, so that the bodies
could be taken out of the city.

Dambusters raid

- **The nerve centre of RAF Bomber Command** was the operations room at Naphill, England. It was deep inside a concrete bunker, known as 'The Hole'.

- **The inside walls were covered** with giant maps of Europe and blackboards with the Order of Battle, showing which squadrons were in action.

- **Targets were decided every morning** and by midday the squadron commanders knew which crews and which planes would be flying that night.

- **On 17 May 1943**, the crews of 617 Squadron knew they had an unusual target.

- **Dams in the Ruhr and Eder valleys** of Germany were to be bombed. If the dams broke, water from their vast reservoirs would flood factories in industrial cities such as Dortmund.

▼ *Water pours through the breach in the Mohne Dam, four hours after the Dambusters raid.*

▶ *The Lancaster was a four-engined heavy bomber. Pilots recorded each mission with a painted symbol on the nose.*

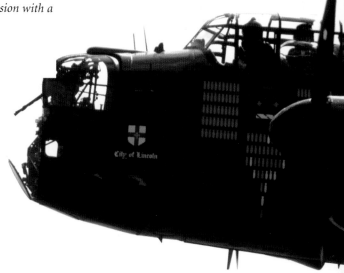

City of Lincoln

● **The commander of 617 Squadron** was Guy Gibson. He and his aircrew had trained for this special mission in Lancaster bombers adapted to carry an unusual weapon.

● **Inventor Barnes Wallis had designed** a bouncing bomb, that if dropped correctly would spin and skip across the water, to hit the dam wall. It would then sink and explode, blasting a hole.

● **The Dambusters raid** took place at night. The Lancasters had to roar in low over the water to drop their bombs at exactly the right height. Some planes were lost to heavy AA fire.

● **However, the bombers blew up** the Mohne and Eder dams. They wrecked a power station and flooded factories in Mulheim and Dortmund.

● **The Dambusters raid was a big boost** to morale in Britain and inspired a 1950s film.

The big bombers

▼ *The Lancaster was one of the main Allied weapons of the war. The bomb-aimer peered through the glass 'bubble' on the underside of the aircraft's nose.*

● **The Avro Lancaster was the RAF's** best big bomber. It had four Merlin engines, the same type as in the Spitfire fighter. Its top speed was about 442 km/h and it had a range of 2730 km.

● **A Lancaster usually carried** 5500 kg of bombs. By 1944, Lancasters could drop the enormous Grand Slam bomb of 10,000 kg.

> **. . . . FASCINATING FACT . . .**
> Gunners in a B-17 wore electrically heated suits to keep warm. Until late 1943, when tail and waist gun-turrets were enclosed, gunners froze in hurricane-force winds.

- **For defence, the Lancaster** had machine guns in rotating turrets in the nose, on top and in the tail. It had a crew of seven.

- **By 1943**, Lancasters were bombing targets deep inside Germany. During the war, this aircraft flew over 156,000 missions – 3345 Lancasters were lost.

- **The American Boeing B-17** was slightly faster than the Lancaster. Designed for daylight raids, the Flying Fortress had 13 machine guns and steel armour.

- **The Americans believed that a group** of 50 or more B-17s with their heavy armament could fight off German fighters.

- **B-17s flew from Britain** to bomb targets in occupied Europe. In January 1943, 64 B-17s bombed the town of Wilhemshaven – their first big raid on Germany.

- **Flying a B-17** was tough. Fliers suffered from altitude sickness and frostbite because they flew high to avoid German fighters.

- **Inside a B-17, the only place** a tall crewman could stand upright was in the radio room.

▲ *The Flying Fortress was aptly named – the B-17 bristled with guns. B-17s flew by day, in tight formation, while Lancasters normally bombed at night.*

Children at war

● **In Britain, gas masks and air raid drills** became part of classroom routine. Children hurried to the air raid shelter when the sirens sounded.

● **In the shelter**, children listened to stories or went on with their lessons until the all clear siren. Then teachers and children went back to the classroom.

● **Home life was affected** by the war. Some marriages broke up because of long separations. Many children missed fathers who were away in the forces.

● **Fathers who became POWs** (see page 142) were away for five years or more. Men taken prisoner in 1939–40 did not return home until 1945.

▲ *Anne Frank kept a diary while her family lived in hiding, in secret rooms behind an office in Amsterdam.*

● **Anne Frank, a Jewish girl**, spent two years hiding from the Nazis in the Netherlands (1942–44). She was 15 years old in June 1944. In August, she and her family were captured. Anne died in Bergen-Belsen concentration camp in 1945. She left her diary, which told her story.

...FASCINATING FACT...
In spite of food rationing, British children stayed surprisingly healthy in wartime. They ate fewer sweets and drank more milk, cod-liver oil and fruit juice.

● **Children helped the war effort** by collecting paper, glass and scrap metal for recycling. They saved leftover school dinners and knitted woolly hats, gloves and scarves for soldiers and refugees.

● **Toy shops had few factory-made toys** to sell, so people made their own – wooden planes and tanks were popular presents. Books were smaller, because paper was rationed.

● **Cinemas stayed open**, and many children enjoyed a weekly treat at the pictures. Bombed buildings made exciting playgrounds, but children were warned to stay away.

● **From school**, many young people went straight into the war. Many RAF pilots in the Battle of Britain had left school only a year or two before.

▶ *Many children were left scarred by the war. These two were photographed in Naples, Italy in 1944.*

North African victory

- **The French still had over 120,000 troops** in their North African colonies and the Allies were keen to make sure none of them helped the Germans.

- **Admiral Darlan**, commanding the French naval forces in North Africa, was not trusted by the Allies who thought he was pro-Nazi.

- **Darlan agreed to make French bases**, including the port of Dakar in West Africa, available to the Allies. He was murdered at the end of 1942.

▲ *Anti-aircraft 'tracer' fire lights up the night sky above the city of Algiers, during a German air raid.*

- **In January 1943**, Churchill and Roosevelt met at Casablanca. Their aim was to drive the Germans and Italians from North Africa, then land in Sicily.

- **Operation Torch** (see page 110) had landed Allied troops in North Africa. The landings were under the command of US General Dwight Eisenhower.

- **The Germans had reinforced** their Afrika Korps in Tunisia to meet the threat from the west. They had new Tiger tanks – the most powerful in the world.

- **US troops in Morocco and Algeria** got their first taste of serious fighting when they fought German troops in tank and infantry battles.

- **The Germans were now sandwiched** between two Allied armies. After victory at Alamein (see page 110), British forces pushed westward to link up with US troops in Tunisia in April 1943.

- **German General Rommel**, a sick man, left North Africa. The Allies swept forwards and German and Italian troops surrendered on 13 May 1943.

- **About 240,000 Axis prisoners** were taken. The way was clear for the Allies to invade Italy.

▼ *US President Roosevelt and British Prime Minister Churchill discuss events at Casablanca, January 1943.*

Tanks at war

- **The biggest tank battles** of World War II were in Russia. When Germany invaded the USSR in 1941, some 3400 German tanks knocked out most of the 17,000 Soviet tanks hurled against them.

- **The best Soviet tank** was the T-34/76. It was simple but rugged, and armed with a 76-mm gun.

- **However, by 1943 the Germans had the new Panther**, which could travel at 50 km/h and had a 75-mm gun. The 56-tonne Tiger was slower, but had an 88-mm gun, the best big gun of World War II.

- **British and American tanks** had inferior guns, thinner armour and broke down too often. The best new US tank was the Sherman. By 1943, British tank units also had the Churchill, an improvement on earlier British tanks.

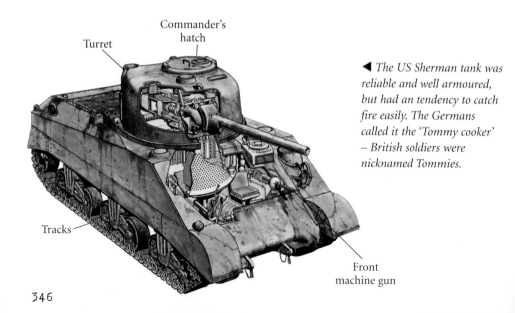

Turret

Commander's hatch

Tracks

Front machine gun

◄ *The US Sherman tank was reliable and well armoured, but had an tendency to catch fire easily. The Germans called it the 'Tommy cooker' – British soldiers were nicknamed Tommies.*

▶ *Infantry advance behind their tanks, under artillery fire, as the Russians attack in the Kursk 'bulge'.*

● **In 1943,** the Russians threw into combat their new T-34/85 tank – it weighed 32 tonnes and stood a better chance against the German Panther.

● **In June 1943**, the Germans attacked the town of Kursk, in Russia. The Russians had used 300,000 workers to build anti-tank defences with thousands of land mines and 6000 anti-tank guns.

● **Kursk was the biggest tank battle** of World War II. The Germans had around 2500 tanks, the Russians about 3300. The Germans failed to blast their way through the Russian defences.

● **In one fight**, 32 Tigers and 96 Panthers destroyed 184 Soviet T-34s, the battle lasting into the night by the glow of burning vehicles.

● **The Russians** kept coming. In the autumn of 1943, they crossed the river Dnieper with 2.5 million men, 51,000 guns and 2400 tanks. It was slow going, less than 250 km in four months of fighting.

...**FASCINATING FACT**...
Tank crews had little chance of escaping if their tank was hit and caught fire. British tank crews grimly called this 'brewing up'.

Italy invaded

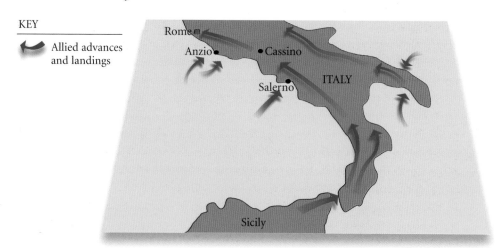

KEY

Allied advances and landings

Rome
Anzio
Cassino
Salerno
ITALY
Sicily

▲ *The Allies began their attack on Italy by landing troops on the island of Sicily. Allied commanders hoped Italy would be the soft underbelly of Nazi-occupied Europe, but it proved a tough campaign.*

- **Having driven the Axis Forces** from North Africa (see page 136), the Allies planned to attack Italy. They hoped to push the Italians out of the war.

- **In July 1943**, Allied troops began landing in Sicily. The Germans fought stubbornly and managed to move most of their troops to the mainland.

- **The Allied forces included the British 8th Army**, led by General Montgomery, and the US/British 5th Army, led by US General Mark Clark.

- **In July 1943**, Mussolini was ousted as Italy's Fascist leader and arrested. A new government led by Marshal Badoglio was appointed.

- **On 3 September**, British 8th Army troops crossed from Sicily to Calabria, in southern Italy. The Italians secretly made a ceasefire agreement with the Allies.

- **In September 1943**, Mussolini was rescued by German paratroops on Hitler's orders. German troops marched into Rome, to show that they were not letting Italy go easily.

- **On 9 September**, Allied troops of the 5th Army landed at the town of Salerno, near Naples. The landings went well and by the end of September, cheering Italians welcomed Allied troops in Naples.

- **The Germans took up defensive positions** along the Gustav Line, barring the way north to Rome. Winter weather with heavy rain slowed down the Allied advance.

- **Winston Churchill described** the Allies' fragile position as being 'like a bug in one leg'. The Apennines mountains were a formidable barrier.

- **Tired and muddy**, Allied troops met yet one more obstacle as the winter of 1943–44 set in. The Germans had fortified the mountains around Monte Cassino into a fortress.

▶ *Bernard Montgomery, commander of the British 8th Army. His success in North Africa, notably at El Alamein, made him an obvious choice for another challenge. He had an unswerving belief in his own ability – a trait that did not always endear him to other commanders.*

Prisoners of war

▼ *Prisoners of the Japanese were lucky to survive. These emaciated Dutch captives were photographed after captivity in the East Indies (Indonesia).*

- **Prisoners of war (POWs)** were servicemen captured while in uniform. The Geneva Convention governed their correct treatment.

- **A prisoner was required only to give his name**, rank and service number. He was not supposed to be interrogated or tortured.

- **The Geneva rules** were not always followed. On the Eastern Front, Germans and Russians sometimes shot prisoners. The Japanese ill-treated Allied prisoners, forcing them to work and starving them.

- **Prisoners of war** were held in camps. German and Italian prisoners captured in western Europe were sent to camps in Britain and Canada.

- **In a POW camp in Germany**, 'Appell' was roll-call, a 'bash' was a decent meal, a 'goon' a German and a 'goon-box' a watch-tower.

- **Some POWs organized entertainment**, sport and education. Others set up committees to plan escapes – they tried digging tunnels under camp fences, slipping away from working parties or escaping in rubbish trucks.

- **POWs were ingenious at making fake guns**, ID papers and clothes, even German uniforms, for escape attempts.

- **The Great Escape took place** from Stalag Luft III in Germany. In March 1944, 76 Allied POWs tunnelled out. Three reached England. Fifty were shot by the Gestapo after recapture.

- **For the Great Escape**, the POWs dug three tunnels, named Tom, Dick and Harry. They hoped that over 200 men would get out through Harry.

- **Colditz Castle in Germany** was a special camp for determined escapers and special prisoners. It had once been a mental asylum.

Burma and China

◀ A British army tin hat, as worn by troops in the Burma battles, though in the jungle many men preferred soft hats.

● **From 1943**, Admiral Louis Mountbatten, a relative of King George VI, was Allied supreme commander in Southeast Asia. He was an enthusiast for combined operations.

● **By late 1943**, the war in China and Burma was entering a crucial stage. Both sides thought that they were winning.

● **The Japanese planned to attack** across the river Chindwin in Burma, to advance on India.

● **The Allies attacked them** from China, with US General Stilwell's Chinese army and Merrill's Marauders, who were Americans trained to fight like the British Chindits.

● **The British 14th Army** in Burma was commanded by General Slim. He told his men that even if they were surrounded by the Japanese, supplies would reach them by air.

● **Slim knew that one reason** for Japan's success in the jungle was how their troops infiltrated through Allied lines and slipped round behind them.

● **The Allies were stronger in tanks** and aircraft. Air power helped drive back Japanese troops attacking the towns of Imphal and Kohima on the India–Burma frontier.

▲ *A Chinese soldier guards a line of US P-40 fighters of the American Volunteer group, the Flying Tigers, who fought the Japanese in a largely unsung war.*

● **In March 1944**, Orde Wingate, the officer who planned the first Chindit raids into the jungle, was killed in an air crash.

● **In May 1944**, Chinese forces crossed the river Salween into Burma to attack the Japanese. Myitkina airbase was captured by the Allies on 17 May, and the town itself in August.

● **Most of northern Burma** was in Allied hands, but the Japanese were not beaten. They seized several airfields in China, which the Allies had wanted to use for bombing raids on Japan.

353

Second front

● **Since 1943, the Soviet Union** had urged the Allies to open a second front in Europe – by attacking Hitler from the west.

● **To help the Russians,** the Allies sent guns, planes and food in convoys of ships (see page 148). Stalin wanted more. He wanted the second front.

● **In August 1943, the Allies agreed** that an invasion of France could not take place before 1944. The code name for the invasion was Operation Overlord.

● **By the end of 1943,** thousands of US and Canadian troops were arriving in England to begin training for a huge Allied sea and air invasion of France.

● **During 1943,** the Allies gained a foothold in Italy and Italian forces began to surrender (see page 140). On 12 October 1943, Italy declared war on its former ally, Germany.

● **The Allies told the Russians** that Hitler was holding back troops in the west. They arrived to defend Italy and prepare to counter Operation Overlord, so German armies on the Eastern Front would be weaker.

● **America, Britain and Russia** disagreed about some war aims. All three wanted Germany defeated, but the Russians were not yet at war with Japan.

● **Stalin wanted to control Eastern Europe** after the war and make Poland virtually part of the Soviet Union. The Polish government-in-exile in London insisted Poland must be free.

▶ *General Dwight D Eisenhower, US Army, was appointed to command the invasion of Western Europe. He was a skilful 'man-manager'.*

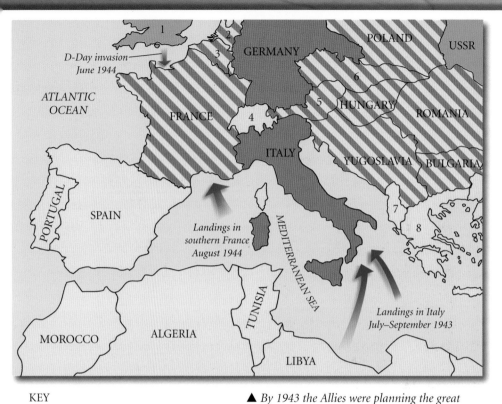

D-Day invasion
June 1944

ATLANTIC
OCEAN

Landings in
southern France
August 1944

Landings in Italy
July–September 1943

KEY

 Occupied by
Axis forces

Allies

Axis forces

1 United Kingdom
2 Netherlands

3 Belgium
4 Switzerland
5 Austria
6 Czechoslovakia
7 Albania
8 Greece

▲ *By 1943 the Allies were planning the great invasion to liberate France. This would open a second front in the west. The Axis forces were fighting the Russians on the eastern front, but much of Europe was occupied by the Nazis.*

● **Churchill felt that the Americans** were too eager to make concessions to Stalin. Churchill hated Communism and did not trust the Soviet leader.

● **In Britain, there was a lot of support** for the Russians as they fought valiantly on their own soil. Demands for the second front came from all sides.

Arctic convoys

- **The Allies began sending convoys** of cargo ships, with naval escorts, around northern Norway to the Russian ports of Murmansk and Archangel.

- **In winter**, it was almost always dark. In summer, 24-hour daylight helped German planes find and attack the convoys.

- **It was so cold that ice** sheathed the ship's decks and seamen wore their overcoats in bed.

- **The Germans attacked** the convoys with warships, U-boats and aircraft.

- **The British feared** that the German battleship *Tirpitz* (see page 170) would leave its Norwegian base to attack convoys. In September 1943, Midget submarines put *Tirpitz* out of action for six months.

...FASCINATING FACT...

One seaman remembered that after an escort dropped depth charges to attack a U-boat, the dead fish that floated to the surface were frozen – it was so cold.

- **The German battle-cruiser** *Scharnhorst* attacked a convoy in December 1943, but was sunk by British warships. One of these was HMS *Belfast*, now moored near Tower Bridge in London.

  - **The worst convoy disaster** was when convoy PQ 17 was attacked in July 1942 – 23 of its 34 ships were sunk.

    - **More than 3000 Merchant Navy seamen** were lost in Arctic waters between 1941 and 1945. Veterans parade in white berets to remind people of the snow and ice they braved.

      - **Altogether there were** 78 Arctic convoys. The last sailed to Russia in May 1945. The dangerous voyage was made by 720 ships, delivering 5000 tanks and 7000 aircraft.

◀ *A ship almost encased in ice and snow while on Arctic convoy escort duty in 1943, and (below) a wrapped-up seaman.*

357

Italy liberated

- **The Allies hoped that the Germans** would withdraw from Italy after the fall of Mussolini.

- **However, the Germans held on,** even though the Allies controlled the seas and air.

- **Allied troops pushed north,** but were held up by Germans in the town of Monte Cassino in January 1944. Fighting around this monastery was fierce. Allied bombs and guns destroyed the monastery on the hilltop.

- **On 22 January 1944,** the Allies landed more troops at the town of Anzio, hoping to cut off the German retreat northwards and speed up their liberation of Rome.

- **Not until May 1944** did British and Polish troops capture what was left of Monte Cassino. Two days later, Allied troops broke out from their Anzio beachhead to join other Allied forces.

- **Allied troops were still finding** it tough going. The Germans used new weapons such as radio-controlled glider-bombs against Allied ships.

- **On 4 June,** Allied troops reached Rome. The Germans retreated and the city was taken without much fighting. Hitler told his generals to blow up bridges across the river Tiber, but they ignored the order.

- **On 5 June,** King Victor Emmanuel of Italy gave up the throne and his son Umberto became king.

- **Italians welcomed the Allies** as liberators. On 4 August Florence was taken by Allied troops and the Germans withdrew.

- **The Allied commander, General Alexander,** told his men that 'we are going to destroy the German armies in Italy'. However, the Germans still held northern Italy and Mussolini was still alive.

▼ *A German soldier stands amid the ruins of Monte Cassino monastery, April 1944.*

D-Day

● **By the spring of 1944**, southern England was crammed with 3 million men. Convoys jammed roads and 20,000 trains steamed to and from the coast.

● **The Supreme Allied commander** was US General Dwight Eisenhower. His number two was General Montgomery.

● **The Allies used tricks** and deception to confuse the Germans. They sent fake messages, and built dummy airfields, plywood ships and inflatable aircraft.

● **The Germans knew invasion was coming**, but not when or where. They expected the Allies to attack the Pas de Calais, the shortest crossing.

● **The Allies chose Normandy**, where beaches would be less heavily defended than those around Calais. Allied troops would attack by sea and from the air.

◀ *Eisenhower has a parting word with airborne troops before they set off for France on 5 June 1944. The troops are kitted out for a night landing with blackened faces.*

...FASCINATING FACT...

An actor was hired to impersonate British General Montgomery to fool the Germans into thinking that he was in Italy, not England.

● **Hitler called his defences** the 'Atlantic Wall', but some German commanders feared they would only hold up the Allies for 24 hours.

● **Operation Overlord depended on air** and naval supremacy and fine weather.

● **D-Day was set for 5 June**, but the weather forecast was so bad that the invasion was postponed for 24 hours. Confident that invasion was not imminent, German General Rommel went back to Berlin for his wife's birthday.

● **Eisenhower listened** to the weather forecast. Hearing that good weather was expected, he fixed D-Day for 6 June.

▶ *Eisenhower's good luck message to the Allied forces.*

SUPREME HEADQUARTERS
ALLIED EXPEDITIONARY FORCE

Soldiers, Sailors and Airmen of the Allied Expeditionary Force!

You are about to embark upon the Great Crusade, toward which we have striven these many months. The eyes of the world are upon you. The hopes and prayers of liberty-loving people everywhere march with you. In company with our brave Allies and brothers-in-arms on other Fronts, you will bring about the destruction of the German war machine, the elimination of Nazi tyranny over the oppressed peoples of Europe, and security for ourselves in a free world.

Your task will not be an easy one. Your enemy is well trained, well equipped and battle-hardened. He will fight savagely.

But this is the year 1944! Much has happened since the Nazi triumphs of 1940-41. The United Nations have inflicted upon the Germans great defeats, in open battle, man-to-man. Our air offensive has seriously reduced their strength in the air and their capacity to wage war on the ground. Our Home Fronts have given us an overwhelming superiority in weapons and munitions of war, and placed at our disposal great reserves of trained fighting men. The tide has turned! The free men of the world are marching together to Victory!

I have full confidence in your courage, devotion to duty and skill in battle. We will accept nothing less than full Victory!

Good Luck! And let us all beseech the blessing of Almighty God upon this great and noble undertaking.

Dwight D Eisenhower

Invasion armada

● **An armada of 4000 ships** converged on northern France. The D-Day fleet included battleships like HMS *Warspite* and cruisers like HMS *Belfast.* Their big guns were used to bombard German defences.

● **The landing craft were packed** with soldiers. By the time they got to France, many of the troops were seasick after hours at sea. Special landing craft carried tanks and heavy equipment.

● **US General Eisenhower said the German army** was, "the most professionally skilful army of all time." Before the invasion began, he said, "If any blame or fault attaches to the attempt, it is mine alone."

▼ *US troops wait for the ramp of the landing craft to drop.*

▶ *When the ramp falls, men wade ashore towards the enemy-held beach.*

● **The BBC broadcast coded messages** to the French Resistance telling them that the invasion had begun.

● **On 5 June, Allied airborne troops** began boarding planes and gliders at 9 p.m. The air armada consisted of 1366 tow-planes and parachute-droppers and 3520 gliders, each carrying assault troops.

● **The first airborne landings** by US and British troops were made at 12.20 a.m. on 6 June. The object was to capture key bridges and canals.

● **At daybreak, the invasion fleet** could be seen by the startled Germans guarding the beaches.

● **In the skies above flew** nearly 8000 aircraft – all with wings painted in black-and-white stripes for identification.

● **Specialized tanks were designed**, such as Crabs – with flails to blow up land mines, Crocodiles – flame throwers, and D-Ds – amphibious Sherman tanks.

● **Dummy paratroopers, known as Ruperts**, were dropped from planes over Normandy to confuse the Germans.

Battle for the beaches

● **The first wave** of the invasion army consisted of 156,000 Allied troops. There were 20 US divisions, 14 British, three Canadian, one Polish and one French.

● **Midget submarines were waiting close inshore** to guide the troops in. Some crews had spent 48 hours inside their tiny craft, which was less than 20 m long.

● **The Allies landed on five** further beaches. US troops headed for Utah and Omaha. The British and Canadians landed on Gold, Juno and Sword.

● **US troops began landing** at the most westerly beach, Utah, at 6.30 a.m. on 6 June. They met little resistance.

- **However at Omaha beach**, many US troops were shot dead before they even reached the sand. The defences there were far stronger than expected.

- **Losses on land and at sea off Omaha** were over 2000 – more than all the other beaches put together.

- **There were further setbacks** as the US 82nd and 101st Airborne Divisions lost many men dropped in the sea or in marshes flooded by the Germans.

- **John Steele of the 82nd Airborne Division** found himself dangling from his parachute cords from the church tower in Sainte-Mere-Eglise.

- **The landings at Sword**, Juno and Gold beaches went relatively smoothly.

- **Two temporary harbours**, known as Mulberry harbours, were towed across the Channel. On 19 June the one at Omaha was wrecked by a storm.

▼ *Getting off Omaha Beach. US reinforcements walk inland from the beach where many first-wave troops were killed.*

Allied air power

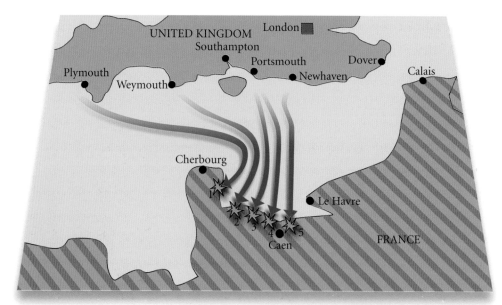

KEY

Allied air and
seabourne forces

Beach battles

Occupied by Axis forces

1 Utah
2 Omaha
3 Gold
4 Juno
5 Sword

▲ *The Allied landing beaches, Omaha, Utah, Gold, Juno and Sword, were protected by a vast armada of warships and an even more numerous air fleet as reinforcements poured in from England.*

● **By the end of June,** 500,000 Allied troops had been landed in France. This success owed much to Allied control of the skies. The German air force had few planes or pilots left.

● **Allied bombers targeted cities,** factories and troops on the move. It was difficult for the Germans to send reinforcements because trucks and trains were attacked by Allied planes.

- **Fast fighter-bombers flew low** over France to surprise the Germans. The RAF's Typhoon was good at 'train-busting' – shooting trains and trucks with rockets.

- **Allied factories were building large numbers** of fast bombers such as the B-26 Marauder and Mosquito, and fighters such as the Thunderbolt, Mustang and Lightning.

- **The plan was for Allied soldiers** to move inland fast. Normandy's small fields and thick hedges slowed them down, aiding the German defence.

- **In tank battles, Allied tanks were outgunned** by German Panthers and Tigers. At Villers-Bocage in Normandy, one Tiger knocked out 25 Allied tanks and 28 other vehicles.

- **Air power helped the Allies** knock out German tanks and hit their fuel supplies, leaving them helpless.

- **Allied bombing** caused severe damage. The Norman city of Caen was almost obliterated during a fierce battle in the summer of 1944.

- **German troops were squeezed** between Allied armies into an area known as the Falaise Pocket. Thousands were killed and huge amounts of weaponry destroyed by air attacks.

...FASCINATING FACT...
The Germans were still building new aircraft, despite the Allied air raids on German factories. They had the first jet fighter, the Me 262 (see page 174) and also a rocket-powered plane, the Me 163.

Flying bombs

● **As the Allied invasion** gathered momentum, Hitler unleashed his first 'revenge weapon' – the V-1 flying bomb.

● **The V-1 was launched** by a catapult from a ramp, before its impulse-engine, a kind of jet engine, began to work.

● **The bomb was 6.5 m in length** and flew at over 560 km/h. The warhead in the nose was packed with 1060 kg of high explosive.

● **The V-1 was guided** by a pre-set automatic pilot. A small propeller in the nose counted back every 30 revolutions making a counter move back. When the counter reached zero, the engine cut out.

● **The V-1 had a range** of about 250 km. The first one fell on London on 12 June 1944. German High Command claimed that the whole of southern England was shrouded in smoke from V-1 attacks.

● **When the engine stopped**, the V-1 dived, crashed and exploded. People could see and hear it coming. Its 'put-put' engine earned it the nickname of 'doodlebug' and 'buzz-bomb'.

● **V-1s flying over the Channel** and southern England were chased by the RAF's fastest fighters, the Tempest and the new Meteor jet.

● **During the V-1 onslaught**, Hitler survived an assassination attempt. In July 1944, a bomb in a briefcase was placed under a table.

● **By the end of 1944**, the threat from the V-1s had passed because the Allies had overrun or destroyed all the landing sites from which the V-1s could reach England.

▼ *The V-1 flying bomb was easy to spot in flight, and as it flew in a straight line, relatively easy to shoot down. The top-scoring flying bomb ace was RAF pilot Joseph Berry who shot down 60 V-1s during 1944.*

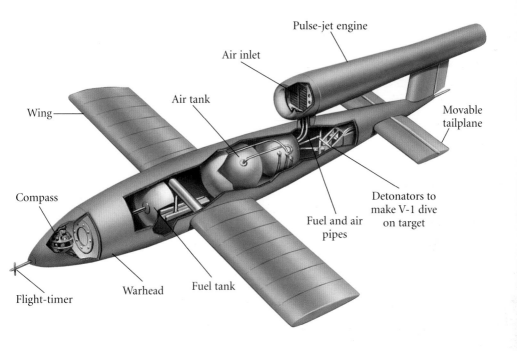

Pulse-jet engine

Air inlet

Air tank

Wing

Movable tailplane

Compass

Detonators to make V-1 dive on target

Fuel and air pipes

Warhead

Fuel tank

Flight-timer

......FASCINATING FACT......
Fighter pilots either shot at the flying bombs or tipped their wings over with their own wing, causing the V-1 to crash in the sea or over fields.

Paris free

- **The Free French government** had been based in London since 1940. Free French troops took part in the liberation of France in the summer of 1944.

- **General de Gaulle, leader of the Free French**, landed in Normandy soon after D-Day. On 20 June 1944, he was greeted in the town of Bayeux.

...FASCINATING FACT...
French people had been told of liberation by the BBC, which broadcast coded 'family messages' in French from England.

- **Churchill visited the Cherbourg Peninsula**, where the key port of Cherbourg was captured on 27 June.

- **Among many German weapons** captured by the Allies were several very large guns mounted on railway trucks.

- **Villages in Normandy had been terribly damaged** by the heavy fighting. People in Paris wondered what would happen to their city.

- **On 14–15 August**, Allied troops landed in the south of France. Resistance fighters began fighting the Vichy militia and German troops.

- **On 18–19 August**, Resistance groups in Paris began firing on the Germans. Collaborators and Nazis were either killed or fled. German snipers fired from rooftops and windows.

- **Fighting stopped on 24 August**, and on 25 August the French 2nd Armoured Division drove into the city. The German commander, General Scholitz, surrendered.

- **There was rejoicing as De Gaulle walked through Paris** and crowds welcomed liberation. But there was also revenge. Collaborators who had worked for the Nazis were shot. French girlfriends of German soldiers were paraded with shaven heads to be jeered at.

◀ *US troops line up on the barrel of a mammoth railway gun left behind as the German armies retreated towards Germany.*

371

Arnhem

- **On 3 September 1944**, British troops liberated Brussels, the capital of Belgium. The Allies were also speeding through France towards the river Rhine and by 10 September, they had arrived in Germany.

- **Allied generals** decided to 'leapfrog' over the river Rhine. The German armies were still reeling from the speed of the D-Day invasion.

- **On 17 September 1944**, thousands of US, British and Polish paratroops floated down from planes to land around the towns of Arnhem and Nijmegen in the Netherlands.

- **More troops were flown in by gliders**, towed by planes. The gliders were released from the tow line and flew down to land in the fields.

- **The plan of Operation Market Garden** was to seize crossings over the rivers Waal and Leck, two branches of the river Rhine, to stop the Germans from blowing up the bridges.

- **The airborne troops were successful** at Nijmegen, but at Arnhem soon found themselves under attack from strong German forces.

- **Bad weather prevented the Allied air forces** from flying and the tanks that was supposed to help the men at Arnhem were held up on the way by German resistance.

- **By 25–26 September**, it was clear that the Arnhem mission had failed. More than 1100 Allied troops were killed and 6000 taken prisoner.

- **The good news was that US forces** to the south were still moving fast and by 15 December they were almost at the river Rhine.

...FASCINATING FACT...
Mike Dauncey, a British pilot at Arnhem, remembered the welcome he
received from the Dutch, "everyone wanted to give us apples." He was
wounded in the fighting and became a POW, but escaped.

▼ *Gliders with their black-and-white invasion markings lie empty,*
as more Allied troops land by parachute.

V-2s hit London

- **The V-2 was Germany's ultimate** 'vengeance weapon'. It was a single-stage rocket with a range of about 320 km, carrying a warhead of 725 kg.

- **Smaller rockets were fired** by armies in World War II as mobile launch systems for battlefield use at close range.

- **The German 6-tube** *Nebelwerfer* was nicknamed the 'Moaning Minnie' by Allied troops because of its distinctive sound. It had a range of 5500 m.

- **The Russians had the Katyusha** rocket. They launched up to 48 at a time from a boxlike launcher nicknamed the 'Stalin Organ'.

- **The V-2 was much bigger** than battlefield rockets. Officially called the A-4, it was designed by Wernher von Braun with a team of scientists at Peenemunde in Germany.

- **The V-2 flew at supersonic speed**, so there was no warning of its coming. Nor was there any defence.

- **The first V-2 was fired against Paris** on 6 September 1944 and on 8 September another hit London. Over 4000 V-2s were fired during the closing months of World War II.

- **In February–March 1945**, V-2s were hitting at the rate of 60 a week. Several V-2 attacks killed more than 100 people.

- **V-2 launch sites were bombed** by Allied planes – this was the only way to stop the threat.

- **When the war ended**, the US captured more than 60 V-2s and Wernher von Braun, who later worked on NASA's space programme.

◀ *V-2 rockets stand on their launch platforms. The threat from the first ballistic missiles, against which there was no defence, worried Allied leaders. Their reaction was to target the V-2 launch sites and the factories producing the rockets.*

Back to the Philippines

● **The Allied plan in the Pacific** was to 'island hop', to wear down Japanese resources and manpower (see pages 126 and 178).

● **US troops occupied Kwajalein Atoll** in January 1944 and Eniwetok in February. They also raided the Japanese base at Truk, in the Caroline Islands.

● **Their next target was the Marianas Islands**, which the Americans attacked with 500 ships and 125,000 troops.

▼ *General MacArthur (centre) wades ashore as US forces land to liberate the Philippines.*

► *US troops destroy one of the last Japanese strongholds on tiny Kwajalein Atoll in February 1944. Each island group captured became a base for the Allies' next attack.*

● **The Japanese devised a counter attack** using 1000 aircraft and nine aircraft carriers.

● **In April 1944,** the Allies drove the Japanese out of western New Guinea, and in June they attacked Saipan in the Marianas.

● **At Saipan, many Japanese defenders** were in caves and underground bunkers. They made a last suicidal counter attack in July.

● **When news of the defeat** reached the prime minister of Japan, Tojo Hideki, he resigned.

● **In November 1944,** the US began flying huge B-29 bombers from Saipan to attack Japan.

● **A Japanese fleet then took on a superior US force** at the Battle of the Philippine Sea. The Japanese lost three carriers and almost 400 planes.

● **In October 1944,** the US landed in the Philippines to begin the liberation of the islands, captured in 1942.

Sinking Tirpitz

- **The battleship *Admiral von Tirpitz*,** launched in April 1939, was called 'the pride of the German Navy'. It was a sister ship to *Bismarck* (see page 70).

- ***Tirpitz's* steel armour was up to 32 cm thick** to stop shells and bombs. The Germans boasted that it was unsinkable.

- **The battleship's main armament** was eight 38-cm guns in four turrets, but it also carried over 50 smaller guns, torpedoes and four seaplanes.

- **The Royal Navy feared** *Tirpitz* would attack Arctic convoys (see page 148), but the huge ship never ventured further than a Norwegian fjord.

- **The British were desperate** to sink *Tirpitz*. They tried using bombers, aircraft-carriers, submarines, torpedoes and even versions of the Dambusters' bouncing bombs.

- **From 1942–44,** they tried 27 different aircraft types of the RAF and Fleet Air Arm to damage or sink *Tirpitz*.

- **In 1944, Barnes Wallis designed** a 5-tonne Tallboy bomb (6 m in length), designed to penetrate a target before exploding.

- **In September 1944,** RAF Lancasters flew to Russia, to attack *Tirpitz* from Yagodnik near Archangel. In two raids, on 15 September and 12 November 1944, Tallboy bombs ended the threat from *Tirpitz*.

- **On the last attack,** *Tirpitz* capsized as a result of explosives 'blowing away' the water beneath the ship, which turned over and sank.

....FASCINATING FACT....
Norwegians watched the attack on *Tirpitz* from the town of Tromso, where the noise of exploding bombs produced a deep trembling.

The British had long feared Tirpitz *would one day come out of hiding. Newspapers could at last celebrate the end of 'the beast', as Churchill called the German battleship, and describe how 29 Lancasters bombed* Tirpitz *out of a war it had never really got seriously involved in.*

Battle of the Bulge

▼ *A US soldier watches over two German prisoners, after the battle at Bastogne.*

● **The US commander of the 3rd Army**, General Patton, was known for his aggressive tactics. His men called him 'Blood and Guts' Patton.

● **By December 1944**, Patton's army was so close to the river Rhine that the Germans decided on one last desperate gamble – a winter counter attack.

● **Hitler would not hear** of surrender. He was out of touch, seemed mad to some, and seldom left of his Berlin HQ. His orders were to keep fighting.

● **Von Rundstedt, commander of the German armies** in the west, called on all his reserves and massed all the tanks, infantry and planes he had left.

● **On 16 December**, they began attacks through the Ardennes forest in Belgium. They drove through the tired US 1st Army.

● **In three days, the Germans opened** up a gap or bulge in the Allied lines. The battle became known as the Battle of the Bulge.

● **Bad weather grounded Allied planes** and the Germans covered 80 km.

● **As the Germans began to run low** on fuel and supplies, the weather cleared and Allied aircraft could begin attacks.

● **By January 1945**, the Germans had pulled back from the bulge. They had lost 90,000 men either killed, wounded or captured.

...FASCINATING FACT...
At Bastogne, the American defenders fought back fiercely. When asked if he wanted to surrender, the US commander gave a one-word reply, "Nuts."

German jets

- **Germany had pioneered jet aircraft**, flying the Heinkel He 178 on 27 August 1939. This was the first jet plane to fly.

- **The first jet engine**, built by Frank Whittle in Britain, was tested in April 1937, but the first British jet plane did not fly until May 1941.

- **The Germans had already tested** their Messerschmitt 262 jet in April 1941.

- **The Me 262** was named *Sturmvogel*, meaning stormbird. It had a top speed of over 860 km/h and was ready for combat in 1944.

- **Hitler was convinced that the jets** would destroy the Allied invasion (see pages 152–156), so he ordered the Me 262 to be fitted with bombs.

- **This was a mistake,** for heavy bombs slowed down the jet. The first Me 262s began combat missions in France in July 1944.

- **Me 262s carrying bombs** could be shot down by slower propeller-driven fighters. The first Me 262 was downed by US fighters on 28 August 1944.

- **A faster fighter version**, the *Schwalbe*, meaning swallow, came into service in October 1944. It could outfly the fastest Allied fighters and attacked Allied bombers raiding Germany.

- **Me 262s were fitted with 24 unguided rockets**, which the pilots fired into formations of US bombers.

- **The Germans also built** the world's first jet bombers, such as the Arado A-234 Blitz in 1944. However, jets came too late to stop them losing the war.

▶ *The fighter-bomber version of the twin-engined Me 262 jet was heavier and thus slower, making it less effective in combat than enemy fighter jets.*

Pacific decider

▼ *US might at sea – the*
battleships USS Pennsylvania
and Colorado *lead the way.*

- **After the US invaded** the Philippines in October 1944 (see page 168), the Japanese made determined air attacks on US ships and troops.

- **The Japanese navy had fewer aircraft carriers**, planes and pilots than the US Navy. Even so, Japanese commanders hoped to win a decisive victory.

- **The Japanese hoped to lure** the US fleet into a trap and even up the odds, using their battleships as well as aircraft carriers.

- **The giant battleship** *Musashi*, a sister-ship of the *Yamato* and the largest warship afloat, was sunk by US air attacks on 23 October 1944.

- **A huge naval-air battle was fought** in the Leyte Gulf, off the Philippines, on 25 October. The result was a disaster for Japan.

- **At Leyte Gulf, the biggest sea battle of the war**, the Japanese lost three battleships, four carriers, ten cruisers and 11 destroyers.

- **The US lost three carriers**, but these were small escorts, less vital than the big fleet carriers that carried most warplanes.

- **The US fleet was commanded** by Admiral Halsey. The Japanese commander at Leyte Gulf, Admiral Kurita, had to be rescued when his ship was sunk early in the battle.

- **In the battle**, 282 ships took part. Towards the end, desperate Japanese pilots made suicide attacks, called kamikaze, meaning divine wind.

...FASCINATING FACT...
The Japanese battleship, *Musashi*, was so enormous that it capsized and sank after only being hit by 19 torpedoes and 17 bombs.

Island hopping

- **During 1944**, the Allies had fought hard to push the Japanese out of the Solomon Islands and New Guinea.

- **At its peak, Japanese control** in the Pacific had stretched from Wake Island in the north to Rabaul in the south – only minutes flying time from Australia. Now they were beginning to give ground.

- **The Japanese did not believe** in surrendering. Even small garrisons of troops on small islands would fight to the last man, at great cost in lives to both sides.

- **Many lives would be lost** if every island had to be fought over. So the Allies decided to 'hop' from one island to another, using sea power and aircraft. Other islands occupied by the Japanese would be left alone.

- **The Allied strategy was to knock out** the Japanese navy and especially its aircraft carriers. They wanted island air bases, for bombing attacks on the Philippines, still held by Japan, and Japan itself.

- **The main ground forces** used in the island-hopping attacks were US Marines, who fought from ships and also had their own aircraft.

- **In September 1944**, US forces landed on the Palau Islands, only 700 km from the Philippines. In 12 days of fighting, the Japanese lost 10,000 men.

- **On 12–13 September 1944**, US battleships bombarded the island of Saipan, a Japanese base in the Marianas Islands. Then US troops landed – the Allies now had a base only 1500 km from Tokyo.

- **The loss of Saipan and of other islands** such as the Marshalls in February 1945 came as a shock to people in Japan. Prime Minister General Tojo told Parliament that the war situation was very grave.

- **Island battles** were savage. Japanese troops in caves and tunnels were killed by bombs, grenades and flame throwers as they defended every inch of ground.

▼ *The Pacific battles took a heavy toll of US army and marines. These marines were photographed on Bougainville Island in 1944. Many of their comrades were dead or wounded.*

The Dresden raid

- **By 1945**, the Allies were winning. Romania was out of the war by August 1944, depriving Germany of vital oilfields. The Russians and Tito's partisans had taken Belgrade, capital of Yugoslavia. Greece had been liberated.

- **Germany was now the key target** in the west. By 1945, the RAF had shifted from 'area bombing' (see page 106) to oil targets inside Germany.

- **By January 1945**, the 8th USAAF had over 1800 bombers, the RAF over 1500.

- **Bomber Command dropped more bombs** in October–December 1944 than during the whole of 1943.

- **German air defences** were much weaker. Even when the *Luftwaffe* managed to send up 300 fighters, they were beaten off by twice that number of Allied fighters escorting the day's bomber streams.

- **Stalin still called for more bombing** of Germany itself, as the Russians attacked from the east through Poland.

- **On 27 January 1945**, RAF Bomber Command was ordered to resume area bombing, as well as targeting oil depots and communications.

- **In February** a large force of RAF and USAAF bombers attacked the German city of Dresden. The target was the centre of the historic city, which had no great military importance. The aim was to cause havoc and disrupt the transport that was supplying German armies fighting the Russians.

- **So intense was the bombing** that it created a firestorm, devastating much of the heart of Dresden and killing civilians.

- **People were burned to death** and suffocated as the fire consumed all the oxygen in the air. The death toll is estimated to range from 35,000 to 150,000.

▶ *Dresden after the firestorm. Most of the city centre was in ruins when the bombers left, and the fires died down.*

Iwo Jima

● **With the Philippines almost liberated** the Americans planned to step up the bombing of Japan.

● **B-29s, the newest bombers in the US armoury,** were flying to Japan from Saipan island. It was a long trip of over 2000 km and US commanders wanted a base closer to Japan.

● **They chose Iwo Jima,** a small volcanic island in the Bonin group, being used as a Japanese base.

● **To attack it, the US assembled** a naval force to bombard the Japanese, who had dug themselves into caves and hilltops.

● **The 20,000 Japanese on Iwo Jima** survived an intensive air and sea bombardment before US Marines landed on the island on 19 February.

◀ *Marines help wounded comrades at Iwo Jima.*

- **The Marines met** stiff resistance. Iwo Jima became one of the bloodiest battles of the war.

- **US Marines raised the American flag** on Mount Suribachi on 23 February, but fighting continued until 16 March.

- **The raising of the US flag** by Marines at Iwo Jima became one of the most powerful and evocative images of the war.

- **The Marines lost** nearly 6000 men. Almost all the 20,000 Japanese troops on Iwo Jima died.

- **Once secured, Iwo Jima's air base** was used by B-29s and their US fighter escorts.

◀ *The Stars and Stripes flag is raised on Mount Suribachi, 23 February 1945.*

Okinawa

- **The Japanese vowed to defend** their homeland to the death. The casualty costs of a D-Day style invasion of Japan would be great.

- **President Roosevelt did not wish to throw away** the lives of Allied troops. His commanders told him that bombing might force the Japanese to surrender.

◀ *A Marine dashes across 'Death Valley' during the battle for Okinawa.*

- **The last island** 'stepping stone' towards Japan was Okinawa. This small island, 108 km long and 26 km wide, was heavily defended.

- **Okinawa was bombed by Allied planes** to weaken its defences while a large amphibious invasion force was gathered.

- **On 26 March 1945** came the first landings on small islands west of Okinawa itself and on 1 April, 60,000 US troops landed on Okinawa's west coast.

- **Japan's government resigned over the disgrace** of the invasions. For US troops to set foot on Okinawa was seen as a national humiliation.

- **The Japanese navy sent** the giant battleship, *Yamato*, on a desperate attack, with only enough fuel for a one-way mission. It was sunk on 7 April.

- **Japanese pilots made kamikaze attacks**, as pilots crash-landed their planes onto Allied warships.

- **The battle for Okinawa** did not end until 2 July 1945, by which time the Japanese commander had already committed suicide.

- **Japanese losses at Okinawa** were about 100,000 dead. The US forces lost about 12,000 dead and 36,000 wounded.

Germany crumbles

- **In January 1945**, the Russians gathered a huge army on the Eastern Front for the assault on Germany. Hitler at first refused to transfer German troops from the west to the east.

- **When the Russian advance** began, the Germans faced the new Stalin tank, armed with a 122-mm gun that was even bigger than the Tiger's 88 mm.

- **The Russians broke through** into Poland and by the end of January, their armies were only 150 km from Berlin.

- **On 13 February**, the Russians captured Budapest, capital of Hungary. On 13 April they were in Vienna, Austria.

- **The Germans were also losing** in northern Italy. On 28 April, Mussolini was caught and the next day executed by partisans near Lake Como. On 29 April, German forces in Italy surrendered.

- **In the west** US tanks captured the Rhine bridge at Remagen. US General Patton and British General Montgomery sent troops across the river Rhine on 21–23 March, using boats, amphibious tanks and airborne troops.

- **On 12 April**, US President Roosevelt died. German Propaganda Minister, Joseph Goebbels, phoned Hitler to say, "God has not abandoned us." Hitler was trapped in his underground bunker HQ in Berlin.

- **Apparently thinking Hitler was dead**, Heinrich Himmler, commander of the SS, offered a secret peace deal, which was refused by the Allies.

- **On 1 May, German radio announced** that Hitler was dead. He and his newly wed wife, Eva Braun, had killed themselves. Also dead was Goebbels, along with his wife and children.

- **On 2 May 1945**, Berlin was surrendered to the Russians. Most of the city was in ruins. Those who could, had fled west towards the Americans and British.

▲ On 2 May 1945, newspaper headlines carried the news that Hitler was dead, three days after Mussolini. Admiral Doenitz had been named as the German leader's successor. The German army or Wehrmacht was still fighting, but most readers knew that the end of the war in Europe could not be far off.

Death camps

- **As the Russians swept across Germany**, they met up with US troops on the banks of the river Elbe. Both sides had seen for the first time the horrors of Nazi rule.

- **At Auschwitz in Poland**, the Russians uncovered evidence of Hitler's Final Solution to 'the Jewish problem' – the gas chambers.

- **US troops entered Buchenwald concentration camp** on 11 April 1945. British troops liberated Bergen-Belsen camp on 15 April.

- **The camps were filled with the dead** and dying. At Bergen-Belsen, the Allies found 40,000 prisoners dying of hunger and ill-treatment. Many of the living were so thin they could hardly stand.

- **At Dachau camp**, officers lost control of US troops, who machine-gunned 120 German camp guards.

◀ *Slave labourers in Buchenwald camp, April 1945. Cameramen entering the death camps with Allied troops took the first pictures to reveal the full extent of Nazi cruelty.*

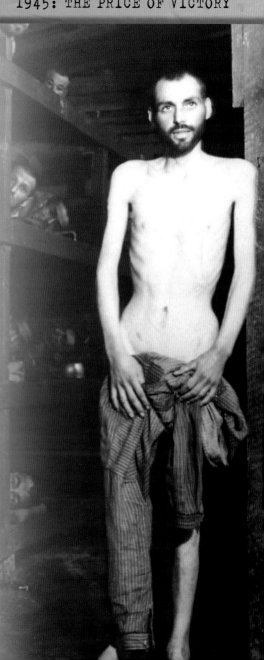

● **Journalists and photographers recorded** the horrors. They saw cremation ovens, gas chambers and laboratories where prisoners had been used in medical experiments.

● **When film of the camps was shown** in cinemas in Allied nations, people wept. German civilians were ordered to visit Bergen-Belsen and other camps to witness the horrors for themselves.

● **In the Holocaust**, as it is now known, about 6 million Jews were put to death by the Nazis.

● **The Nazis had planned to kill all Europe's Jews** – men, women and children. Many victims had walked naked into the gas chambers after being told they were to have a shower.

● **Allied troops were shocked by the sight** of mass graves. Many of the camp survivors were past help and died soon after liberation. But enough survived to tell their stories.

▶ *Walking skeletons, but still alive, survivors from Ebensee concentration camp in Austria were freed in May 1945.*

VE Day

- **On 2 May, newspapers in Britain and America** carried the news that Hitler was dead. German troops in Italy surrendered the same day. The Soviet army, known as the Red Army, completed the capture of Berlin.

- **On 3 May,** British General Montgomery accepted the surrender of German generals in northwest Germany.

- **At 2.41 a.m. on 7 May**, General Jodl signed Germany's unconditional surrender at US General Eisenhower's HQ in Rheims, France.

- **In Berlin, Marshal Zhukov of the Red Army** accepted the surrender of German troops on 9 May.

- **Celebrations began around the world** as news spread by radio. The British government announced that 8 May would be VE Day – Victory in Europe Day. On VE Day, street parties took place all over Britain.

- **"This is your victory,"** Churchill told cheering crowds in London. The Royal Family appeared with the Prime Minister on the balcony of Buckingham Palace. Princess Elizabeth, later Queen Elizabeth II, and her sister Margaret joined the crowds in the London streets.

- **Shoppers in London could buy** Victory scarves, ribbons and rosettes.

- **In the Channel Islands,** two British destroyers arrived to receive the German surrender, liberating the only part of the British Isles to be occupied.

- **In The Hague, the Netherlands,** a Dutch family emerged from hiding after three years to find Canadian soldiers on their doorstep.

- **In Moscow,** 1000 guns fired 30 shells each to celebrate the victory, and in New York, paper cascaded from skyscraper windows in tickertape parades.

▶ *The hero of the hour – Churchill (centre, with raised arm) is mobbed by a rejoicing crowd in Whitehall, London.*

Japan fights on

● **By the spring of 1945**, Japan was short of planes, pilots, ships, fuel and food. The war in Asia was now clearly lost, but the Japanese fought on.

● **In Burma**, the British 14th Army captured Mandalay and then, in May, the Burmese capital, Rangoon.

● **In the Philippines**, Japanese troops fought off invading Allied forces, but were outflanked by amphibious landings by seaborne troops.

● **Manila in the Philippines** was liberated by the Americans on 3 March 1945, though some Japanese fought on in the mountains. Australian forces recaptured Borneo and Brunei by June 1945.

● **The Japanese expected the Allies** to invade Japan. The fierce battles on Okinawa (see page 184) had cost thousands of lives.

● **The US commanders**, General MacArthur and Admiral Nimitz, received welcome reinforcements as British warships arrived from Europe, where they were no longer needed.

● **The Americans used B-29 Superfortress bombers** to raid Japan. The biggest bomber of the war, the B-29 carried over 7 tonnes of bombs at over 500 km/h and flew at 12,000 m high.

● **On 9 March 1945**, 279 bombers dropped fire-bombs on Tokyo. A quarter of the city went up in flames and over 150,000 people died.

● **Japanese suicide pilots made kamikaze attacks** on US ships and bombers. Kamikaze pilots vowed to die in defence of Japan.

● **On 1 April 1945**, the Japanese introduced a new weapon – the Okha rocket-bomb, guided by a pilot to crash onto Allied ships.

▼ *Japanese defenders seldom surrendered. These US tanks are using flame throwers to eliminate pockets of resistance.*

The atom bomb

- **The Allies had learned** from bitter experience how hard it was to defeat the Japanese. By May 1945, they were poised to attack Japan.

- **Thousands of mines had been scattered** around the Japanese islands, to sink what was left of Japan's shipping.

- **B-29 bombers were pounding** Japanese cities such as Osaka, Nagoya and Kobe. Leaflets explaining where the next raid would be spread panic among Japanese civilians.

- **Allied commanders still feared** that the invasion of Japan would be much worse, in terms of casualties, than anything so far.

▶ *The mushroom cloud of the atomic bomb signalled a new era of potential mass destruction.*

> **...FASCINATING FACT...**
> The first controlled nuclear reaction to make atomic energy had taken
> place in Chicago, USA, on 2 December 1942.

● **New US President**, Harry S Truman, learned that Allied scientists had been developing a new weapon that could end the war.

● **In July 1945**, Truman, Stalin and Churchill met at Potsdam in Germany. During the talks, Churchill was passed a note that read 'babies satisfactorily born' – this meant that an atomic bomb had been successfully tested.

● **The Allies feared that German scientists** were also working to build an atomic bomb and speeded up their research at the Los Alamos laboratory in New Mexico, USA.

● **Scientists from several countries** worked at Los Alamos. The first bomb was tested at 5.30 a.m. on 16 July 1945 at the Alamogordo air base.

● **It was placed on top** of a metal tower. There was a huge explosion, a blinding flash, a mushroom cloud – the tower was vaporized and sand around it turned to glass.

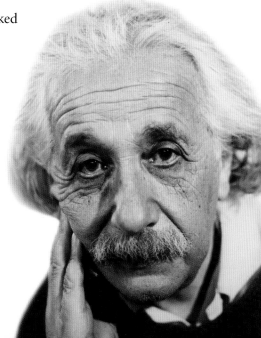

▶ *Albert Einstein (1879–1955) wrote to President Roosevelt warning of the danger should Germany make an atomic bomb. His letter helped persuade the Allies to build the bomb themselves.*

Hiroshima and Nagasaki

- **The world's most brilliant scientists**, including Einstein, knew how destructive nuclear weapons could be. Some scientists thought the atomic bomb must never be used.

- **Allied leaders decided that using the atomic bomb** against Japan was the quickest way to end the war and save lives.

- **Two targets were selected** – the cities of Hiroshima and Nagasaki. The first bomb was dropped from a B-29 bomber on 6 August 1945.

- **The aircraft that dropped** the Hiroshima bomb was *Enola Gay* and its captain was Colonel Paul Tibbets Jr.

- **The explosion was equal to 20,000 tonnes** of high explosive and flattened the centre of Hiroshima. Around 66,000 people were killed outright and 69,000 injured.

- **Many more of the city's 343,000 inhabitants** were to die later from the after-effects of the bomb's poisonous radiation.

- **On 9 August, a second bomb** was dropped on Nagasaki. Here the casualties were 39,000 killed and 25,000 injured.

- **The captain of the second B-29** was Major Charles W Sweeney. His aircraft was *Bock's Car*.

- **Few people in Japan understood** what had happened, but the Japanese government realized that it could not fight this new and terrible weapon.

- **Fighting did not stop** immediately. Japanese pilots were still flying suicide missions on 15 August, after the ceasefire order had been given.

▼ *Survivors wander through an unrecognizable landscape of bombed Nagasaki.*

VJ Day

● **After VE Day, the Allies began** moving troops, ships and planes from Europe to the Pacific, to finish the war against Japan. People with relatives or friends fighting in the Pacific, or prisoners of the Japanese, could not celebrate VE Day. The war was not yet won.

● **The atomic bombs dropped on Hiroshima** and Nagasaki on 6 and 9 August 1945 made headline news around the world.

● **Russia declared war on Japan** on 8 August and immediately invaded Manchuria. This alarmed the western Allies, who did not want Stalin interfering in post-war Japan.

● **Keeping Stalin out of the Pacific** peace settlement had been one reason why the Americans wanted the war over quickly – and why perhaps the atomic bombs were dropped.

● **Emperor Hirohito told his government**, "we see only one way left for Japan to save herself." That way was to admit defeat and surrender.

● **On 14 August, Japanese troops** were told to stop fighting. It took days, even weeks, for news of the ceasefire to reach troops scattered on islands across the Pacific.

● **Many Japanese soldiers did not believe** the news at first, they thought it was a trick by the Allies. Thirty years later, Japanese soldiers were still being found hiding in the jungle on remote islands.

● **VJ Day, Victory over Japan Day, was celebrated** on 2 September, when US General MacArthur accepted the Japanese surrender.

● **The Allied nations knew the war was over** and troops began to come home. Allied troops moved in to occupy Japan and begin rebuilding its shattered cities, factories and transport system.

● **Some US commanders** had been against using the atomic bomb, arguing that the Japanese could have been starved into surrender, using Allied sea power. Arguments continue to this day.

▼ *US General Douglas MacArthur signs the official end of the war onboard the battleship USS* Missouri *in Tokyo Bay. The Japanese seat is vacant, as US officers watch this historic moment.*

A new world

- **In April 1945, delegates from 46 countries** met in San Francisco to form the new United Nations Organization. Their aim was to prevent another world war. The new UN Charter was signed on 26 June.

- **The Allies had new leaders** – President Truman in the USA and in Britain, Clement Attlee became prime minister.

- **On 26 July 1945, Britain had a general election** – Winston Churchill and the Conservatives were defeated. The new Labour government was headed by Attlee, who took Churchill's place at the Potsdam Conference.

- **The new Western leaders** knew problems lay ahead. Stalin told them that he would control Eastern Europe, where there would be no free elections.

- **Soviet troops now occupied** Hungary, Czechoslovakia, Romania and Poland. Stalin also controlled half of Germany and the German capital, Berlin.

- **In 1946, Churchill spoke of a new Iron Curtain** – a boundary symbolically, ideologically and physically dividing Europe. It was the start of the Cold War.

- **Servicemen in Britain began to come home** as they were demobilized at the rate of 150,000 a month by August 1945.

- **The British government warned people** that victory did not mean plenty. There would be years of cutback because Britain was practically bankrupt.

- **People learned of the horrors** of the Holocaust and Japanese ill-treatment of POWs. Everyone knew the war had been fought against terrible evils.

- **India was promised swift independence** from British rule to acknowledge its contribution to the war. Other colonies in French Indo-China, Dutch East Indies and in Africa also looked towards independence.

KEY

- ☐ East Germany
- ◩ West Germany
- ■ Soviet Bloc
- ▨ Occupied by Allies
- 1 Norway
- 2 Sweden
- 3 Denmark
- 4 Estonia
- 5 Latvia
- 6 Lithuania
- 7 East Prussia
- 8 Netherlands
- 9 Belgium
- 10 Luxembourg
- 11 Switzerland
- 12 Austria
- 13 Hungary
- 14 Albania
- 15 Greece
- 16 Under Polish control

▲ *The new map of post-war Europe. Soviet armies controlled much of Eastern Europe. Germany was divided. The Iron Curtain was descending.*

War crimes

- **Wartime atrocities shocked** the world. The Allies decided to put former war leaders from Germany and Japan on trial for war crimes.

- **On 28 May 1945,** the Nazi propaganda broadcaster, William Joyce, was captured. He was tried for treason and hanged on 3 January 1946.

- **In Paris, Marshal Petain** and Pierre Laval, the Vichy chief and Nazi puppet ruler of France, were put on trial. Laval was shot on 15 October and Petain was sent to prison.

- **SS boss Heinrich Himmler was arrested** on 23 May in Germany. He bit into a concealed cyanide poison capsule and killed himself.

- **In Japan, former Prime Minister Tojo,** tried to shoot himself on 8 September as he was arrested. He was tried before the Japanese War Crimes tribunal and later executed, along with six other Japanese leaders.

- **In November 1945, Nazi leaders appeared** in a special war crimes tribunal at Nuremberg, Germany.

◀ *Marshal Petain, a World War I hero, had thought that collaboration with Germany was best for France. He was put on trial as a traitor, but spared the death penalty because of his age of 89 years old. He died in 1951.*

- **Former *Luftwaffe* chief Hermann Goering cheated** the hangman by taking poison hours before his execution, on 16 October 1946.

- **Ten other top Nazis were hanged** on 16 October. Among them were Foreign Minister Ribbentrop and Field Marshal Keitel.

- **Rudolf Hess, a Nazi leader who flew to Britain** secretly in 1941 to try to fix a peace deal, remained in Spandau Prison until his death in 1987.

- **Martin Bormann, Hitler's deputy, was hunted** for years, but is now thought to have died in May 1945 during the last battles around Hitler's bunker HQ.

▼ *Nuremberg defendants in the dock.*
Far left is Goering, beside him Rudolf Hess,
Ribbentrop and Keitel.

Counting the cost

● **The human cost of World War II** was incalculable. Of 70 million people who served in the armed forces, about 17 million were killed.

● **The Soviet Union lost over 7 million** fighting men and women – far more than any other country. Britain and America lost around 700,000 between them.

● **Germany lost 3.5 million servicemen** dead and Japan about 1.3 million. In post-war Berlin, women outnumbered men by three to one.

◀ *A grave marker in a battlefield. The ground has been churned up by tanks and constant artillery fire.*

- **Civilian casualties raised the figures** even higher. The Soviet Union may have lost as many as 19 million civilians and China around 10 million.

- **Poland lost 20 percent** of its population – the highest proportion in Europe, 60 percent of its schools and 30 percent of its farms.

- **Germany and Japan were both in ruins** in 1945, but were rebuilt with amazing speed, thanks largely to the Marshall Aid Plan of 1948.

- **China was still torn by civil war**, which lasted until 1949 when the Communists seized power.

- **In Britain, 30 percent of homes** were damaged. Factory-built concrete 'prefabs' were a short-term answer to the housing shortage. Bombed city centres were rebuilt in the 50s and 60s.

- **Across Europe**, there were 21 million refugees. As late as 1955, over one million German POWs were listed as missing in the Soviet Union.

- **Many Jewish survivors** of the death camps had lost their entire families. Some left Europe, and made new homes in the state of Israel.

▲ *US sailors salute over the freshly dug grave of a dead comrade.*

Rebuilding

- **Millions of people** across the world set about rebuilding their lives and repairing the damage done by World War II.

- **The United Nations symbolized hope** for a better future. People hoped that the UN would become a world peacemaker.

- **The United States and the Soviet Union** were suspicious of each other and began to build up stocks of new weapons. US troops remained in Europe and the Far East.

- **In Britain, house-building was started**, but there was little money for industry. Under the Labour government (1945–50), railways, coalmines and steelworks were state-owned.

- **By the 1950s**, the British Empire was evolving into the Commonwealth, as more colonies in Africa and Asia gained their independence.

- **Germany stayed divided** into East and West for 40 years, until the collapse of Communism in Europe in the 1980s.

- **West Germany and France** became friends and partners in the new European Common Market, set up in the 1950s. This is now the 25-nation European Union.

- **Japan made** the most startling recovery. By the 1950s, rebuilt factories were building cars, motorbikes, radios and TVs, making Japan the new 'workshop of the world'.

- **The new state of Israel**, to which many Jews emigrated, did not enjoy peace and security. It fought several wars with its Arab neighbours.

- **Bombed cities in Poland and Germany**, including Dresden, were rebuilt, to look much as they had before.

▼ *Prisoners of war, in Europe and Asia, celebrated liberation – and survival. British and US flags are waved together by these ex-POWs in the Far East.*

CHRONOLOGY

 WORLD WAR 1 1914-1918

 WORLD WAR II 1939-1945

The following pages chart the momentous events of World Wars I and II. Each month of every year of both wars is broken down, and major incidents around the world are highlighted. Day-by-day accounts of troop movements, key battles and diplomatic negotiations provide a running commentary of important events, giving a remarkable insight into the strategies of war.

WESTERN FRONT

■ 25. Kaiser Wilhelm II of Germany informs France and Britain that he will mobilize the entire German armed forces unless Russia agrees to cease its partial mobilization within three days.

■ 30. The Netherlands declares that it will remain neutral in any war resulting from the murder of Archduke Franz Ferdinand.

■ 31. Germany asks France to explain what its position would be if war were to break out between Germany and Russia.

EASTERN FRONT

■ 23. Austria–Hungary delivers an ultimatum to Serbia following the murder in June of Austrian Archduke Franz Ferdinand by a Serb. If accepted, this would give Austria–Hungary control over Serbia.

■ 25. Serbia accepts nine of the ten terms of the ultimatum. Austria–Hungary refuses.

■ 25. Tzar Nicholas II of Russia orders a partial mobilization. Russian troops march towards Serbia to defend against the Austro-Hungarian invasion.

■ 28. Austria–Hungary declares war on Serbia.

■ 29. Bulgaria declares itself neutral in the dispute between Serbia and Austria–Hungary.

★ 30. The first shots of the war are fired when Austro-Hungarian warships on the river Danube open fire on the Serbian capital of Belgrade.

■ 30. Germany warns Russia to demobilize its army or risk war.

THE MED & MIDDLE EAST

■ 25. Italy, a partner with Germany and Austria–Hungary in the Triple Alliance, does not join with Germany in diplomatic moves to put pressure on Russia.

REST OF THE WORLD

● 28. British First Lord of the Admiralty, Winston Churchill, orders the Royal Navy to steam to prearranged war stations and to prepare for action.

● 29. The German High Seas Fleet is ordered to take up battle stations.

KEY: ■ DIPLOMACY ◆ HOME ● NAVAL ▲ SECRET WAR ★ BATTLE

■ 1. Belgium declares that it will remain neutral.

■ 1. France orders a general mobilization.

★ 2. Germany invades neutral Luxembourg.

■ 2. Germany asks Belgium for permission to use Belgian roads. Belgium refuses.

■ 2. Germany declares war on France.

■ 4. Germany declares war on Belgium.

★ 4. German armies invade Belgium.

■ 4. Britain demands that German armies retreat from Belgium. No reply is received, so Britain declares war on Germany.

★ 8. Battle of Mulhouse. French armies invade Germany.

■ 10. France declares war on Austria–Hungary. Britain follows.

★ 18. Belgian army retreats to Antwerp.

★ 23. British forces at Mons in Belgium are attacked by German forces.

★ 25. French invasion of Germany halted.

★ 25. Retreat from Mons. British forces fall back into France.

★ 25. Battle of Marne begins.

■ 1. Germany declares war on Russia.

■ 3. Romania declares that it will remain neutral.

■ 5. Austria–Hungary declares war on Russia.

■ 5. Montenegro declares war on Austria–Hungary.

■ 5. Serbia declares war on Germany.

★ 12. Battle of river Jadar. Austro-Hungarian armies invade Serbia.

★ 21. Battle of river Jadar. Serbian forces halt the Austro-Hungarian armies.

★ 20. Russian armies invade Germany near Gumbinnen. Kaiser Wilhelm II appoints General Paul von Hindenburg to command the defence, assisted by General Erich Ludendorff.

★ 23. Battle of Krasnik. Austria–Hungary invades Russia.

★ 23. Battle of Tannenberg. German armies crush the Russian 2nd Army, inflicting massive losses and halting the Russian invasion of Germany.

▲ 2. Germany signs a secret treaty with Turkey. Under the treaty, Germany promises to aid Turkey if war should break out with Russia. Turkey promises to shelter German warships.

■ 3. Italy declares that it will remain neutral in the war despite the Triple Alliance.

★ 4. German warships *Breslau* and *Goeben* open fire on the ports of Bône and Philippeville in French Algeria.

■ 10. German warships *Breslau* and *Goeben* take refuge in Turkish waters.

● 6. German cruiser *Königsberg* sinks British cruiser *Pegasus* off Mombasa in East Africa.

■ 15. Japan demands that Germany hand over the port of Tsingtao on the Chinese coast.

■ 15. Japan later declares war on Germany.

★ 20. British troops from Nigeria invade German Cameroons and later capture German Togoland.

WESTERN FRONT

★ 4. Battle of the Marne. British and French armies begin to counter attack Germans along the river Marne.

★ 7. Battle of the Marne. German counter attack is halted when French General Joseph Gallieni rushes reinforcements to the front from Paris in taxi cabs.

★ 9. Battle of the Marne. British forces cross the river Marne to push deep into German lines near Chateau Thierry. Belgian armies attack the Germans near Antwerp.

★ 9. Battle of the Aisne. British and French forces are halted as the German retreat stops on the river Aisne.

★ 17. British aircraft bomb German airship bases at Cologne and Düsseldorf.

★ 22. Race to the Sea. British and French armies seek to outflank German armies in Picardy. The Germans respond by marching north towards Péronne.

★ 27. Race to the Sea. German armies attack at Artois in an attempt to outflank the British. French armies march up to block the move.

EASTERN FRONT

★ 3. Battle of Rava Ruska. Austro-Hungarian invasion of Russia ceases and is thrown back with a loss of 350,000 men.

★ 11. Battle of Rava Ruska. Austro-Hungarian forces retreat, evacuating Lemberg.

★ 11. Battle of the river Drina. Austro-Hungarian forces invade Serbia and march towards Belgrade.

▲ 17. The Germans learn of Russian plans to invade the key coal-mining area of Silesia. German troops are rushed south by rail.

★ 28. Battle of the Vistula. German armies led by Hindenburg attack Russian armies along the river Vistula. Although outnumbered by three to one, the Germans advance steadily. Russia calls off plans for the invasion of Silesia.

★ 30. Battle of the Vistula. Hindenburg calls off the German attack.

THE MED & MIDDLE EAST

REST OF THE WORLD

■ 17. Australia pledges to support Britain 'to the last man and the last shilling'.

● 22. German U-boat U-9 sinks three British cruisers in about 30 minutes off the Dutch coast.

KEY: ■ DIPLOMACY ◆ HOME ● NAVAL ▲ SECRET WAR ★ BATTLE

★ 6. Siege of Antwerp. Belgian forces begin to evacuate the city.

★ 10. Siege of Antwerp. The remaining Belgian forces in the city surrender to the Germans.

◆ 13. The first Canadian troops land in Plymouth, England. They will later be moved to France to fight on the Western Front.

★ 18. Battle of the Yser. Sir John French orders his British forces to attack across the river Yser towards Lille and Menin. The move is designed to protect the key transport centre of Ypres.

◆ 19. King Albert of Belgium orders the sea defences to be breached, flooding large areas of northern Belgium in an attempt to halt the German advance towards Nieuport.

★ 29. First Battle of Ypres. German commander in chief Erich von Falkenhayn launches a major assault on the Belgian city of Ypres, held by the British.

★ 31. First Battle of Ypres. British troops stop the German attack at Gheluvelt.

★ 3. Austro-Hungarian armies advance from Galicia to support Hindenburg's right wing.

★ 9. Massive Russian reinforcements begin to arrive on the river Vistula.

★ 17. Hindenburg orders the German and Austro-Hungarian armies to retreat from the river Vistula before the expected Russian attack takes place. The retreating troops are ordered to steal all food and burn all buildings as they retreat so as to hinder the Russian advance.

◆ 11. Ethnic Armenians serving in the Turkish army begin to desert in large numbers.

▲ 17. Turkish secret service agents report that weapons are being smuggled over the border from Russia to arm Armenian rebels.

★ 23. Units of the British–Indian army invade Mesopotamia, part of the Turkish Empire to protect British oil supplies.

■ 29. Turkey declares war on Britain and Russia, then closes the Dardanelles to ships.

◆ 16. The first New Zealand troops leave Wellington to steam to Britain for war service.

◆ 20. The first Australian troops leave Sydney to steam to Britain.

● 20. German U-boat U-17 sinks British cargo ship *Glitra* off the Norwegian coast. This is the first merchant ship ever to be sunk by a submarine.

WESTERN FRONT

★ 3. First Battle of Ypres. The Germans renew their attack and capture Dixmunde, north of Ypres.

◆ 3. German warships attack British east coast towns.

★ 12. First Battle of Ypres. Heavy snows bring an end to the German attack.

▲ 8. British intelligence establishes 'Room 40', an organization that cracks the codes of German military radio signals.

★ 15. Battle of Champagne. Joint British and French attack fails to achieve much success against the newly constructed German trenches.

▲ 25. Christmas Truce. At several sections of the Western Front an unofficial truce takes place. Fighting ceases as soldiers sing carols, swap presents and cook festive meals. German and British regiments organize international football matches. In most places the truce ends on Boxing Day.

EASTERN FRONT

★ 5. Battle of Belgrade. Renewed Austro-Hungarian assault on the Serb capital begins. Belgrade is captured after three weeks.

★ 11. Battle of Lodz. An offensive by German 9th Army led by General von Mackensen is halted. A Russian counter attack surrounds the German attack forces. The battle ends in deep snow on 25 November when the German survivors fight their way out of the trap.

★ 9. Battle of Belgrade. Serb forces recapture Belgrade and drive Austro-Hungarian armies out of Serbia. The fighting for Belgrade has cost the Austro-Hungarians 230,000 killed, wounded or captured, and the Serbs 170,000 – almost half their army.

THE MED & MIDDLE EAST

★ 4. Battle of Qurna. British forces land from the sea and capture the Turkish town.

■ 18. Britain declares it will take temporary control of Egypt and moves troops to the area.

REST OF THE WORLD

● 1. Battle of Coronel. German Pacific Fleet sinks two British cruisers off Chile.

★ 10. Japan captures German base of Tsingtao in China.

● 8. Battle of the Falklands. German Pacific Fleet is attacked by British South Atlantic Squadron. Only one of the five German ships escapes – the cruiser *Dresden*.

◆ 19. German Zeppelin airships bomb several towns in England. British aircraft are unable to fly as high as the Zeppelins.

■ 13. The British War Cabinet decides that priority must be given to forcing Turkey to reopen the Dardanelles. Since the sea lane was blocked, Russian exports have collapsed and it has become almost impossible for Britain or France to send weapons and supplies to Russia. First Lord of the Admiralty Winston Churchill is given the task of drawing up a plan.

◆ 1. The German government starts to ration bread as Britain's naval blockade of German ports takes effect.

■ 20. Austria–Hungary is forced to withdraw troops from the Eastern Front to the Alps as relations with Italy become increasingly difficult.

★ 13. Battle of Bolimov. Poison gas is used for the first time in warfare by the German 9th Army under General von Mackensen. Problems with the weather make the gas ineffective and the German attack towards Warsaw is halted with comparative ease by the Russians after four weeks of fighting.

★ 7. Battle of the Masurian Lakes. The Germans under Hindenburg in East Prussia drive back the Russians by 110 km and capture 90,000 prisoners.

★ 7. Bad weather and poor supply systems halt an Austro-Hungarian attack on the Russians in Gallicia.

◆ 1. The Austro-Hungarian government starts to ration bread.

★ 3. Battle of Sarikamish. A Turkish attack on Kars is defeated by the Russians. Turkish commander Enver Pasha resigns.

■ 11. Greece refuses to join the Allies, despite being offered Turkish territory in return.

★ 3. Battle of Suez. Turkish assault on the Suez Canal is driven off by British troops in Egypt.

◆ 14. The Turkish government begins a murderous crackdown on Armenian rebels.

● 24. Battle of Dogger Bank. British and German battle-cruiser fleets meet in the North Sea. The German battle-cruiser *Blücher* is sunk.

■ 4. Germany announces that all merchant ships heading towards Britain will be sunk.

▲ 22. South Africa sends spies into the German colony of Southwest Africa.

WESTERN FRONT

★ 10. Battle of Neuve-Chappelle. British commander in France, Sir John French, begins a limited four-day attack to test new weapons and tactics. The attack captures key areas around Neuve-Chappelle.

◆ 27. The Shell Scandal. Sir John French announces that the British army is dangerously short of ammunition, particularly artillery shells. A major political row develops with national newspapers launching serious criticism of the government.

★ 10. Battle of St Mihiel. French attacks at St Mihiel near the Meuse begin well, but soon falter as German defences prove too strong.

▲ 19. German engineers invent an interrupter gear to allow machine guns to fire forwards through an aircraft propeller. This allows the Germans to develop an effective fighter aircraft and to dominate the skies.

★ 22. Second Battle of Ypres. German attack on the British at Ypres opens with a successful gas attack.

EASTERN FRONT

★ 22. Siege of Przemysl. The key Austro-Hungarian strategic transport centre of Przemysl, which has been under siege for weeks, finally surrenders to the Russians.

THE MED & MIDDLE EAST

★ 18. The British Mediterranean Fleet fails to force a passage through the Dardanelles, losing three ships. The British government orders Admiral de Robeck to make a second attempt using land forces as well as warships.

◆ Turkish troops begin a series of massacres of suspected rebels in Armenia.

★ 25. Gallipoli. The British–French landings at Gallipoli beside the Dardanelles begin, but poor organization leads to confusion.

REST OF THE WORLD

★ 18. South Africa invades German Southwest Africa (Namibia) with 21,000 troops led by General Louis Botha.

★ 6. Second Battle of Ypres. British counter attacks fail to succeed. The area is given a new commander – General Herbert Plummer.

★ 9. Battle of Artois. A French offensive begins with an advance of 6 km in two hours, but the key Vimy Ridge is not captured.

★ 25. Second Battle of Ypres. German attacks end in failure, but the British front line is now only 5 km in front of Ypres.

◆ 25. A new British coalition government is formed under Liberal Herbert Asquith.

◆ 1. British government allows women to work in munitions factories for the first time.

■ 1. Germany issues a formal apology to the USA for the sinking of an American merchant ship.

★ 16. Battle of Artois. The French offensive climaxes with an assault by 20 divisions, but Vimy Ridge is still in German hands.

▲ 24. Chantilly Conference. Senior British and French commanders in France meet to decide on future strategy. They decide to launch a major offensive in September.

★ 1. The Germans begin a joint attack with the Austro-Hungarians in Galicia on a 45-km-wide front. After five days of fighting, the Russian 3rd Army collapses.

★ 6. The Germans capture the city of Gorlice from the Russians.

★ 3. The joint German-Austro-Hungarian attack in Galicia continues with the recapture of the key fortress city of Przemysl.

★ 22. The Austro-Hungarians recapture Lemburg in Galicia. The Hungarian city has been in Russian hands for nine months.

★ 6. Gallipoli. The Turks halt the British attack.

★ 19. Gallipoli. Australian and New Zealand Army Corps (ANZAC) halt a Turkish attack.

■ 23. Italy declares war on Austria–Hungary over a border dispute in the Alps.

★ 4. Gallipoli. Turkish forces halt a renewed ANZAC attack.

★ 30. First Battle of Isonzo. Italians drive the Austro-Hungarians back to the river Isonzo, but fail to cross it.

● 7. British liner *Lusitania* is sunk off Ireland by a German U-boat – 124 Americans are killed.

★ 11. South African troops capture Windhoek in German Southwest Africa.

WESTERN FRONT

◆ 9. British secretary for war, Lord Kitchener, begins a major recruitment drive. Over 2 million men volunteer within three weeks.

▲ 1. The Fokker Scourge. The German interrupter gear claims its first aircraft victim. Fokker aircraft gain superiority over British and French air forces.

▲ 4. The Germans arrest British nurse Edith Cavell on charges of espionage.

▲ 12. British engineers begin work on the armoured vehicle moving on tracks that will later become known as the tank.

EASTERN FRONT

★ 13. Battle of Warsaw begins as the German 12th Army attacks from East Prussia.

▲ 17. Bulgaria signs a secret treaty with Germany promising to attack Russia. Germany promises to give Bulgaria parts of neighbouring countries if they win the war.

◆ 21. Russia's Tzar Nicholas II sacks his commander in chief and takes command of the Russian armed forces. He moves to the military command post, leaving domestic government to his wife and ministers.

★ 25. Battle of Warsaw. German advance on Warsaw continues with the capture of the city of Brest-Litovsk.

■ 28. Germany offers Russia peace, the Tzar refuses unless all German troops retreat.

THE MED & MIDDLE EAST

★ 18. Second Battle of Isonzo. A new Italian attack again fails to cross the river Isonzo.

★ 24. Battle of Nasiriya. A British army marching through Mesopotamia towards Baghdad defeats Turkish resistance.

★ 6. Gallipoli. New British landings at Suvla Bay attempt to break the deadlock, but fail due to poor organization.

■ 20. Italy declares war on Turkey.

REST OF THE WORLD

★ 9. German forces in Southwest Africa surrender to South Africa.

● 11. German cruiser *Königsberg* is destroyed off East Africa, but the crew escape.

● 26. After renewed US protests, Germany ends the practice of attacking merchant ships without warning.

KEY: ■ DIPLOMACY ◆ HOME ● NAVAL ▲ SECRET WAR ★ BATTLE

★ 25. Second Battle of Champagne begins. Major French attack breaks through German trenches, but reinforcements do not arrive in time to exploit the success.

★ 25. Third Battle of Artois begins. Major French attack again fails to capture Vimy Ridge.

★ 25. Battle of Loos begins. Major British attack fails to advance against strong German field fortifications.

▲ 7. The Germans execute British nurse Edith Cavell despite many international calls for mercy.

★ 6. Second Battle of Champagne. A renewed French attack collapses in failure.

★ 13. Battle of Loos. A fresh British attack succeeds in capturing the German Hohenzollern Redoubt fortress.

■ 22. Bulgaria begins to mobilize its army.

★ 25. Battle of Warsaw. German advance reaches Vilna.

★ Battle of Warsaw. Heavy rains bring a halt to the German offensive.

★ 6. A new joint German and Austro-Hungarian invasion of Serbia begins.

■ 14. Bulgaria declares war on Serbia and invades, attacking the Serb army from the rear.

■ 15. France, Britain and Montenegro declare war on Bulgaria.

■ 19. Italy and Russia declare war on Bulgaria.

★ 16. The British forces in Mesopotamia reach the key river town of Kut-el-Armana.

■ 27. Greece agrees to allow the Allies to use the port of Salonika as a supply base.

★ 28. British forces capture Kut-el-Armana.

★ 18. Third Battle of Isonzo. Sudden heavy rains halt a new Italian attack.

WESTERN FRONT

◆ 3. The government appoints General Joseph Joffre to command all French forces on the Western Front.

▲ 6. Second Chantilly Conference. Senior British and French commanders in France decide to launch a major offensive in the summer of 1916.

◆ 17. Sir John French is sacked as commander of British forces on the Western Front and replaced by Douglas Haig.

◆ 28. Britain introduces conscription of able-bodied men into the armed forces.

EASTERN FRONT

★ 5. Bulgarian forces capture Serb city of Nis, threatening the rear of the Serb army.

★ 23. The Serb army abandons all attempts to defeat their enemies. The 71-year-old King Peter refuses to surrender and announces he will walk over the snow-capped mountains to neutral Albania. Most of his army decides to follow. Having destroyed all vehicles and artillery to stop them being captured, the Serbs disappear into the snow. Pursuing Bulgarian forces refuse to follow.

★ 15. The Serb army begins to arrive in the Albanian town of Scutari, which they fortify. It is estimated that about one-third of the Serbs died on the march.

THE MED & MIDDLE EAST

★ 10. Fourth Battle of Isonzo begins. Another Italian attack fails to break Austro-Hungarian lines.

★ 22. British forces in Mesopotamia fail to capture Ctesiphon and fall back to Kut.

★ 10. Fourth Battle of Isonzo ends. The city of Gorizia is totally destroyed.

★ 7. British forces at Kut are surrounded.

★ 8. Gallipoli. British and Anzac forces begin to evacuate their positions.

REST OF THE WORLD

KEY: ■ DIPLOMACY ◆ HOME ● NAVAL ▲ SECRET WAR ★ BATTLE

▲ 24. Newly appointed Admiral Reinhard Scheer, commander of the German navy, formulates a plan to ambush and destroy the British Grand Fleet in the North Sea.

▲ 27. General Erich von Falkenhayn, German senior commander, informs Kaiser Wilhelm II of plans to inflict massive casualties on the French with a strategy of controlled attrition at the fortress city of Verdun.

▲ 19. The first trials take place of the British secret weapon codenamed 'Mother', later to be called the tank.

★ 1. Seven German Zeppelin airships launch the largest air raid on Britain so far.

▲ 14. British and French commanders agree to begin their major offensive on 1 July.

★ 21. Verdun. A German artillery barrage is followed by an attack with 150,000 men.

★ 24. Verdun. German troops break the second of three lines of French defences.

★ 25. Verdun. French commander General Henri-Philippe Pétain takes command. He states, "They shall not pass."

★ 5. Austro-Hungarians invade Montenegro. The Montenegrin army falls back to join the Serbs in the Albanian town of Scutari.

★ 22. Austro-Hungarians capture Scutari. The Montenegrins and Serbs march south to the port of Valona.

▲ 4. Top secret Austro-Hungarian government report states that the Allies will win the war.

★ 9. The British navy transports the surviving Montenegrian and Serb soldiers to Salonika.

▲ Hussein, Sherif of Mecca, will rebel against the Turks if sent weapons by Britain.

★ 4. British forces leave Basra to relieve Kut.

★ 8. Gallipoli. Allied evacuation is completed.

★ 10. Russia invades Turkey at Erzerum.

★ 16. Russian troops advance from Erzerum into Turkish Armenia. Armenian rebels tell him that one million Armenians have been massacred by the Turks. The Turks say that only a few thousand rebels were killed in fighting and all civilians were spared.

★ 1. British forces capture Yaunde, capital of the German colony of Cameroons.

■ 23. Portugal objects to German attacks on neutral shipping and announces that all Portuguese ports, including colonial ports, are closed to German ships.

WESTERN FRONT

★ 2. Verdun. French forts Vaux and Douaumont are now in German hands.

■ 9. Germany declares war on Portugal.

★ 9. Verdun. Renewed German assaults begin on Dead Man Ridge. French losses rise alarmingly under attack from German artillery and poison gas.

▲ 21. The Easter Rising. Irish nationalists start a rebellion in Dublin aimed at achieving Irish independence from Britain.

EASTERN FRONT

★ 18. Battle of Lake Naroch. Russian attack with 350,000 men begins against 75,000 Germans near Vilna.

★ 14. Battle of Lake Naroch. Russian attack is called off by Tzar Nicholas II after suffering 122,000 casualties, compared to 20,000 German losses.

THE MED & MIDDLE EAST

★ 2. Fifth Battle of Isonzo. An Italian offensive fails against the Austro-Hungarians.

★ 11. British advance on Kut is halted.

★ 6. British advance to relieve the forces at Kut restarts.

★ 18. Russian troops capture key port of Trebizond in Turkey.

★ 29. British forces at Kut surrender.

REST OF THE WORLD

▲ 1. The Easter Rising. The British crush the Irish rebellion in Dublin and execute 14 rebels.

★ 1. Verdun. New French commander General Robert Nivelle begins to plan counteroffensive.

★ 2. Another major raid by eight German Zeppelin airships hits ports along the East Coast.

★ 23. Verdun. Renewed German attack near Fort Vaux moves towards Fort Souville, which dominates the only supply route open to the French in Verdun.

★ 24. Battle of the Somme. Around 2000 British artillery guns open fire on German defences around the river Somme, firing an estimated 1.5 million shells each day for the next six days.

★ 4. The Brusilov Offensive begins as Russian troops attack on a 320-km-wide front against Austro-Hungarians south of the Pripet Marshes, led by General Aleksey Brusilov. Brusilov devises new tactics.

★ 10. The Brusilov Offensive. Austro-Hungarian armies collapse at Lutsk and Kovel.

★ 18. The Brusilov Offensive. German reinforcements slow down the Russian attack, but fail to stop Brusilov's advance.

★ 2. Multinational Allied force marches from Salonika towards the Serb border.

★ 5. Hussein of Mecca starts the Arab Revolt.

★ 15. A major Austro-Hungarian attack at Trentino smashes the Italian 1st Army.

■ 3. The Allied force at Salonika arrests Greek officials. Greece mobilizes its army.

★ 8. Austro-Hungarian attack is halted due to supply problems in the Alps.

■ 14. China agrees to allow the Allies to recruit labourers to work on construction projects.

● 31. Battle of Jutland. The main British and German warfleets clash in the North Sea.

● 1. Battle of Jutland. German fleet returns to port due to severe damage, despite sinking several British warships. The Germans never again dare face the British fleet.

WESTERN FRONT

★ 1. Battle of the Somme. The British, supported by the French, advance on a 40-km-wide front around the river Somme. Despite a heavy artillery bombardment, the strong German defences are mostly intact. By nightfall the British have suffered almost 60,000 casualties, 20,000 of them killed. The Germans have lost just 8000 men.

★ 2. Battle of the Somme. British commander Douglas Haig, misled by early reports, orders massive new attacks to take place, causing more heavy casualties.

★ 3. Battle of the Somme. British commander Douglas Haig orders new attacks, but heavy rain makes them impossible. Haig later learns of the massive losses and small advances achieved. He orders a halt to the attacks.

★ 14. Battle of the Somme. Haig orders fresh British attacks on a smaller scale. Local successes encourage him to extend the concept of small, sudden attacks.

★ 23. Battle of the Somme. The new British tactics lead to the capture of Pozières, but a major breakthrough is not achieved.

EASTERN FRONT

★ 2. First recorded attack by Serb guerrillas against Austro-Hungarian occupation troops.

★ 25. Brusilov Offensive. After a pause to reorganize, the Russians renew the attack, but are now faced by fresh German forces. The Russians continue to advance, but at a slower rate and for higher casualties.

THE MED & MIDDLE EAST

▲ 3. Austro-Hungarians sink the Italian battleship *Leonardo da Vinci* in Taranto.

★ 19. Turkish forces launch a surprise attack towards the Suez Canal. They reach within sight of the railway that supplies the canal, then halt and dig in.

★ 25. Turkish attack in Armenia is halted by the Russians at Erzincan.

REST OF THE WORLD

  KEY: ■ DIPLOMACY ◆ HOME ● NAVAL ▲ SECRET WAR ★ BATTLE

★ 2. A major raid by Zeppelin airships on England ends when one is shot down.

▲ 13. Battle of the Somme. British commander Douglas Haig writes to the British government accepting that he will not break through the German defences, but promising to continue the smaller attacks to wear down German defences and inflict casualties.

▲ 28. Battle of the Somme. General Haig is ordered to mount a new, large attack to tie down German reserves on the Somme so that they cannot be moved to attack Romania.

◆ 29. General Erich von Falkenhayn is replaced by Field Marshal Paul von Hindenburg as German Chief of the General Staff in overall command of the war. Hindenburg has General Eric Ludendorff as his deputy. Hindenburg begins a series of meeting with German industrialists with the aim of tripling the output of weapons and ammunition within six months.

★ 12. Brusilov Offensive. General Brusilov announces that during his Russian attack, his troops have captured 375,000 enemy troops and almost 40,000 sq km of territory.

▲ 17. Russian secret agents open talks with King Ferdinand of Romania, using Brusilov's announcement as proof that the Russians would win the war. They hope to persuade King Ferdinand to attack Bulgaria.

★ 17. Bulgarian troops invade Greece to attack Allied forces around Salonika.

■ 27. King Ferdinand of Romania decides to join the Allies. Romania declares war on Austria–Hungary and invades Transylvania, which has a large ethnic Romanian population.

■ 29. Germany and Bulgaria declare war on Romania.

★ 4. Sixth Battle of the Isonzo. Italian troops finally take the ruins of Gorizia, their main target of the previous summer.

★ 4. Anzac troops halt a renewed Turkish attack on the Suez Canal.

★ 5. In Armenia, the Turks capture Mus.

■ 28. Italy declares war on Germany.

▲ 17. British codebreakers intercept German radio signals that reveal a force of German warships is to attack the British town of Sunderland. The British fleet is ordered to sea.

● 19. German U-boats sight the British fleet and sink two cruisers. The German fleet turns back to Germany rather than risk a major battle.

WESTERN FRONT

★ 3. Battle of the Somme. The fresh British attack takes place at Guillemont and High Wood with mixed results.

▲ 8. Hindenburg visits the Somme and Verdun. He is appalled by the scale of German casualties and issues new orders that positions should be abandoned if they become too costly to defend.

★ 15. Battle of the Somme. The British use tanks for the first time, but most break down before they achieve much.

◆ 5. The French government temporarily nationalizes all agricultural land to increase food output.

★ 24. Verdun. A major French offensive begins in dense fog, which masks the attackers from German artillery and machine guns. The attack is aimed at pushing German artillery out of range of Verdun. On the first day, the French capture Fort Douaumont and 6000 prisoners.

EASTERN FRONT

★ 3. A joint German–Bulgarian army invades Romania from the south.

★ 3. Allied forces at Salonika push invading Bulgarian forces out of Greece.

★ 16. The German–Bulgarian invasion of Romania is halted while secure supply lines are established.

★ 10. Brusilov Offensive. Tzar Nicholas II orders the end to the Russian attacks as tough German resistance makes the assaults too costly.

★ 19. The German–Bulgarian invasion of Romania restarts along the Black Sea coast.

★ 22. German troops capture the key Romanian port of Constanza on the Black Sea coast.

THE MED & MIDDLE EAST

★ 14. Seventh Battle of the Isonzo. The Italians launch a short, three-day battle that succeeds in capturing limited objectives.

★ 17. Anzac troops drive the Turks back 50 km from the Suez Canal.

★ 9. Eighth Battle of the Isonzo. The Italians launch another short attack with limited objectives, but this time fail to take them.

▲ 16. British officer T E Lawrence takes over as British liaison officer with the Arabs.

REST OF THE WORLD

■ 6. Germany announces that it will again sink all merchant ships heading for British ports, including those of neutral countries.

★ 2. Verdun. The Germans retreat from several exposed positions, including Fort Vaux.

★ 12. Battle of the Somme. A fresh British attack lasting five days captures Beaumont Hamel, an objective of the attack on 1 July.

◆ 15. The German government announces the early call up of men due to be conscripted in 1918.

★ 18. Battle of the Somme ends.

★ 18. Verdun. A final French attack by General Nivelle recaptures most of the land lost.

◆ 5. British Prime Minister Herbert Asquith resigns amid worries over heavy losses and lack of success. The new prime minister is David Lloyd George.

◆ 12. The French government sacks General Joffre as commander in chief and replaces him with General Nivelle, who organized the successful counter attacks at Verdun.

■ 12. The Peace Note. Germany sends a diplomatic note to all its enemies proposing peace, but on German terms.

■ 30. The Peace Note is rejected.

■ 5. Germany and Austria–Hungary announce that Polish-speaking areas of Russia are to be an independent country. Thousands of Poles join the German army.

★ 23. A second German–Bulgarian invasion of Romania begins over the river Danube, while a third crosses the Transylvanian mountains from Austria–Hungary. Both forces make rapid progress as the 500,000-strong Romanian army retreats in confusion.

■ 1. The Romanian army abandons the capital Bucharest. The German commander General von Mackensen announces a three-day truce to allow civilians to flee before his army enters the city.

★ 6. The German army holds a victory parade in Bucharest, then begins the pursuit of the Romanian army, which is retreating towards the Russian border.

★ 1. Ninth Battle of the Isonzo. The Italians begin an attack similar to that in October, with similar disappointing results.

■ 4. Hussein is crowned King of Mecca.

■ 23. Greece declares war on Bulgaria.

★ 13. A fresh British advance in Mesopotamia begins. The advance of 50,000 men is supported by numerous river transports, some converted to be armoured gunboats. Only 20,000 Turks oppose them.

■ 13. Germany asks Mexico for permission to use Mexican ports to supply U-boats. Mexico refuses.

WESTERN FRONT

★ 23. German forces along the Western Front start withdrawing from the line of trenches. As they fall back, they demolish all buildings and plant mines. The British and French troops advance cautiously over territory that they have fought hard to win. The Germans halt their retreat after 30 km on a line of strong prepared defences known as 'The Hindenburg Line'.

■ 24. British diplomats hand the US ambassador an intercepted copy of the Zimmermann Telegram.

EASTERN FRONT

THE MED & MIDDLE EAST

★ 9. Battle of Magruntein. British forces drive Turks out of western Sinai.

★ 22. Second Battle of Kut. British forces defeat Turks near Kut-el-Armana. Turkish commander Kara Bey orders his forces to withdraw towards Baghdad.

REST OF THE WORLD

■ 19. Zimmermann Telegram. German foreign minister Zimmermann sends a telegram suggesting Mexico should attack the USA to recover lands lost in the 19th century.

■ 3. Germany announces that it will sink all merchant ships without warning. China, USA and others cut diplomatic links to Germany.

▲ German airmen spot signs of massive French preparations for an assault in the Aisne and Champagne region along a 60-km front. A German spy captures the top secret documents, revealing details of the planned French assault. The French attack is later named 'Nivelle's Offensive' after the general who planned it.

★ Bloody April. German pilots in new Albatross DIII fighters destroy almost 30 percent of Allied aircraft on the Western Front.

★ 9. Battle of Arras. Canadian troops capture Vimy Ridge, but other British assaults fail to advance very far.

★ 16. Nivelle's Offensive. Over 100,000 French soldiers attack prepared German defences. Casualties are high.

★ 17. Nivelle's Offensive. The French 108th Regiment refuses to attack. The mutiny spreads rapidly.

◆ 8. The March Revolution begins in Russia. A wave of strikes and riots break out in major cities, protesting against food shortages and massive war casualties. The army garrison of Petrograd refuses orders to open fire on rioters.

◆ 15. The March Revolution. Chaos spreads rapidly across Russia. After failing to control the situation, Tzar Nicholas II abdicates. The Duma (parliament) establishes a republic with a provisional government led by Alexander Kerensky.

◆ The March Revolution. The Russian army is paralysed by the upheavals taking place behind its back.

★ 11. Advancing from Kut-el-Armana, British forces occupy Baghdad.

★ 26. Advancing from Egypt, British forces attack Gaza in order to invade Palestine, but are driven off and suffer from water shortages.

★ 17. A renewed British attack on the Turkish forces at Gaza is again defeated with heavy losses. The British commanders are sacked by the furious Prime Minister Lloyd George.

■ 1. The Zimmermann Telegram is published in the USA, stoking anti-German feeling. US President Woodrow Wilson announces that US merchant ships will be armed against U-boats.

■ 6. The USA declares war on Germany following the sinking of several US merchant ships by U-boats.

WESTERN FRONT

▲ 1 Nivelle's Offensive. The French army mutiny that began in April has now spread to 68 of the 112 divisions in the French army. The massive casualties and minor gains of the attack cause widespread alarm. The extent of the rioting and unrest is kept secret.

★ 9. Nivelle's Offensive. The offensive is halted – nothing has been achieved and there are 187,000 French casualties. Nivelle is sacked and replaced by General Pétain. Pétain calls off all attacks and concentrates on restoring morale and discipline.

★ 7. Organized by the innovative General Herbert Plummer, the British 2nd Army captures the strategic Messines Ridge with relatively few losses.

★ 14. First German air raid in London by bomber planes.

◆ 24. The first US troops land in France, commanded by General John Pershing. They begin several weeks of training in trench warfare before they enter the front line.

EASTERN FRONT

◆ 4. The new Russian Republican government appoints General Alexi Brusilov as the new army commander in chief with orders to stabilize the front and reform the army.

THE MED & MIDDLE EAST

★ 9. Serb and French troops at Salonika attack Macedonia, but make little progress in two weeks of fighting.

★ 12. Tenth Battle of the Isonzo. Italian forces once again fail to break through.

◆ 13. King Constantine of Greece is forced to abdicate in favour of his son, Alexander, who favours the Allied cause. Eleutherios Venizelos becomes prime minister.

■ 27. Greece joins the Allies.

REST OF THE WORLD

● 10. The British Royal Navy forces all merchant ships in the North Atlantic to travel in escorted convoys. Losses to German U-boats fall dramatically.

★ 13. Battle of Passchendaele. The British offensive begins with massed air attacks to drive the Germans from the skies, followed by a massive two-week artillery barrage.

▲ 24. Dutch-born dancer Mata Hari is put on trial by the French as a German spy. The glamorous international star of the stage is found guilty and executed.

★ 31. Battle of Passchendaele. The British offensive begins to the north of Ypres, near Passchendaele, with the aim of breaking through to the coast.

★ 2. Battle of Passchendaele. Sudden and unexpected heavy storms and torrential rain halt the British attack as the low-lying ground around Passchendaele turns to mud.

★ 16. Battle of Passchendaele. With dry ground, the British attack begins again, but the element of surprise has been lost and the Germans are ready. Progress is slow and casualties are high. Once again, Haig reverts to his tactic of limited objectives and small-scale attacks.

★ 1. Kerensky Offensive. Ordered by Russian Defence Minister Alexander Kerensky, the new Russian defence minister, a fresh offensive takes the Germans and Austro-Hungarians by surprise. The Russians begin well, but the attack falters as resistance stiffens.

★ 19. Kerensky Offensive. A German counter attack drives back the Russian army, which begins to disintegrate. Fresh Romanian troops are rushed up to halt the German attack.

◆ 4. The Russian Republican government, now with Kerensky as prime minister, sacks General Brusilov as the commander in chief and replaces him with General Lavr Kornilov. Kornilov has orders to stop the mutinies, desertions and rebellions that are afflicting the Russian army.

★ 12. Eleventh Battle of the Isonzo. A new attack sees Italian forces finally break through towards Trieste. The Austro-Hungarians manage to halt the drive, but realize their armies are exhausted and appeal to Germany for help in any future battle.

WESTERN FRONT

★ 18. Battle of Passchendaele. British commander Haig orders a new attack by Plummer's 2nd Army on the higher, drier ground south of Ypres. Plummer uses new tactics and gains key hills before more heavy rain again turns the area into thick mud. Haig orders the attacks to continue, but the mud makes supply and movement difficult.

★ 9. Battle of Passchendaele. British commander Haig decides to limit his offensive to the capture of Passchendaele Ridge. A three-day attack by Australian troops begins, but ends in failure.

★ 28. Battle of Passchendaele. The British make a renewed assault on Passchendaele Ridge, spearheaded by Canadian troops. Progress is slow and casualties are high, but Haig insists the attacks must continue.

EASTERN FRONT

★ 1. Using new 'stormtrooper' tactics, the Germans attack towards Riga. The Russian 12th Army collapses, allowing the Germans to sweep forwards with few casualties.

◆ 9. Russian commander Lavr Kornilov uses the army to mount a coup against the republican government. The coup fails when armed workers attack the few soldiers who support Kornilov. The victory by the workers militia gives added power and prestige to the Bolshevik Communists.

THE MED & MIDDLE EAST

★ 27. Battle of Ramadi. British forces advancing northwest from Baghdad defeat the local Turkish forces, then continue along the river Tigris.

★ 24. Battle of Caporetto. A joint German and Austro-Hungarian attack in foggy conditions breaks through the Italian front on the river Isonzo. The Italian commander General Cadorna, orders his men to retreat to the river Tagliamento.

REST OF THE WORLD

● 17. Two German light cruisers attack and destroy a British convoy off Scotland.

■ 26. Brazil declares war on Germany after Brazilian ships are sunk by U-boats.

KEY: ■ DIPLOMACY ◆ HOME ● NAVAL ▲ SECRET WAR ★ BATTLE

★ 6. Battle of Passchendaele. British and Canadian troops finally capture and fortify the Passchendaele Ridge. Haig calls off the battle – it has cost him 310,000 casualties, and the Germans 260,000. Haig is criticized for not calling off the attack earlier.

★ 20. Battle of Cambrai. A small British attack is led by 476 tanks that break through the German lines with ease. However, the tanks run out of fuel and reinforcements are slow in arriving. Within ten days, elite formations of German troops have halted the attack.

★ 4. Battle of Cambrai. British commander Haig orders his forces to retreat to prepared defences, abandoning all gains made in the battle. He calls off all major attacks to study the results of this, the first major use of tanks in warfare.

◆ 6. The Russian Revolution. Led by Leon Trotsky and Vladimir Lenin, the Bolshevik Communists launch a successful coup that overthrows the Russian Republican government. Disorder and rioting break out in several cities. Desertion from the army reaches massive proportions. Lenin announces an immediate armistice with the Germans and Austro-Hungarians.

■ 3. German and Russian diplomats meet in the border city of Brest-Litovsk to discuss a peace treaty.

■ 9. Abandoned by the Russians, the Romanians agree a ceasefire with Germany.

◆ 9. The new Communist government nationalizes land in Russia, sparking a revolt by Don Cossack peasants. It is the start of a civil war that will spread to engulf most of Russia.

★ 1. Battle of Beersheba. Australian cavalry capture Beersheba. The British invasion of Palestine begins.

★ 2. Battle of Caporetto. Germans cross the Tagliamento, causing the Italians to flee so fast, the Germans are unable to keep up.

★ 1. Battle of Caporetto. New Italian troops dig in along the river Piave, halting the German and Austro-Hungarian advance just outside Venice. Short of supplies, the invaders stop to reorganize.

★ 27. Battle of Mahiwa. Colonial British forces defeat the German colonial forces of General von Lettow-Vorbeck in German East Africa. The Germans begin a guerrilla campaign.

★ 27. Battle of Vladivostok. Japan invades eastern Russia to seize the strategic port of Vladivostok.

WESTERN FRONT

▲ German commanders Hindenburg and Ludendorff fear that with the vast industrial might and manpower of the USA, the Allies will have an overwhelming advantage. They plan to defeat France and Britain before the Americans arrive in force, expected to be in autumn 1918. They lay detailed plans for a series of massive offensives in France, but first they need the troops tied down in Russia.

EASTERN FRONT

◆ 1. Finland becomes independent of Russia, but soon collapses into civil war between Bolshevik Communists and traditionalist factions.

◆ 28. Estonia, which has also declared itself to be independent of Russia, is invaded by Bolshevik Russian troops. The Estoninans appeal to the Germans for help. A German army is sent to help, marking an end to the Russian–German ceasefire agreed the previous November.

■ 18. German diplomats in Brest-Litovsk call off talks with the Russians in protest at the Russian refusal to agree a peace deal.

★ 19. The Germans launch a major offensive into the Ukraine to seize the vast and prosperous agricultural area. They hope to commandeer enough food to feed the German civilians, and put pressure on the Russian government to agree a quick peace agreement.

THE MED & MIDDLE EAST

● 20. Two Turkish warships steam into the Aegean Sea, but are driven back by minefields and air attacks.

■ 27. A British army is sent from Baghdad to Baku to take control of Russian oilfields.

★ 24. The Turks launch a major offensive in Armenia to drive the Russians out of Turkey. The longer term aim is to cross the Caucasus Mountains to seize the oilfields around Baku.

REST OF THE WORLD

■ 8. US President Woodrow Wilson announces his '14 Points for Peace', including self-government for nations and the setting up of an international body to prevent wars.

   KEY: ■ DIPLOMACY ◆ HOME ● NAVAL ▲ SECRET WAR ★ BATTLE

★ 21. Operation Michael. After a short, intense artillery bombardment, 63 German divisions attack 26 British divisions south of Arras. The German units are led by elite stormtroopers who infiltrate British defences. The British line collapses on a front 48 km wide.

★ 25. Operation Michael. The Germans are 40 km from their start lines.

◆ 26. French General Ferdinand Foch is appointed supreme commander of all British and French armies on the Western Front.

★ 5. Operation Michael. The Germans halt their attack as Allied defences strengthen.

★ 9. Operation Georgette. The Germans unleash a second massive assault along the river Lys. Portuguese and British defenders fall back in disorder.

★ 12. Operation Georgette. British commander Haig orders his men to fight, "with our backs to the wall." By 17 April, the German attacks have been halted.

★ 23. Zeebrugge Raid. British amphibious assault destroys a U-boat base at Zeebrugge.

■ 3. Treaty of Brest-Litovsk. Under pressure of German military advances, the new Bolshevik Communist government of Russia agrees to independence for Poland, Finland, Latvia, Lithuania and Estonia. Germany is to occupy the Ukraine. Germany at once starts moving large numbers of troops to the Western Front.

WESTERN FRONT

★ 27. Operation Blücher. A third German offensive opens as a limited attack on the strategic ridge of Chemin des Dames. French defenders flee in disorder.

★ 28. Operation Blücher. US troops in action for the first time hold the key high ground around Cantigny.

★ 29. Operation Blücher. German forces capture Soissons, following the fleeing French. The next day the Germans are only 60 km from Paris. German commander Ludendorff decides to pour in extra men.

★ 4. Operation Blücher. German forces are blocked at Chateau Thierry by reorganized French and US defences. Ludendorff halts the offensive.

★ 9. Operation Gneisenau. German armies attack near Amiens, damaging the French defences.

★ 13. Operation Gneisenau. The German attack is called off after a successful French counter attack.

EASTERN FRONT

■ 7. Treaty of Bucharest. Romania surrenders to Germany, Austria–Hungary and Bulgaria, which between them occupy 85 percent of Romania. However, King Ferdinand of Romania lives up to his reputation for cunning by finding excuses never to sign the treaty, allowing him to claim that Romania is still a combatant nation when the final peace treaties are being negotiated in 1919.

■ 23. Allied troops land at Archangel to supply anti-Communist Russian forces.

THE MED & MIDDLE EAST

● 9. Austro-Hungarian battleship *Szent Istvan* is sunk in battle against the Italians.

★ 13. Battle of the Piave. A massive Austro-Hungarian attack pushes the Italians back over the Piave, but fails to break through.

REST OF THE WORLD

■ 23. Allied troops land at Vladivostok to prevent a Japanese occupation. A force of Austro-Hungarian prisoners break out of the Russian prison camp to help.

★ 15. German commander Ludendorff begins an attack on the Marne to draw Allied forces away from the north, where he intends to capture the Channel ports. The attack lasts two days, but fails to reach its objectives.

★ 18. Second Battle of the Marne. A joint French, British and US counter attack takes the Germans by surprise. Ludendorff moves his reserves from the north to halt the new threat.

★ 2. Second Battle of the Marne. French soldiers recapture Soissons as the Germans fall back towards defences along the river Vesle.

★ 8. British forces attack east of Amiens, spearheaded by a large force of tanks. The Germans surrender or retreat without offering any resistance. Ludendorff calls this 'The Black Day of the German army'. The British advance continues for two weeks, when it is halted as supplies can no longer keep up with the advancing troops.

■ 11. Newly independent Lithuania chooses Prince Wilhelm of Urach to be their King under the name of Mindove.

◆ 16. The former Tzar Nicholas II of Russia and his entire family are shot dead by Bolshevik Communists who have been holding them prisoner for some months.

◆ 26. Breaking out of their prison camps in the Urals, a force of Austro-Hungarian soldiers find themselves amid the chaos of the Russian civil war. They begin the journey home.

WESTERN FRONT

★ 3. Expecting further Allied attacks, German General Ludendorff orders a retreat to the Hindenburg Line. The move takes two weeks to complete.

★ 26. The Argonne Offensive. A joint French–US attack begins north of Verdun towards Sedan. The Germans are fighting on territory that they have occupied for over three years with strongly defended fortifications. Allied progress is slow.

★ 27. Fourth Battle of Ypres. A British advance pushes the Germans back more than 15 km.

■ 6. German Prince Max contacts US President Wilson to ask for terms of an armistice.

★ 14. The Argonne Offensive. The French–US attack captures the final German defences, but halts for reinforcements to arrive.

★ 22. Fourth Battle of Ypres. The British drive the Germans across the river Selle and continue to advance steadily.

EASTERN FRONT

■ 14. A large Turkish army arrives at the key Russian oilfields around Baku. The British force that has been occupying the area is driven out.

THE MED & MIDDLE EAST

★ 15. Battle of the river Vardar. Allied troops from Salonika invade Bulgaria.

■ 30. Bulgaria agrees to an armistice.

★ 15. Battle of Megiddo. British and Arab forces destroy Turkish forces in Palestine.

★ 15. British and Arab forces enter Damascus as Turkish forces flee north.

★ 23. Battle of Vittorio Veneto. Italian armies drive across the river Piave.

■ 30. Turkey agrees to an armistice.

REST OF THE WORLD

● 29. The Kiel Mutiny. German sailors of the High Seas Fleet at Kiel refuse to obey orders to go to sea.

★ 6. The Argonne Offensive. Advancing French–US forces capture Sedan. German resistance is almost non-existent.

■ 7. Led by Matthias Erzberger, German diplomats meet French Marshal Foch to discuss an armistice. Foch's demands are so severe that Erzberger contacts Berlin for advice.

★ 8. The British forces advancing from Ypres cross the river Scheldt, meeting little resistance as German forces surrender or break up.

◆ 9. German Kaiser Wilhelm II abdicates. Germany becomes a republic.

■ 11. Germany agrees to an armistice. It comes into force at 11 a.m.

◆ 17. German forces begin to march home and disband. The new German state is allowed to keep some men under arms to control Communist and other extremist uprisings.

● 21. The German fleet surrenders to the British.

■ 2. Lithuania ousts its new German king and proclaims itself to be a republic as Russian Communist forces prepare to invade.

■ 4. Under the terms of the Turkish armistice, the Turkish army occupying the Russian oilfields around Baku surrenders to the returning British force.

◆ 11. Austro-Hungarian Emperor Karl abdicates.

◆ 11. General Jozef Pilsudski becomes the first president of an independent Poland.

◆ 12. The Austro-Hungarian state collapses as both Austria and Hungary declare themselves to be independent republics. The other constituent parts of the empire soon follow suit.

◆ 15. German troops that have been occupying Ukraine return home. Ukraine collapses into civil war as Bolsheviks invade. Civil war spreads across Russia.

■ 4. The Austro-Hungarian government agrees to an armistice with Italy pending the negotiation of a final peace treaty with the other Allies. No peace treaty is ever signed as the Austro-Hungarian Empire ceases to exist.

◆ 25. The final German surrender takes place at Abercorn in Northern Rhodesia when the guerrillas receive news of the armistice and surrender to British colonial troops.

WESTERN FRONT

■ 1. Denmark, Norway, Finland and Sweden declare themselves neutral.

■ 3. Britain, France, Australia, New Zealand and India declare war on Germany.

■ 3. Belgium announces it will remain neutral in any European war.

● 3. First U-boat victim of the war, the British liner *Athenia*. A total of 112 civilians are killed, 28 of them Americans.

■ 6. South Africa declares war on Germany.

★ 7. Battle of the Saar. French forces invade Germany in Saar valley, advancing 8 km.

■ 10. Canada declares war on Germany.

● 15. First convoy of merchant ships protected by naval warships sets out from Jamaica for Britain.

★ 30. Battle of the Saar. French forces retreat from occupied areas of Germany and return to the pre-war border.

● 30. German battleship *Graf Spee* begins sinking merchant ships in the South Atlantic.

PACIFIC & FAR EAST

■ 4. Japan announces it will remain neutral in any European war. Japan is already fighting a war against China.

EASTERN FRONT

★ 1. Germany invades Poland.

■ 1. Poland declares war on Germany and appeals to Britain and France for help.

★ 9. Battle of the Bzura. Polish counter attack lasting six days fails to halt advance of German panzers on Warsaw.

★ 17. Russian invasion of Poland. Soviets seize eastern parts of Poland.

■ 30. Polish government flees to France.

THE MED & MIDDLE EAST

■ 1. Italy declares itself neutral in the war between its ally Germany, and Poland.

■ 2. All American countries (except Canada) declare themselves neutral and ban fighting warships from entering to within 1000 km of their coasts.

● 5. Britain and France send out naval flotillas to hunt the German battleship *Graf Spee*.

■ 6. Adolf Hitler offers to convene a 'Peace Conference' with Britain and France. The offer is rejected unless German troops evacuate Poland.

◆ 7. British Expeditionary Force of 161,000 men completes arrival in France.

● 14. German submarine U-47 sinks British battleship HMS *Royal Oak* inside naval base of Scapa Flow.

● 20. Germany announces that merchant ships of any nationality in Allied convoys will be sunk without warning.

★ 6. Final Polish army surrenders to Germans at Kock, near Warsaw.

▲ 14. Polish agents escape to France with a German Enigma code machine. Work begins on cracking German coded radio signals.

★ 16. Germans announce official end to Polish campaign.

■ 28. Soviet leader Josef Stalin demands that Finland hand over border territories.

▲ 24. Polish gold reserves arrive in France.

■ 19. Britain and France sign a treaty of friendship with Turkey.

● 25. Three German U-boats are sent to the Mediterranean to attack Allied shipping.

WESTERN FRONT

■ 1. The Netherlands declares itself neutral, but mobilizes army and navy.

■ 7. Belgium and Netherlands issue joint offer of mediation to find a path to peace.

◆ 8. Assassination attempt on Hitler by left-wing activist fails.

★ 12. First German air raid on Britain.

■ 15. Germany rejects Belgian–Dutch offer.

● 23. British merchant cruiser *Rawalpindi* sunk by German battleship *Scharnhorst*.

◆ 8. Polish squadrons that escaped the fall of Poland are absorbed into the British Royal Air Force (RAF).

★ 9. First British soldier killed in action, Corporal Thomas Priday on patrol in France.

★ 13. Battle of the river Plate. Three British cruisers clash with the German battleship *Graf Spee* off South America. *Graf Spee* is damaged and is scuttled four days later.

PACIFIC & FAR EAST

★ 27. Japanese capture key transport centre of Nanning in China.

★ 28. Japan launches heavy bombing raids on Chinese city of Lanchow in attempt to halt production of ammunition in the city's factories.

EASTERN FRONT

◆ 1. Poland is officially partitioned between Germany and Russia.

★ 30. Russia invades Finland. Russian armies advance on four fronts and bomb Finnish capital of Helsinki.

★ 2. Finnish forces fall back to prepared defences on the Mannerheim Line.

■ 3. International Olympic Committee cancel 1940 Olympics, due to be held in Finland.

★ 16. Finns repel Russian attacks at Summa.

THE MED & MIDDLE EAST

KEY: ■ DIPLOMACY ◆ HOME ● NAVAL ▲ SECRET WAR ★ BATTLE

◆ 3. British government takes over all merchant shipping for the duration of the war.

▲ 10. German aircraft carrying complete set of plans for German invasion of France lands by mistake in Belgium during a snowstorm. Belgian authorities pass the plans to France. Hitler orders that new plans be drawn up.

● 29. German air force (*Luftwaffe*) begins campaign against British merchant ships in the North Sea.

◆ 31. French government announces second month without major land fighting.

★ 8. French patrol captures a German patrol in the Forbach Forest. No other land fighting reported in February.

● 9. German destroyers make first of several night voyages to lay mines off the east coast of England.

● 12. British navy capture German U-33, complete with code books.

● 16. *Altmark* Incident. British warships pursue German merchant ship *Altmark* into Norwegian waters to rescue British prisoners. Norway objects.

■ 21. *Asama Maru* incident. British warship stops and searches the Japanese merchant ship *Asama Maru*. They find and arrest 21 German weapons technicians. The incident leads to long-running diplomatic dispute between Britain and Japan.

★ 5. Finns surround and destroy Russian 18th Division near Lake Ladoga.

★ 11. Finns crush Russian attack near Salla.

★ 25. Finns repel renewed Russian attacks in the Lake Ladoga area.

★ 1. Battle of Sama. Major Russian assault begins on the Mannerheim Line at Sama.

★ 16. Battle of Sama. Finns withdraw to new defensive positions having inflicted huge losses on the Russians.

■ 21. *Orazio* incident. French warships race to rescue survivors when Italian liner *Orazio* catches fire off Spain.

WESTERN FRONT

★ 2. Germans capture British patrol on the Franco-German border.

◆ 11. Britain introduces rationing of meat.

★ 16. Germans launch major air raid on British naval base at Scapa Flow. One cruiser is badly damaged.

★ 17. British launch reprisal air raid on German naval base at Sylt. No serious damage is caused.

◆ 20. French government falls over criticism of policy towards Finland. New Prime Minister is Paul Reynaud.

★ 24. German patrols active along entire Western Front. French respond with artillery fire on German positions.

▲ 28. British government agrees to suggestion by First Lord of the Admiralty, Winston Churchill, that neutral Norwegian waters should be mined to stop merchant ships carrying iron ore to Germany. France objects, then agrees only if the move is delayed by one week.

PACIFIC & FAR EAST

EASTERN FRONT

★ 1. Battle of Viipuri. Largest Russian attack of the Finnish War opens with determined assaults on the city of Viipuri.

★ 10. Battle of Viipuri. Final Finnish reserves committed. Marshal Mannerheim advises Finnish government to make peace.

■ 12. Treaty of Moscow. Finland retains independence, but hands over extensive border territory to Russia. Finns have lost 25,000 men, the Russians 210,000.

THE MED & MIDDLE EAST

● 7. Coal Ships Incident. British Mediterranean Fleet seizes Italian coal ships. Diplomatic row ends with ships being returned to Italy, but Britain retains right to stop and search Italian ships.

■ 18. Hitler and Mussolini meet at Brenner. Mussolini is vague about joining the war.

KEY: ■ DIPLOMACY ◆ HOME ● NAVAL ▲ SECRET WAR ★ BATTLE

★ 2. German air raid on British naval bases.

● 7. British ships leave to begin mining Norwegian waters.

● 8. British destroyer *Glowworm* meets major German naval fleet off Norway and is sunk.

★ 9. Germany invades Denmark.

★ 9. Germany invades Norway. Norwegian artillery sinks German battle-cruiser *Blücher* off Oslo. British and German warships exchange fire off Narvik and Kristiansand.

■ 10. Denmark surrenders to Germany. Iceland declares itself independent of Denmark.

● 3. Two Russian merchant ships arrive in Hong Kong under escort by British warships. The ships are carrying cargoes that the British believe is to be transported along the Trans-Siberian Railway to Germany. Russia objects. The British release the ships, but retain the cargoes.

◆ 1. More than 450,000 Finns are expelled from occupied areas by Russians. They are marched to Helsinki and all their possessions confiscated by the Russian government.

★ 13. Battle of Narvik. British battleship *Warspite* sinks eight German destroyers.

■ 15. King Haakon of Norway says he will, "save the freedom of our beloved country."

★ 14. British troops land near Narvik.

★ 17. British warships begin series of bombardments of German coastal positions in Norway.

★ 26. Norwegians halt German advance along Gudbrandsbal Valley.

WESTERN FRONT

▲ 6. Norway's gold reserves arrive in Britain.

◆ 7. British Parliament debates the conduct of the war. Prime Minister Neville Chamberlain is severely criticized and three days later resigns to be replaced by Winston Churchill.

★ 10. Germany invades Belgium, Netherlands and Luxembourg. British and French armies march into Belgium.

★ 12. Fresh French troops land at Narvik.

★ 13. German panzers cross the river Meuse at Sedan and Dinant opening a gap 80 km wide in the French defences.

★ 14. Central Rotterdam is destroyed by German bombing.

■ 14. The Netherlands surrender to Germany.

★ 20. German panzers reach the Channel coast at Abbéville. British retreat begins.

★ 26. Operation Dynamo. Evacuation of British and French troops from Dunkirk begins under heavy attack by *Luftwaffe*.

■ 28. Belgium surrenders to Germany.

PACIFIC & FAR EAST

■ 11. Japan warns that it will not tolerate occupation of the Dutch East Indies (Indonesia) by the armed forces of any nation other than the Netherlands.

EASTERN FRONT

THE MED & MIDDLE EAST

■ 26. Benito Mussolini believes Germany will win the war. He decides to join Germany, hoping to gain glory and diplomatic advantage. He also wants to annex border territory from France.

★ 3. Operation Dynamo ends. In all, 210,000 British and 120,000 French troops are successfully evacuated from Dunkirk.

★ 5. Battle of France. Reorganized German forces strike in the south over the Somme. French front collapses after 24 hours.

★ 8. Battle of France. German panzer spearheads reach the river Seine.

▲ 8. King Haakon leaves Norway for Britain.

■ 9. Norwegian army surrenders. Norwegian navy to continue the war from Britain.

★ 14. Battle of France. GermanS march into Paris, which is undefended by the French.

◆ 16. New French government formed under Marshal Pétain, hero of World War I.

★ 14. Battle of France. French resistance collapses. German panzers advance 250 km in one day.

◆ 18. French warships leave France for ports in French colonies.

■ 22. France surrenders.

★ 14. Japanese air force begins series of fire bomb raids on Chinese city of Chungking.

★ 15. Russia invades Lithuania without declaring war.

★ 17. Russia invades Latvia and Estonia without declaring war.

★ 28. Russia invades Romania without declaring war.

■ Romania surrenders after three days. Border provinces of Bessarabia and Bukovina are annexed to Russia.

■ 30. Communist governments are imposed on Lithuania, Estonia and Latvia by Russia.

■ 10. Italy declares war on France and Britain. Italians invade southern France.

★ 14. Italian warships shell British coastal positions in Egypt.

★ 23. Italians capture French city of Menton.

★ 28. Air fights take place between Italian and British forces over Libyan–Egyptian border.

WESTERN FRONT

◆ 1. French government sets up office in Vichy. Most of northern and western France is occupied by the Germans.

● 3. Britain seizes all French ships in British and colonial ports, including 59 warships.

★ 10. Battle of Britain. Massed German air attacks on British ports and shipping begin.

■ 19. Hitler offers peace to Britain. The offer is rejected.

◆ 21. Britain forms the Home Guard, a voluntary local defence militia.

▲ 1. Hitler sets 15 September as date for invasion of Britain.

★ 10. Battle of Britain. Massed German air attacks on British ports and shipping reach a peak, then strikes begin on RAF bases.

★ 15. Battle of Britain. Heaviest German air attacks yet pound RAF bases across Britain.

★ 16. Battle of Britain. RAF base at Tangmere is put out of action by German attacks.

★ 24. Battle of Britain. RAF base at Manton is put out of action by German attacks.

PACIFIC & FAR EAST

■ 19. Under pressure from Japan, British authorities in Burma, a British colony, agree to stop military supplies passing through Burma to China.

■ 25. Britain withdraws its small garrisons from various Chinese towns, such as Shanghai and Tientsin. The garrisons had been introduced to ensure the safety of British merchants and goods. However, trade has collapsed since the China–Japan war began and the men are needed elsewhere.

EASTERN FRONT

◆ 4. Under pressure from Germany, Romania expels the British from the oil fields.

■ 21. Communist parliaments in Estonia, Latvia and Lithuania vote to join USSR.

■ 21. Bulgaria takes Dobrudja from Romania.

THE MED & MIDDLE EAST

● 3. British warships sink French warships at Mers-el-Kebir to prevent their capture.

● 19. Battle of Cape Spada. The British sink one Italian cruiser, but sustain heavy damage.

★ 3. Italians invade British colonies of Sudan and Somaliland from Ethiopia.

★ 20. Italians begin blockade of Malta.

★ 1. Battle of Britain. Major German attacks on RAF bases continue. British losses are heavy.

★ 7. The Blitz. First major air raid on London.

★ 14. Battle of Britain. British bombers attack German invasion fleet in Belgian ports.

★ 15. Battle of Britain. Largest German attacks of the battle take place day and night.

★ 17. Hitler abandons invasion of Britain.

● 20. 'Wolf Pack' tactics by German U-boats gain first success with sinking of 12 ships from British convoy HX72 in a single night.

★ 4. The Blitz. Night raid on London by 130 German bombers. Raids continue on London and other cities almost every night throughout the autumn and winter.

★ 14. The Blitz. RAF bombs Berlin. *Luftwaffe* bombs London.

● 17. British and German destroyers clash off the Cornish coast.

■ 23. Hitler meets with Spanish dictator General Franco in the Pyrenees. Franco expresses support, but refuses to join the war.

★ 13. Japanese bomb Chungking, using the Zero fighter for the first time.

■ 22. Vichy French government agrees to Japanese demand to use air and naval bases in French colonies of Indo-China (now Vietnam, Laos and Cambodia). Local French garrison at Da Nang refuse to comply and fighting breaks out.

■ 27. Japan signs the political and economic Tripartite Pact with Germany and Italy.

★ 13. Italians invade Egypt from Libya. The British fall back to prepared defences.

★ 17. Italian advance into Egypt halts at Sidi Barrani.

● 1. British cruisers break Italian blockade to land troops and supplies on Malta.

★ 28. Italy invades Greece at three points from Italian-occupied Albania.

WESTERN FRONT

● 5. German battleship *Admiral Scheer* attacks British Atlantic convoy, sinking six ships. All convoys cancelled for two weeks.

★ 14. Massed attack by 440 German aircraft on Coventry guided by new navigational equipment destroys the city centre, burns the medieval cathedral and kills 600 people.

★ 19. Heavy raid by German aircraft on Birmingham leaves 3000 dead or injured.

★ 28. Heavy raid by German aircraft on Liverpool is thwarted by navigational problems.

★ 12. Heavy raid by German aircraft on Sheffield badly hits iron foundries.

★ 16. RAF launch 'area' raid on Mannheim. One aircraft bombs Basle in Switzerland.

● 25. German cruiser *Admiral Hipper* attacks British Atlantic convoy off Spain, but is driven off by British cruiser *Berwick*.

★ 29. *Luftwaffe* drop 30,000 incendiary bombs on central London. Large areas of the historic city go up in flames.

● Allies lost 1059 merchant ships in 1940.

PACIFIC & FAR EAST

● 9. German raider *Passat* lays mines off Australian coast, sinking two merchant ships. Port of Melbourne is closed until minesweepers can be brought into action.

● 21. German raider *Komet* lands prisoners taken from sunk merchant ships on the remote island of Emirau, then radios the location to the Australian navy to arrange rescue.

EASTERN FRONT

■ 20. Hungary signs military alliance with Germany and Italy.

■ 22. Romania signs military alliance with Germany, Italy and Hungary. Romania wants to regain lands annexed by Russia.

■ 12. Hungary signs friendship treaty with Yugoslavia.

▲ 18. Hitler orders his military staff to draw up plans for a German invasion of Russia to start in June.

THE MED & MIDDLE EAST

★ 3. Greeks halt Italian attacks in the Pindus Mountains, but fall back on the coast.

● 11. British naval aircraft attack Taranto, crippling three Italian battleships.

◆ 1. Italy begins rationing of pasta.

★ 3. Greeks drive Italians into Albania.

★ 9. British launch surprise attack at Sidi Barrani. Italians retreat back to Libya.

KEY: ■ DIPLOMACY ◆ HOME ● NAVAL ▲ SECRET WAR ★ BATTLE

★ 3. Night raid by *Luftwaffe* on Bristol destroys huge stocks of grain and flour.

■ 9. Senior US diplomat, Harry Hopkins, arrives in Britain on a mission from US President Roosevelt to discuss how the USA can help Britain.

★ 10. *Luftwaffe* drop incendiary bombs on Portsmouth, destroying large area of town.

● 22. Powerful German warships *Gneisenau* and *Scharnhorst* leave Kiel. They evade British patrols in the North Sea and enter the Atlantic to attack British shipping.

● 17. Battle of Koh Chang. Attempted Thai invasion of French Indo-China halted when Vichy French fleet crushes Thai fleet, sinking three ships.

◆ 21. Pro-German faction launches coup in Romania. The coup is put down by General Antonescu who imposes army rule.

★ 3. Italian counteroffensive in Albania fails.

★ 5. British take 45,000 Italians at Bardia.

★ 22. British capture Tobruk in Libya.

● 9. German long range Condor bombers attack Atlantic convoy and sink 5 ships.

● 11. British ships shell Ostend docks.

● 12. German cruiser *Admiral Hipper* attacks Atlantic convoy, sinking seven ships.

● 22. German battleships *Gneisenau* and *Scharnhorst* attack convoy off Canadian coast, sinking five ships.

★ 5. Battle of Beda Fomm. British surround and capture 100,000 Italians. Benghazi falls two days later.

★ 25. British conquer Italian Somaliland.

WESTERN FRONT

★ 4. Lofoten Islands Raid. British commandos destroy German weather station and fish-oil factories, and sink six merchant ships.

■ 11. Britain and USA agree Lend-Lease, an arrangement by which Britain can acquire weapons from the USA on credit.

★ 13. Heavy German raids on Glasgow leave 35,000 homeless and 460 dead.

● 22. German warships *Gneisenau* and *Scharnhorst* return after sinking 22 ships.

● 29. US government impounds all German ships in retaliation for American ships sunk.

▲ 2. Germans test world's first jet fighter, the Heinkel 280.

★ 9. British RAF launches successful night raid on Berlin.

■ 10. Greenland (part of Denmark) puts itself under USA protection.

★ 15. Germans launch heavy night raid on Belfast, killing 500 people.

★ 21. Germans begin five consecutive night raids on Plymouth that destroy the town centre, kill 750 and make 30,000 homeless.

PACIFIC & FAR EAST

■ 13. Russia and Japan sign a five year non-aggression treaty. The treaty does nothing to solve territorial disputes between the two countries, but merely defers them.

EASTERN FRONT

■ 1. Bulgaria signs military alliance with Germany and Italy.

■ 23. Russia makes official diplomatic protest to Germany about reconnaissance flights by German aircraft over the Russian border.

■ 24. Hitler meets with Hungarian leader, Admiral Horthy, who agrees to join the war.

THE MED & MIDDLE EAST

★ 5. British troops land in Greece.

★ 24. German Afrika Korps opens attack in North Africa, capturing El Agheila.

◆ 27. Anti-German coup in Yugoslavia.

★ 6. Germany, Italy and Bulgaria invade Yugoslavia and Greece.

■ 17. Yugoslavia surrenders to Germany.

■ 22. Greece surrenders to Germany.

★ 1. Germans begin eight nights of raids on Liverpool that kill 1450, leave 76,000 homeless and destroy much of the docks area.

▲ 5. British recover secret radio-navigation equipment from German bomber.

★ 10. Heaviest night raid on London.

■ 10. Deputy leader of Germany, Rudolf Hess, flies to Scotland on mysterious mission.

● 18. German battleship *Bismarck* puts to sea to attack British convoys in the Atlantic.

● 27. German battleship *Bismarck* sunk by British warships.

★ 1. Germans accidentally bomb neutral Dublin while trying to find Bristol.

★ 11. Germans drop propaganda leaflets across Britain boasting of U-boat success against merchant ships and threatening to starve Britain into surrender.

■ 14. USA freezes assets of Germany, Italy, Hungary, Romania and Bulgaria and expels German diplomats.

★ 31. British RAF launches low-level daylight raid on German ships in Bremen harbour.

■ 22. Germany, Italy and Romania declare war on Russia and invade with a joint army of 3.2 million men and 3300 tanks.

■ 26. Finland declares war on Russia.

■ 27. Hungary declares war on Russia.

★ 3. Italians in Ethiopia defeated by British.

★ 16. Rommel's advance in North Africa reaches Sollum. British in Tobruk under siege.

★ 20. German airborne invasion of Crete.

★ 8. British and Free French invade Vichy French possessions of Syria and Lebanon.

★ 14. Operation Battleaxe. British attempt to relieve Tobruk from siege ends in defeat.

WESTERN FRONT

◆ 7. US Marines land in Iceland to establish air and naval bases for use against U-boats.

■ 19. Germany and Switzerland, now surrounded by Axis states, sign a trade treaty.

◆ 1. Nazi chief Herman Goering issues orders for 'the final solution of the Jewish question' – the extermination of all Jews.

■ 12. Britain and USA sign the Atlantic Charter, a statement of war aims.

● 21. First convoy carries US weapons to Russia round the north of Norway.

PACIFIC & FAR EAST

■ 28. Dutch government in exile instructs authorities in the Dutch East Indies to halt all oil exports. The move is supported by the USA and is aimed primarily at Japan, which imports most of its oil from this source. It is hoped that a lack of oil will hamper the Japanese war effort in China.

■ 30. US warships in the Pacific begin boarding Japanese fishing boats, several of which are found to be carrying a naval intelligence officer.

★ 6. Japanese begin series of 40 air raids on Chungking in China.

■ 25. Japan protests to Russia about passage of merchant ships carrying weapons to Vladivostok through waters claimed by Japan. Russia rejects the protest on the grounds that it claims the waters for its own.

EASTERN FRONT

★ 1. German columns reach rivers Berezina and Dvina as Russians collapse.

★ 15. Germans surround and capture 300,000 Russians at Smolensk.

★ 21. First of 73 German air raids on Moscow.

★ 5. Romanians lay siege to Odessa.

▲ 12. Hitler postpones direct drive on Moscow to divert troops to the Ukraine.

★ 25. Finns attack Hango and Viipuri.

★ 28. Germans capture Tallinn, Estonia.

THE MED & MIDDLE EAST

■ 8. Yugoslavia is divided between Italy, Hungary and newly independent Croatia.

■ 14. Vichy French forces in Syria and Lebanon surrender to Free French.

★ 24. British ships begin extensive mining of Italian waters.

★ 25. Joint British–Russian occupation of Iran takes place to safeguard oil supplies.

KEY: ■ DIPLOMACY ◆ HOME ● NAVAL ▲ SECRET WAR ★ BATTLE

● 4. *Greer* Incident. US destroyer *Greer* attacked by German U-boat U-652 off Iceland. Neither vessel is damaged.

● 17. US warships take up convoy escort duties between Canada and Iceland.

★ 29. Major British air raid on rail works at Amiens is met by formidable new German fighter, the FW190.

● 12. German E-boats, fast torpedo boats, sink two British merchant ships within sight of Cromer, Norfolk.

● 22. German U-boats sink a British destroyer and fuel tanker during convoy battles.

◆ 25. Germans shoot 100 Frenchmen at Bordeaux in reprisal for French Resistance shooting of two Germans.

● 10. New Zealand warships, previously serving as part of the British Royal Navy, now reorganized as the Royal New Zealand Navy.

● 12. Japanese navy begins a series of extensive naval exercises in the Pacific.

▲ 16. Japanese arrest Richard Sorge, a Russian spy working in Tokyo. They execute him one month later.

◆ 18. New Japanese government takes office. It is led by General Tojo who is known for his hard-line attitude to China and to relations with the USA and Britain.

★ 8. Siege of Leningrad begins. Russia's second city surrounded by Axis forces.

★ 15. Battle of Kiev. GermanS surround four Russian armies and take 600,000 prisoners.

★ 27. GermanS reach industrial Donets area.

★ 1. Operation Typhoon, Germans begin drive to capture Moscow.

★ 6. Germans encircle and destroy six Russian armies at Vyasma.

★ 23. Germans capture Kharkov.

● 27. Italian torpedo bombers severely damage British battleship HMS *Nelson*.

● 2. The British lay a minefield that temporarily closes Piraeus, the main port of Greece.

● 25. German bombers sink British cruiser HMS *Latona*.

WESTERN FRONT

★ 7. The British launch raid on Berlin, losing 12 percent of aircraft due to bad weather and poor planning. When he learns the facts of the disaster, Churchill sacks head of RAF Bomber Command. The new commander is Arthur 'Bomber' Harris.

● 22. British cruiser HMS *Devonshire* sinks German raider *Atlantis* off Ascension Island, ending a career that has claimed 22 merchant ships in 19 months.

● 24. British cruiser HMS *Dunedin* sunk by German U-boat U-124.

● 25. British battleship HMS *Barham* sunk by German U-boat U-331.

PACIFIC & FAR EAST

■ 5. Japan sends special diplomatic mission to USA to seek peaceful resolution to differences between the two nations, particularly the oil embargo.

■ 14. USA agrees to withdraw US Marines from Peking and Shanghai at the request of Japan.

● 19. Battle of Shark Bay, Australia. German raider *Kormorant* and Australian cruiser *Sydney* sink each other.

■ 20. Japanese diplomatic mission to USA demands immediate resolution or threatens to break off talks.

▲ 24. US Government instructs all US merchant ships in Pacific to stay in port unless steaming convoy escorted by US Navy warships.

● 26. Large Japanese fleet leaves Japan for secret destination with sealed orders. It is heading for US naval base of Pearl Harbor.

EASTERN FRONT

★ 3. Germans capture Kursk.

◆ 6. Stalin makes key speech calling for defence of Russia.

★ 9. Germans capture Yalta.

★ 14. Romanian–German attack on Sebastopol.

★ 24. Germans capture Solnechaya, less than 50 km from Moscow.

★ 27. Germans halted 30 km from Moscow by heavy snow and lack of supplies.

THE MED & MIDDLE EAST

● 14. British aircraft carrier HMS *Ark Royal* sunk off Gibraltar by German U-boat.

▲ 17. Raid by Colonel Keyes captures Rommel's HQ, but Rommel is not present.

★ 18. Operation Crusader. British 8th Army drives back German–Italian army in North Africa and relieves Tobruk.

● 21. Two Italian cruisers sunk by British.

KEY: ■ DIPLOMACY ◆ HOME ● NAVAL ▲ SECRET WAR ★ BATTLE

■ 5. Britain declares war on Finland, Romania and Hungary.

■ 11. Germany and Italy declare war on USA.

● 19. First action by fighters flying off small 'escort carriers'. US Martlet fighters (built in British service) shoot down two German Condor long-range bombers attacking an Atlantic convoy. The escort carrier is sunk by German U-boat 24 hours later.

■ 22. First Washington Conference. British chiefs of staff meet with US chiefs of staff to decide war strategy and aims.

★ 24. Free French forces occupy Vichy French colonies off the Canadian coast.

● Allies lost 1299 merchant ships in 1941.

● 3. British Force Z of one battleship, one battle-cruiser and four destroyers reaches Singapore.

● 5. Large Japanese fleet, including troop transports, leaves ports in southern China, heading south.

● 7. Pearl Harbor. Aircraft launched from Japanese aircraft carriers launch surprise attack on US naval base at Pearl Harbor in Hawaii. The Japanese sink five US battleships, cripple three more and sink ten other warships as well as destroying 188 aircraft and killing 2403 servicemen. The Japanese lose 29 aircraft.

★ 7. Japanese invade Malaya, landing on northeast coast near Kota Bharu.

■ 7. Japan declares war on USA and Britain.

★ 8. Japanese invade the Philippines.

● 10. British Force Z sunk by Japanese.

★ 16. Japanese invade Dutch East Indies.

★ 25. Japanese capture Hong Kong.

★ 1. Germans begin panzer attack aimed to surround Moscow. They enter Moscow suburbs on 4 December.

★ 5. Russians launch surprise counter attack against Germans north of Moscow.

★ 13. Russians begin general offensive on Germans around Moscow.

★ 17. Hitler issues 'Halt Order' forbidding any retreat in face of the Russian attack.

★ 27. Russians recapture Kaluga.

● 14. British torpedo and damage Italian battleship *Vittorio Veneto* off Sicily.

● 15. German U-boat U-557 sinks British cruiser HMS *Galatea* off Egypt.

● 18. British lose one battleship, two cruisers and one destroyer to Italian mini submarines.

★ 25. British 8th Army captures Benghazi and continues drive west along the coast.

WESTERN FRONT

● 9. German submarines mine the Thames, sinking British destroyer HMS *Vimiera*.

● 11. Operation Drumbeat. German U-boats begin operating in US coastal waters, sinking large numbers of merchant ships steaming singly rather than in convoys.

◆ 20. German SS chief Reinhard Heydrich organizes the Wansee Conference to prepare for mass extermination of Jews, gypsies and other races deemed to be 'undesirable'.

■ 1. King Koadio of Ivory Coast declares for Free French and ousts Vichy French officials.

● 12. The Channel Dash. German battleships *Gneisenau*, *Scharnhorst* and cruiser *Prinz Eugen* race up the English Channel to safety in Germany. The British are caught by surprise and fail to stop the ships.

● 28. Operation Drumbeat. Germans announce their U-boats have sunk 69 ships in US waters during February.

PACIFIC & FAR EAST

★ 2. Japanese capture Manila, capital of the Philippines. Filipino and US forces now under siege in Corregidor and Bataan.

★ 7. Battle of Changsha sees Japanese attack halted by Chinese.

★ 8. Japanese land on Borneo.

★ 10. Japanese begin ten-day assault on Filipino and US forces on Bataan Peninsula.

★ 15. Japanese capture Kuala Lumpur.

★ 20. Japanese invade Burma.

★ 4. Japanese lay siege to major British army and naval base of Singapore, Malaya.

■ 5. Thailand declares war on USA.

★ 15. Japanese capture Singapore, along with 80,000 British and Empire prisoners.

★ 19. Japanese aircraft from Dutch East Indies bomb Darwin, northern Australia. Dozens of other raids follow.

★ 21. British begin retreat from Burma.

★ 24. US carrier aircraft raid Wake Island.

EASTERN FRONT

★ 9. Russians begin 12-day assault that drives 100 km into German lines west of Moscow.

◆ 22. 500,000 evacuated from Leningrad.

★ 23. Russians break through German lines near Smolensk and surge forwards.

★ 20. Russians surround German 16th Army at Demyansk, but fail to capture it.

★ 23. Russians reach the river Dneiper, but fail to break German resistance.

THE MED & MIDDLE EAST

★ 17. British capture Halfaya Pass.

★ 29. Surprise counter attack by German–Italians under Rommel recaptures Benghazi and begins British retreat.

★ 5. Rommel's offensive halts at Gazala.

▲ 6. Suitcase bomb explodes in Spanish Morocco. Local newspaper blames British, leading to widespread anti-British rioting.

● 25. Italian submarine *Pietro Calvi* sinks five merchant ships off Brazil.

● 27. St Nazaire Raid. British commando raid destroys dock and harbour gates being used by German naval craft.

★ 28. RAF bombers strike the German port of Lübeck. The medieval wooden city centre is destroyed by fire.

● 29. Convoy PQ13 is attacked by German U-boats, destroyers and bombers off Norway. The Germans sink five merchant ships and cripple the cruiser HMS *Trinidad*.

♦ 6. German government cuts food rations.

▲ 8. German agents land on Iceland to spy on US military bases.

♦ 15. French Resistance attack German army HQ in Arras with grenades.

▲ 17. Anti-Vichy French General Henri Giraud escapes from prison camp in Germany and reaches Switzerland.

● 1. Scattered naval battles around Java result in loss of nine Allied warships an 13 merchant ships. Japanese suffer no losses.

♦ 3. Americans intern 110,000 Americans of Japanese ancestry.

★ 8. Japanese capture Rangoon, Burma.

★ 9. Japanese capture Java.

★ 4. Heavy Japanese air raid on Mandalay in Burma destroys town centre and rail yards.

● 5. Japanese carrier aircraft attack Colombo in Ceylon, sinking British cruisers and 19 merchant ships.

★ 9. Japanese capture fortified Bataan Peninsula on the Philippines with 70,000 prisoners, and begin attacks on Corregidor.

● 18. Doolittle Raid. US carrier aircraft bomb Tokyo and four other Japanese cities.

■ 19. Romanian government claims Transylvania from Hungary. Hitler is forced to intervene to solve dispute between his allies.

▲ 30. Germans estimate ten million Russian casualties in the war so far.

■ 11. Entire Bulgarian government resigns in protest at German demands for troops to fight in Russia.

★ 1. Massive air raids on Malta by Italians.

■ 13. British allow grain ships to reach Greece.

● 22. Battle of Sirte. Both Italians and British take heavy losses.

★ 1. Germans begin 11-day bombing attacks on Malta, causing heavy damage.

♦ 7. Exchange of wounded prisoners arranged in Turkey.

WWII	May	June

WESTERN FRONT

★ 3. Heavy German air raid on Exeter badly damages cathedral and city centre.

● 13. US introduce escorted convoys for merchant ships in Atlantic coastal waters.

● 20. German U-boats sink second Mexican merchant ship in ten days. Mexico issues serious protest to Germany.

■ 22. Mexico declares war on Germany.

★ 30. RAF launches 1000 bomber raid on Cologne. City centre is destroyed but the historic cathedral survives.

★ 1. RAF launches 1000 bomber raid on Essen. Bad weather hampers bomb aiming.

★ 25. RAF launches 1000 bomber raid on Bremen. Using new Gee radar navigation system, the attacks destroy the business area.

● 26. Germany announces a U-boat blockade of US east coast and lays mines, but it is a ruse to cover a withdrawal of U-boats from the area.

PACIFIC & FAR EAST

★ 2. Japanese capture Mandalay.

● 3. Battle of the Coral Sea. US carrier fleet intercept Japanese fleet heading for New Guinea. Both sides lose an aircraft carrier and the Japanese abandon invasion.

★ 4. British invade Vichy Madagascar.

★ 6. Japanese capture Corregidor, final US outpost on the Philippines.

▲ 14. American code-breakers intercept Japanese signals about invasion of Midway.

● 4. Battle of Midway. Complex battle lasting three days ends with the Japanese losing four carriers and two cruisers, and the US losing one carrier. The naval advantage in the Pacific now lies with the Americans.

EASTERN FRONT

★ 9. Battle of Kharkhov begins with Russian attack, followed by German counter attack. After six weeks the battle ends inconclusively.

★ 23. Sudden panzer attack at Barvenkovo captures 250,000 Russians.

★ 1. Germans begin siege of Sebastopol.

★ 27. Germans launch major offensive in the Ukraine aimed at capturing Stalingrad and the Caucuses oil fields. Over 100 divisions smash Russian lines.

THE MED & MIDDLE EAST

● 11. Three British destroyers sunk by German bombers off Egyptian coast.

★ 26. Rommel launches Italian–German attack on British at Gazala.

● 12. British convoys to Malta take heavy losses. Malta is dangerously short of supplies.

★ 17. Rommel breaks British defences at Gazala and on 21 June captures Tobruk.

KEY: ■ DIPLOMACY ◆ HOME ● NAVAL ▲ SECRET WAR ★ BATTLE

● 4. British convoy PQ17 is ordered to scatter after German battleship *Tirpitz* approaches. The merchant ships are then picked off by U-boats and bombers – 24 of 38 ships are sunk.

● 10. German U-boats begin new campaign in the Caribbean.

★ 11. RAF bombs U-boat yards at Danzig.

★ 15. RAF Spitfires carry out low-level raids on northern France. Over 200 aircraft take part.

▲ 18. First test flight of the German Me262 jet fighter.

★ 17. First all-American bombing raid in Europe takes place as 12 B-17 Flying Fortresses attack rail yards at Rouen.

★ 19. The Dieppe Raid. Canadian and British forces land around Dieppe to test amphibious assault tactics. The raid ends in disaster with 60 percent casualties and no gains.

■ 13. Brazil declares war on Germany and Italy after U-boats sink Brazilian ships.

◆ 31. Police in Ulster arrest 90 IRA men planning attack on US troops stationed in Northern Ireland.

● 13. Japanese submarines begin five-week campaign off the southeast coast of Australia.

★ 21. Japanese invade New Guinea at Buna and begin overland march to Port Moresby.

★ 30. Chinese capture Tsingtien.

★ 7. US Marines land on Guadalcanal in the Solomon Islands.

● 8. In the Battle of Savo in the Solomons the Allies lose four cruisers and the Japanese one. US Marines on Guadalcanal are now cut off.

★ 21. US Marines on Guadalcanal drive off strong Japanese landing forces.

● 24. In the Battle of the Eastern Solomons, the Japanese lose one carrier and one US carrier is badly damaged.

★ 3. Germans capture Sebastopol.

★ 5. Germans reach the river Don.

★ 17. Germans gain control of the Donets coal field.

★ 25. Germans cross the river Don.

★ 19. German assault on Stalingrad is begun by the 6th Army under Paulus.

★ 23. German air raid on Stalingrad kills 40,000 and destroys city centre.

★ 25. Germans reach Mozduck, Cauccasus.

★ 1. Rommel's advance of 650 km in 35 days into Egypt is halted by the British 8th Army at the five-day First Battle of El Alamein.

● 7. The British Pedestal convoy leaves Gibraltar with 14 merchant ships. Only four ships reach Malta, the escort having lost one carrier, two cruisers and one destroyer.

WESTERN FRONT

★ 4. German bomber attacking Torquay is shot down, crashlanding on the beach.

● 23. First of many hundreds of prefabricated 'Liberty Ship' merchant vessels launched in the USA just 10 days after construction began.

★ 25. RAF launch precision, low-level raid on Gestapo HQ in central Oslo, Norway.

★ 29. German bomber hits a school in Sussex, killing 31 children and injuring 28.

▲ 3. First test launch of German V-2 rocket.

★ 4. Successful British commando raid on Sark, in the occupied Channel Islands.

● 7. German U-boat pack sent to South Africa, where it will sink 28 ships in three weeks.

★ 31. German daylight bomber raid on Canterbury carried out at low level to avoid defences. Heavy damage is caused and ten attackers shot down.

PACIFIC & FAR EAST

★ 5. Major Japanese reinforcements landed on Guadalcanal.

★ 11. Japanese advance on Port Moresby halted by Australian troops on Kakoda Trail.

★ 13. Japanese attack on US Marines on Guadalcanal defeated on 'Bloody Ridge'.

★ 21. British attack at Arakan in Burma begins well, but ends in failure.

● 11. US warships sink a Japanese cruiser in Battle of Cape Esperance, Guadalcanal.

● 13. Japanese battleships shell US Marines on Guadalcanal on the first of three consecutive nights.

■ 17. US agrees to arm 30 Chinese divisions.

★ 23. Japanese launch four-day assault on US positions on Guadalcanal. Attack fails.

● 26. Battle of Santa Cruz end with sinking of a US carrier and a Japanese cruiser.

EASTERN FRONT

★ 4. Germans reach river Volga south of Stalingrad, cutting off Russian defenders.

★ 13. Germans begin major assault on central Stalingrad.

★ 24. Germans reach Volga in Stalingrad.

★ 14. Germans begin new 14-day attack in Stalingrad, capturing key tractor factory.

THE MED & MIDDLE EAST

★ 4. Battle of Alam Halfa ends with the failure of a German attack on the British positions at El Alamein.

★ 14. British raid on Tobruk defeated.

★ 20. Italian bombers heading for Gibraltar bomb Spain by mistake.

★ 23. Second Battle of El Alamein opens with attack by British and Australians.

◆ 11. German and Italian forces occupy Vichy France. Military rule imposed throughout France. Italians seize Corsica.

◆ 15. Church bells rung throughout Britain to celebrate victory at El Alamein. The bells have been kept silent since May 1940 for use as invasion alert signal.

◆ 27. Vichy French Admiral de Laborde orders the scuttling of all French warships to prevent them being seized by Germans. A total of 56 ships are sunk, including one battleship, two battle-cruisers and seven cruisers.

▲ 2. US scientist Enrico Fermi achieves the first controlled nuclear chain reaction.

● 11. British commandos paddle canoes up river Gironde to sink six ships in Bordeaux.

◆ 28. Free French leader General de Gaulle joins with General Giraud in appeal for unity between Free French and ex-Vichy French.

● 31. Battle of the Barents Sea. German warships *Lützow* and *Admiral Hipper* fail to sink helpless convoy due to poor leadership.

● Allies lost 1570 merchant ships in 1942.

★ 1. US Marines counter attack Japanese on Guadalcanal, driving off attackers.

★ 5. Final surrender of Vichy French forces on Madagascar to British and Free French.

● 12. Night action off Guadalcanal sees Japanese lose one battleship and US one cruiser. The following night a second Japanese battleship is sunk.

● 30. Night action off Guadalcanal ends in confusion and defeat for US cruisers.

● 1. Australians capture Gona on New Guinea as they drive the Japanese back.

★ 7. US attack on Guadalcanal timed to mark anniversary of Pearl Harbor.

★ 20. Japanese bomb Calcutta at night.

★ 21. Australian tanks breach Japanese defences at Buna, New Guinea.

★ 11. German assault engineers launch failed bid to crush Russians in Stalingrad.

★ 19. Russians launch pincer attack with 11 armies to surround Germans in Stalingrad.

★ 25. Germans air supply men in Stalingrad.

★ 12. Operation WinterStorm. German attempt to relieve troops trapped in Stalingrad begins, but fails after five days.

★ 23. Renewed German drive to reach Stalingrad halted by Russians at Myshkova.

★ 2. Second Battle of El Alamein ends in victory for British under General Montgomery.

★ 8. Operation Torch. US, British and Free French troops land in Vichy-controlled Algeria.

■ 1. Ethiopia declares war on Germany.

★ 6. German attack at Medjez is defeated.

★ 13. Germans retreat from El Agheila.

WESTERN FRONT

■ 15. Churchill and Roosevelt meet in the Casablanca Conference to decide on war aims for the coming year. They give top priority to defeating the U-boats and agree Sicily is to be invaded in the summer of 1943.

★ 20. Germans launch low-level attack on London docks, causing heavy damage.

● 7. Atlantic convoy SC118 attacked by German U-boats and six ships sunk.

◆ 16. Students riot in Munich after local Nazi leader makes insulting speech. Two students are later executed as traitors.

▲ 18. Test flight of new US B29 Superfortress bomber ends in disastrous crash that kills engineers and chief test pilot.

● 25. German U-boats begin five-day attack on convoy ON166, sinking 15 ships.

PACIFIC & FAR EAST

★ 2. Allies capture Buna and begin drive along north coast of New Guinea.

★ 6. Battle of Huon Gulf. Massed Allied air attacks destroy Japanese troop convoy heading for New Guinea.

★ 17. British launch a second assault into the Arakan region of Burma. As before, the attack begins well, but later fails in the face of Japanese counter attacks.

● 1. Japanese destroyers begin night-time evacuation of surviving troops on Guadalcanal. By 8 February the Americans have total control of the island.

★ 14. British begin first Chindit operation as self-supporting columns penetrate Japanese lines in Burma.

EASTERN FRONT

★ 10. Russians begin attacks on German 6th Army trapped in and around Stalingrad.

★ 13. Russians begin drive south from Kharkhov to cut off German forces in the Caucasus, but are halted and driven back.

★ 2. Battle of Stalingrad ends with surrender of German Field Marshal von Paulus and 100,000 survivors of his 6th Army.

★ 8. Russians recapture Kursk.

THE MED & MIDDLE EAST

★ 19. British 8th Army captures Homs.

★ 20. German attack at Ousseltia driven off by Free French.

★ 23. British 8th Army captures Tripoli.

★ 4. British 8th Army enters Tunisia.

★ 13. Surprise German attack at Battle of Kasserine Pass disrupts Allied advance.

★ 4. British 8th Army takes Medenine.

★ 5. British RAF opens 'Battle of the Ruhr', a sustained campaign of night bombing aimed at destroying German industrial output in the key Ruhr Valley. The campaign lasts until June.

● 6. The largest convoy battle of the war rages for six days around convoys HX228 and HX229. The Allies lose 21 ships while the Germans lose four U-boats.

■ 7. Bolivia declares war on Germany, Italy and Japan.

★ 26. Massive British RAF raid on Duisburg goes wrong in poor weather and most bombs miss their targets.

● 2. Battle of the Bismarck Sea. Allied aircraft and surface ships destroy large Japanese convoy and escort off New Guinea.

★ 13. Chinese begin moderately successful offensive in the Yangtse Valley.

★ 7. Japanese launch massive air strikes on Allied shipping in the Solomons. Two warships and three transports are sunk.

★ 18. Japanese naval commander in chief Admiral Yamamoto is killed when his transport aircraft is shot down by US fighters over Bougainville.

◆ 2. Mussolini withdraws all Italian troops from the Eastern Front.

★ 12. Russians capture Vyazma.

■ 31. Hitler meets King Boris of Bulgaria, but fails to persuade him to join war on Russia.

◆ 12. Germans announce discovery of mass graves of Polish officers murdered in 1940 by Russians in the Katyn Forest.

◆ 19. Jews launch abortive uprising in Warsaw Ghetto. Fighting ends after 27 days.

◆ 9. German Erwin Rommel gives up command in North Africa due to ill health.

★ 28. British 8th Army capture German–Italian defences at Mareth.

★ 6. Battle of Wadi Akarit. British 8th Army break German outer defences.

★ 8. British 8th Army captures port of Sfax.

● 16. British destroyer sunk off Sicily.

WESTERN FRONT

★ 3. German bombers lay extensive minefields off the English east coast.

● 11. Battle around convoy HX237 results in three U-boats sunk for no British loss.

★ 16. The Dambusters Raid. Elite force of 19 RAF Lancasters bomb the dams that supply water to the Ruhr industrial belt. Two dams are destroyed, one damaged.

● 23. Renewed attacks by German U-boats result in nine U-boats sunk, only one ship lost.

● 24. Germany suspends U-boat attacks.

★ 14. Operation Musketry. RAF Coastal Command begin series of daily patrols over Bay of Biscay to find and sink German U-boats before they reach the shipping lanes.

★ 20. First Allied 'shuttle' raid. A force of RAF Lancaster bombers bomb Germany, and then fly on to Algiers. They are refuelled and rearmed to bomb Italy on their return to Britain.

PACIFIC & FAR EAST

★ 4. Japanese counter offensive in the Chinese Yangtse Valley begins.

★ 7. Australians capture Mubo, New Guinea.

★ 20. Japanese counter offensive in the Yangtse Valley halted by determined Chinese resistance.

★ 30. End of Japanese resistance on occupied Attu Island in the Aleutian Islands off Alaska, the only US territory to be occupied during the course of the war.

● 8. Japanese battleship *Mutsu* mysteriously explodes in Hiroshima harbour.

● 16. German raider *Michel* begins attacking ships west of Australia.

★ 16. Of 94 Japanese aircraft raiding Guadalcanal, 93 are shot down.

★ 30. Americans begin Operation Cartwheel – a complex series of naval and amphibious operations to isolate major Japanese base on Rabaul.

EASTERN FRONT

★ 1. Russians begin extended series of bombing raids on rail junctions and yards behind German lines in Russia.

THE MED & MIDDLE EAST

★ 6. Massive Allied attack strikes German-Italian defences around Tunis.

★ 12. Surrender of German-Italian forces at Tunis. There are no Axis forces left in Africa.

★ 11. Italian island of Pantellaria surrenders after ten-day bombardment.

★ 12. Italian island of Lampedusa surrenders to RAF pilot who crash lands.

★ 24. Operation Gomorrah. Sustained heavy RAF raids on Hamburg lasting four nights result in horrific firestorm, killing 42,000, injuring 37,000 and destroying 600 factories. Nazi propaganda chief reviews the destruction and reports to Hitler that Germany could lose the war if such raids continue.

▲ 24. First test flight of British jet fighter, the Gloster Meteor.

● 12. Battle of Kolombangara. Japanese lose cruiser *Jintsu* while US ships *Honolulu*, *St Louis* and *Gwin* are badly damaged.

★ 16. Australians capture Mount Tambu, New Guinea.

● 27. US battleships *Mississippi* and *Idaho* fight one-sided battle with non-existent Japanese fleet due to malfunction of radar on the *Mississippi*. Event becomes known as Battle of the Pips.

★ 5. Battle of Kursk opens with massive German attacks north and south of Kursk.

★ 12. German attacks at Kursk halted in largest tank battle in history, south of Kursk.

★ 15. Russian counter attack takes Orel.

★ 10. Joint US–British invasion of Sicily begins.

★ 22. Americans capture Palermo, Sicily.

◆ 25. Italian dictator Mussolini is sacked and arrested on orders of King Victor Emmanuel.

■ 14. 1st Quebec Conference. Churchill and Roosevelt agree to launch joint invasion of France in summer 1944.

★ 17. The Peenemunde Raid. RAF bombers launch night raid on German weapons development works at Peenemunde.

★ 17. First Schweinfurt Raid. US bombers launch daylight raid on heavily defended ball bearing factory at Schweinfurt. 60 out of 230 aircraft are shot down.

◆ 28. Germans impose martial law on Denmark after civilian government resigns.

● 6. In the Battle of Vella Gulf, US destroyers ambush and sink two of four Japanese destroyers.

★ 17. American carrier aircraft carry out heavy raids on Japanese positions at Wewak, New Guinea.

★ 5. Russians capture Belgorod.

★ 13. Russians launch major offensive near Smolensk.

★ 23. Russians recapture Kharkhov.

★ 26. Russians launch offensive in Ukraine.

■ 2. Italian ambassador in Portugal asks British ambassador for surrender terms.

★ 17. British and Americans complete occupation of Sicily with capture of Messina.

WESTERN FRONT

● 14. Germans finish equipping their U-boats with anti-aircraft guns and acoustic torpedoes. U-boats are sent back to the Atlantic to attack convoys.

● 19. German U-boats attack convoy ON202, sinking seven ships for loss of three U-boats.

● 20. British mini submarines disable German battleship *Tirpitz* in Alta Fjord, Norway.

★ 14. Second Schweinfurt Raid. 60 out of 290 US bombers are shot down. US 8th Air Force temporarily abandons daylight raids over Germany.

● 17. British naval ships land Free Norwegian troops to liberate Norwegian Spitzbergen Island.

◆ 28. In USA, 530,000 coalminers go on strike over pay. President Roosevelt declares martial law in mining areas. Strike collapses after one week.

PACIFIC & FAR EAST

★ 15. Lae, New Guinea, captured by Allies.

● 18. US carrier aircraft attack Japanese positions on Tarawa in the Gilbert Islands.

● 23. US submarine *Trigger* sinks Japanese convoy of oil tankers off Formosa.

● 26. Japanese begin evacuation of the Solomon Islands.

★ 3. Australians take Finschhafen, New Guinea.

★ 6. Japanese evacuate Vella Lavella, sinking two US destroyers that try to intervene.

★ 11. Japanese aircraft bomb Madras.

▲ 20. Japanese carriers transport aircraft to Rabaul to prepare for offensive in Solomons.

■ 21. Japan grants independence to puppet government in the Philippines.

◆ 25. Burma railway completed.

EASTERN FRONT

★ 13. Russians launch offensive north of Smolensk.

★ 15. Russians break through at Desna.

★ 17. Russians capture Bryansk.

★ 22. Russians cross river Dnieper at Kiev.

★ 13. Russians capture Zaporozhe.

★ 30. Russians cross the Dnieper.

★ 30. Russians cut off German forces in the Crimea.

THE MED & MIDDLE EAST

■ 8. Italian surrender announced.

★ 9. Allies invade Italy at Salerno.

★ 9. Germans seize all strategic points in Italy and forcibly disarm Italian forces.

★ 1. Allied 5th Army enters Naples.

★ 3. Germans seize Italian bases in Greece.

■ 13. Italy declares war on Germany.

KEY: ■ DIPLOMACY ◆ HOME ● NAVAL ▲ SECRET WAR ★ BATTLE

● 3. German E-boats sink three ships off Hastings.

● 15. Germans abandon U-boat campaign in the Atlantic.

★ 18. Battle of Berlin. British RAF begins five-month-long campaign of night bombing of the German capital that kills 6000 civilians and leave 1.5 million homeless.

★ 21. British and Free Norwegian Commandoes raid Arendal, Norway.

■ 4. Second Cairo Conference between Allies gives priority to Pacific campaign not Burma.

◆ 12. Hitler appoints Field Marshal Rommel to command the defence of western Europe.

◆ 24. Commanders chosen for invasion of France. US General Eisenhower – overall command, British General Montgomery – land forces, Air Marshal Tedder – air forces, and Admiral Ramsay – naval forces.

● 26. Battle of North Cape. German battleship *Scharnhorst* sunk off Norway.

● Allies lost 597 merchant ships in 1943.

★ 1. Americans land on Bougainville, Solomons. Japanese cruiser *Sendai* is sunk.

★ 11. US aircraft launch raids on Rabaul.

★ 20. US Marines land on Tarawa and Betio in the Gilbert Islands. Japanese defenders fight to the death, inflicting heavy casualties.

● 25. Battle of Cape St George. American destroyers annihilate Japanese destroyer squadron.

● 9. American ships attack Nauru and Kwajeilein islands.

★ 27. Australians capture Pimple Hill, New Guinea.

★ 1. Russians land on the Crimea.

★ 6. Russians capture Kiev, then cut strategic Odessa–Leningrad railway.

★ 14. Russians capture Cherkassy.

★ 17. German attack at Kirovograd fails.

◆ 19. Russia adopts a new national anthem in place of the Communist Party song.

◆ 22. Spanish fascist volunteers return home.

★ 4. Americans cross the river Volturno.

★ 19. British establish bridgehead over Sangro.

◆ 21. General Kesselring takes over as German commander in Mediterranean.

★ 6. British 8th Army crosses the river Moro.

★ 28. Canadians capture Ortona after prolonged street fighting.

WESTERN FRONT

◆ 5. Outspoken Danish pastor Kaj Munk shot by Germans for anti-German speeches.

★ 4. Germans launch the 'Little Blitz', a series of heavy raids on London and southeast England. There will be 14 night attacks of about 450 aircraft in the following five weeks.

■ 26. Liberia declares war on Germany and Italy.

★ 20. American 8th Air Force launches 'Big Week' – seven days of heavy co-ordinated raids on German industrial targets, mostly aircraft factories.

★ 22. American bombers lose their way and accidentally bomb Dutch city of Nijmegen, inflicting heavy civilian casualties.

PACIFIC & FAR EAST

★ 10. British capture Maungdaw, Burma.

★ 11. German wolf pack 'Monsoon' begins operations in Indian Ocean. They will sink 17 ships before returning to Germany in March.

★ 31. Americans invade Kwajalein and Majuro in the Marshall Islands.

● 3. Americans begin construction of massive dockyard facilities on remote Majuro Island to serve as forward supply base.

★ 4. Japanese launch major attack in Arakan area of Burma.

● 10. Japanese fleet abandons forward base at Truk after heavy American bombing.

● 13. Japanese submarine sinks British troopship *Khedive Ismail*, killing 2000.

EASTERN FRONT

★ 4. Advancing Russians reach the 1939 Polish border at Olevsk.

★ 14. Russians launch offensive from Leningrad, finally ending the siege.

★ 19. Russians capture Novgorod.

★ 6. Russians cross river Dnieper at Nikopol.

★ 21. Russians capture Krivoi Rog, key iron mining area in the Ukraine.

★ 25. Russians launch heavy bombing raid on Helsinki, capital of Finland.

THE MED & MIDDLE EAST

◆ 11. Italian Count Ciano shot by Fascists.

★ 15. Germans pull back to river Rapido.

★ 22. Allied landings at Anzio begin well, but fail to move inland rapidly.

★ 15. Allies bomb Monte Cassino, destroying medieval monastery but fail to break through.

★ 19. German attack at Anzio is driven off.

★ 6. First major daylight air raid on Berlin carried out by 730 bombers of the US 8th Air Force, protected by 800 new Mustang long-range fighters.

● 13. German U-boat U-852 torpedoes Greek merchant ship *Peleus*, then machine-guns the survivors in their lifeboats. Only three of 35 crew survive.

★ 23. RAF 1000 bomber raid on Berlin.

◆ 24. The Great Escape. 76 Allied airmen escape from prison camp Stalag Lufe III. Fifty are recaptured and shot by the Gestapo.

★ 11. Precision, low-level raid by RAF Mosquitoes destroys Gestapo HQ in The Hague, Netherlands.

★ 13. Allied air forces carry out heavy raids on German coastal defences in France.

★ 18. Germans launch last big air raid on London with 125 bombers.

★ 19. British bombers drop mines along the river Danube.

■ 22. Turkey ceases exports of war materials to Germany and its allies.

★ 7. Japanese launch major offensive over the river Chindwin, Burma, towards India.

★ 20. Chinese troops occupy the Hukawng Valley, northern Burma.

● 20. American warships bombard Emirau and Kavieng in the Bismarck Archipelago.

★ 29. Siege of Imphal. Japanese troops advancing from Burma surround British supply base at Imphal.

★ 6. Siege of Kohima. Japanese troops advancing from Burma surround British outpost at Kohima.

◆ 14. Munitions ship *Fort Stikine* explodes in Bombay harbour, sinking 27 other ships and killing 1500 people.

★ 20. Siege of Kohima. British reinforcements arrive at Kohima.

★ 22. American forces land at Hollandia and Aitape, New Guinea.

★ 15. Russians reach the river Bug, Ukraine.

■ 18. Admiral Horthy visits Hitler to ask that Hungarian troops be withdrawn from Russia. Hitler refuses.

★ 19. Germany invades Hungary.

★ 3. Russian advance reaches Romania.

★ 10. Russians capture Odessa.

■ 16. Nazi puppet government in Hungary announces that all Jews are to be arrested.

★ 16. Russians capture Yalta.

★ 1. New German attack at Anzio begins, but is driven off after four days.

★ 16. New Zealand attack at Cassino makes some gains, but fails to break through.

◆ 4. Free Greek army begins 20-day mutiny against King George in favour of a republic.

WESTERN FRONT

■ 3. Spain agrees to cut exports of metal ores to Germany.

★ 8. 'Oil Offensive' opens with massive American bombing raids on synthetic oil plants in Germany. Lack of oil supplies has been identified as key strategic weakness for German armed forces.

★ 14. Around 90 German bombers raid Bristol.

★ 17. French Resistance destroy ball bearing factory at Ivry-sur-Seine.

◆ 18. Pro-German riots break out in Constantinople. Turkish government imposes martial law.

★ 20. Allied bombers begin massed raids on rail junctions and yards in northern France.

● 26. *Serpa Pinto* Incident. German U-boat U-541 stops neutral Portuguese liner *Serpa Pinto* as it heads for Canada. Crew and passengers are ordered into lifeboats but U-541 leaves without sinking liner. Crew and passengers reboard ship after nine hours, but three die of exposure.

PACIFIC & FAR EAST

★ 4. British capture key junction on the Maungdaw-Buthidaung Road, Burma.

★ 6. Siege of Imphal. British launch offensive to break through to Imphal from India.

★ 17. US–Chinese forces capture Myitkyina Airfield, Burma.

★ 19. US carrier aircraft attack Marcus and Wake islands.

★ 23. Chinese launch offensive in the Honan Province.

★ 27. US forces land on Biak Island, off north coast of New Guinea.

★ 29. Japanese land reinforcements on Biak.

▲ 30. Team of Japanese sabotage agents is landed on Ceylon from submarine, but fail to achieve much damage before they are killed.

EASTERN FRONT

◆ 1. Russian dictator Stalin asks Marshals Zhukov and Vasilevsky to plan final offensive to conquer Germany.

★ 9. Russians capture Sebastopol.

▲ 20. Test firing of German V-2 rocket goes wrong. Rocket is captured by Polish Resistance and smuggled into London.

★ 30. German offensive at Jassy, Romania, makes limited gains.

THE MED & MIDDLE EAST

★ 11. Allied 5th and 8th Armies launch attack on Monte Cassino and Gustav Line defences.

★ 18. Free Polish capture key Monastery Hill at Cassino. The Germans retreat.

★ 20. Canadians break through German defences. Germans retreat from Anzio.

KEY: ■ DIPLOMACY ◆ HOME ● NAVAL ▲ SECRET WAR ★ BATTLE

★ 5. Massive attacks by Allied air forces in Normandy. They target rail lines, bridges and German artillery batteries.

★ 6. D-Day. Allied invasion of France. At dawn, five divisions of British, Canadian and US troops are landed on Normandy beaches while Allied warships and bombers pound German defences. Airborne troops have already landed and seized key targets up to 8 km inland.

★ 7. Normandy. British reach Bayeux. German resistance stiffens.

◆ 7. Germans arrest King Leopold of Belgium and imprison him in Germany.

◆ 10. German SS division hunting for Resistance fighters massacre 642 French civilians at Oradour sur Glane.

★ 12. Normandy. Allied beachheads link up to form continuous front.

★ 13. First V-1 flying bombs hit London.

★ 29. Americans capture Cherbourg.

● 11. American carrier aircraft attack various targets in the Marianas Islands.

● 13. American battleships bombard Saipan, Marianas.

★ 14. First US air raid by B29 Superfortress bombers strikes Japan. The aircraft fly from bases in China.

★ 15. Americans land on Saipan.

★ 18. Japanese offensive captures city of Changsha, China.

● 19. Battle of the Philippine Sea. Three-day naval battle sees the Japanese carrier-based air force effectively destroyed by American pilots from carriers in the Philippine Sea.

★ 22. Siege of Imphal. British break through to besieged garrison. Japanese start to retreat back to Burma.

★ 27. Battle of Hengyang sees Japanese advance halted by the Chinese.

★ 9. Russians launch major offensive against the Finns, north of Leningrad.

★ 20. Russians capture Viipuri, Finland.

★ 20. Russian partisans begin three-day campaign of sabotage against railways in German-occupied Ukraine.

★ 23. Russians launch their largest offensive of the war so far in Byelorussia with 1.2 million men and 5200 tanks. German defences collapse within hours.

● 1. Last German supply ship reaches Crete. Most island garrisons now isolated.

★ 4. Allied 5th Army enters Rome after city is abandoned by German commander

Kesselring without fighting so that the ancient monuments would not be damaged.

★ 17. British 8th Army captures Assissi.

★ 26. South Africans capture Chiusi.

WESTERN FRONT

★ 8. Normandy. British attack at Caen fails.

★ 17. German commander in France, Field Marshal Rommel, is badly wounded by British aircraft. He is taken to hospital in Germany.

◆ 20. July Bomb Plot. Group of German army officers narrowly fail to kill Hitler by planting a bomb in his HQ. Officers in Paris launch coup against Nazis, but this collapses when it is learned that Hitler has survived. Plotters are executed. The Gestapo track down anyone with links to the plot, disrupting German military hierarchy.

★ 1. US 1st Army breaks out of Normandy at Avranches, advancing rapidly to south.

★ 4. First Allied jet aircraft enters combat – the British Gloster Meteor fighter.

★ 11. Americans capture Angers and Nantes.

★ 13. Americans capture Orleans.

★ 15. Germans pummelled by Allied air forces at Falaise.

◆ 19. Paris Uprising. French Resistance, police and civilians attack German garrison.

★ 25. German garrison in Paris surrenders.

PACIFIC & FAR EAST

★ 7. Americans wipe out Japanese defenders of Saipan.

◆ 18. Tojo resigns as Japanese prime minister due to defeats in the Pacific. He is replaced by equally hardline General Koiso.

★ 21. Americans land on Guam.

★ 24. Americans land on Tinian.

★ 28. Americans complete capture of Biak.

★ 30. Americans land at Sansapor, completing occupation of New Guinea.

★ 10. Americans secure control of Guam. Isolated groups of Japanese continue guerrilla warfare from the jungle. Final Japanese soldier surrenders in 1972.

★ 16. Japanese abandon defensive positions along the Burma–India border and pull back to central Burma.

EASTERN FRONT

★ 3. German 4th Army cut off at Minsk.

★ 7. Finns retreat to defensive U Line.

★ 10. Russians begin major offensive in Baltic States. Germans retreat slowly.

★ 11. German 4th Army surrenders.

★ 1. Polish Home Army launch Warsaw Uprising. Russians refuse to help.

■ 23. King Michael of Romania sacks the government and surrenders to Russia.

■ 25. Romania declares war on Germany.

THE MED & MIDDLE EAST

◆ 1. Brazilian Expeditionary Force leaves Brazil to fight in Italy.

★ 17. British 8th Army crosses river Arno.

★ 15. Allied 7th Army lands near Nice and drives rapidly inland.

★ 22. Allied forces in Italy reach Metauro.

★ 27. Germans evacuate Athens.

★ 1. Canadians capture Dieppe, British capture Arras. Americans capture Verdun.

★ 3. British capture Brussels after advancing 360 km in just four days.

★ 8. First German V-2 rocket lands on London, killing three and demolishing several buildings.

★ 11. US 1st Army enters Germany near Trier.

★ 17. British and Polish paratroops seize key bridge across Rhine at Arnhem. Ground attack fails to reach them and most surrender. Allied offensive in the west is halted.

★ 3. RAF bomb Dutch sea dykes, causing extensive flooding behind German lines.

★ 7. US 1st Army breaches German Siegfried Line Defences near Aachen, but fails to achieve significant breakthrough.

★ 14. 2000 RAF bombers raid Duisburg.

◆ 14. Rommel commits suicide after being implicated in July Bomb Plot.

★ 15. US forces begin landing on the Palau Islands.

★ 16. Japanese carrier Unyo sunk by US submarine *Barb* off China.

★ 12. Battle of Formosa. Allied and Japanese fleets clash, but results are inconclusive.

★ 20. Allied forces land on Leyte, Philippines.

★ 24. Battle of Leyte Gulf. Four Japanese fleets converge on the Philippines to destroy Allied fleets and landing forces. Confused three-day battle ends in total defeat for Japanese navy, which loses four carriers, three battleships, ten cruisers and 11 destroyers.

★ 2. Russians reach Bulgarian border.

■ 8. Bulgaria declares war on Germany.

■ 10. Finland surrenders.

★ 22. Russians capture Tallinn, Estonia.

◆ 2. End of Warsaw Uprising. Polish Home Army destroyed by Germans.

★ 4. German Army Group North cut off in Baltic States.

★ 13. Russians capture Riga, Latvia.

★ 24. British land in Greece and begin pursuit of retreating Germans. Naval detachments are sent to occupy Greek islands. Various Greek factions agree temporary unity.

◆ 30. Agreement between Greek factions breaks down as royalist government in exile bans Communist Party.

WESTERN FRONT

★ 2. Liberation of Belgium completed.

★ 5. Allies capture Flushing.

◆ 7. Franklin D Roosevelt re-elected as US president after hiding true extent of his ill health.

★ 8. US 3rd Army begins offensive near Metz.

● 12. German battleship *Tirpitz* sunk in Tromso Fjord, Norway, by RAF bombers.

★ 8. US 1st and 9th Armies begins offensive near Aachen.

★ 25. V-2 kills 160 in London store.

★ 1. US 3rd Army reaches river Saar.

★ 10. Free Norwegian forces destroy rail links to prevent evacuation of German troops from Norway to Germany.

★ 16. Battle of the Bulge. Surprise German attack in the Ardennes smashes US defences and drive west towards Allied supply lines.

★ 21. Germans reach Bastogne, but cannot overcome determined US resistance.

★ 25. Germans halted at Celles.

● Allies lost 205 merchant ships in 1944.

PACIFIC & FAR EAST

★ 24. US launch first B29 Superfortress bombing raid on Tokyo. Aircraft take off from India and refuel in China. It is decided this is not a viable long-term option. Future raids will be flown from Saipan and Tinian.

★ 27. US warships off Philippines attacked by Japanese aircraft, several of which are reported to deliberately crash into the ships. These are the first attacks by Japanese kamikaze pilots.

★ 7. US troops land at Ormoc, Philippines.

● 8. US warships bombard Japanese positions on the strategic island of Iwo Jima.

★ 13. US B29 bombers from Saipan seriously damage Mitsubishi works at Nagoya, Japan.

★ 15. US troops land on Mindoro, Philippines.

★ 16. Chinese capture Bhamo.

EASTERN FRONT

★ 29. Russian forces link up with Yugoslav Communist Resistance fighters at Pecs.

◆ 22. Russians set up puppet Communist government in occupied Hungary.

★ 24. Russians reach Budapest and lay siege to powerful German forces in the city.

THE MED & MIDDLE EAST

★ 4. Liberation of Greece completed.

★ 25. British 8th Army crosses the river Cosina.

◆ 3. British troops break up battle between Greek royalists and Communists in Athens.

◆ 5. Greek Communists attack British troops. Greek civil war begins.

★ 2. Heavy Allied bombing raids strike transport links behind German lines.

★ 8. Allied armies clear German forces from west bank of the Maas.

★ 16. German armies driven back to their position before the Battle of the Bulge.

● 15. German E-boats launch attack on Allied merchant ships in the Thames estuary.

★ 3. Free French liberate Colmar.

★ 3. 1000 US bombers strike Berlin in daylight, destroying airport and rail yards.

■ 9. Ecuador, Peru and Paraguay declare war on Germany.

★13. The Dresden Raid. 1000 British and American bombers obliterate Dresden to destroy transport links. Many German refugees are killed in the resulting firestorm.

■ 22. Saudi Arabia, Turkey and Uruguay declare war on Germany and Japan.

★ 6. 18 US warships, including two battleships, are badly damaged by kamikaze attacks.

★ 9. Americans land at Lingayen, Philippines.

★ 19. US launch heavy B29 raid on aircraft works at Kobe, Japan.

★ 24. British Pacific Fleet attacks Japanese positions in Dutch East Indies.

★ 25. Japanese begin evacuation of inland China.

★ 16. US paratroops capture fortified island of Corregidor, Philippines.

★ 19. US Marines land on Iwo Jima in the face of determined and skilful Japanese resistance.

★ 23. US Marines take Mount Suribachi on Iwo Jima. Flag raising becomes the most famous photo of the war.

★ 12. Russians launch major offensive over the Vistula, advancing 40 km on first day.

★ 17. Russians capture ruins of Warsaw.

★ 23. Russians reach river Oder.

★ 29. Russians besiege Poznan.

■ 4. Yalta Conference. Churchill, Stalin and Roosevelt discuss post-war face of Europe.

★ 4. Russians begin offensive over the Oder.

★ 13. Russians capture Budapest.

★ 24. Russians capture Poznan.

WESTERN FRONT

★ 3. US 1st Army reaches Cologne.

★ 7. US 1st Army captures bridge over the river Rhine at Remagen. Tanks and troops pour across to establish a bridgehead.

★ 11. Precision raid by British bombers halts production at Krupps steel works, Essen.

★ 17. Bridge at Remagen destroyed by attack by German Ar234 jet bombers. Americans have already built replacement pontoon bridges and continue to cross the river Rhine.

★ 22. US 3rd Army crosses the river Rhine at Mainz using hurriedly assembled boats.

★ 23. Operation Plunder. British cross the river Rhine at Wesel in strength. German resistance is at first slight, but soon stiffens.

★ 25. British bombers destroy vast German oil reserves at Hamburg.

★ 29. British armoured forces break out of Wesel bridgehead.

★ 29. US 7th Army capture Heidelberg.

PACIFIC & FAR EAST

★ 3. Americans capture Manila, Philippines.

★ 8. British enter Mandalay, Burma.

★ 9. US B29 bombers from Tinian and Guam launch firestorm raid on Tokyo that kills 84,000 and destroys 26 sq km of the city.

★ 9. In Indo-China, the Japanese arrest or murder French officials and declare a puppet government.

★ 16. Japanese counter attack at Meiktila, Burma, is defeated.

★ 20. British capture Mandalay, Burma, and begin drive south towards Rangoon.

● 25. US naval forces arrive off Okinawa to begin preliminary bombardment and reconnaissance prior to landings.

★ 26. US forces declare Iwo Jima 'secure', although isolated Japanese continue guerrilla actions for some days to come.

EASTERN FRONT

◆ 8. Marshal Tito forms provisional Communist government in Yugoslavia.

★ 11. Russians capture Küstrin and Tczew.

★ 12. Russians capture Zvolen.

★ 18. Poles capture Kolberg.

◆ 19. Hitler orders his army to employ 'scorched earth' policy as they retreat.

★ 22. Russians break German defences at Oppeln, Silesia.

THE MED & MIDDLE EAST

   KEY: ■ DIPLOMACY ◆ HOME ● NAVAL ▲ SECRET WAR ★ BATTLE

★ 1. German Army Group B surrounded in Ruhr Valley by US and British armies.

★ 8. Americans capture Schweinfurt and Essen. Free French capture Pfrozheim.

★ 11. Americans reach river Elbe.

★ 13. Americans capture Jena.

★ 13. Americans capture Nuremburg.

★ 18. Canadians reach the Zuider Zee, Netherlands.

★ 19. German Army Group B – 400,000 men – surrenders in the Ruhr.

★ 25. British bombers attack Hitler's mountain retreat of Berchtesgarten in case he is seeking refuge there.

★ 26. Russian and US forces meet at Torgau on the river Elbe.

★ 1. US 10th Army lands on Okinawa. There is no resistance from the Japanese forces believed to be on the island.

★ 5. US forces on Okinawa meet first Japanese resistance from prepared defences.

★ 6. Massed kamikaze attacks on US fleet off Okinawa inflicts heavy damage.

★ 14. Americans launch first attack on Japanese defences on Motobu Peninsula, Okinawa.

★ 23. Japanese on Okinawa withdraw to defensive positions around Shuri.

★ 27. British reach Toungoo, Burma.

★ 30. German commander in the Netherlands asks for terms of surrender.

★ 3. Russians capture Bratislava.

★ 6. Russians attack Vienna and Königsberg.

★ 13. Russians capture Vienna.

★ 16. Russians begin offensive on Berlin.

★ 21. Russians enter Berlin suburbs.

★ 24. Russians surround central Berlin.

◆ 30. Hitler and other leading Nazis commit suicide at command bunker in Berlin.

★ 8. British 8th Army crosses river Senior.

★ 21. Allies capture Bologna.

★ 22. Allies reach banks of the river Po.

★ 25. Germans evacuate Genoa.

◆ 28. Former Italian dictator Mussolini captured and shot by Communist partisans.

★ 29. One million Germans in Italy surrender.

WESTERN FRONT

◆ 1. German radio announces that Hitler is dead. Admiral Dönitz succeeds him as *Führer* of Germany.

★ 4. All German forces on the Western Front surrender to British General Montgomery.

★ 4. Unconditional surrender of Germany signed by Field Marshal Jodl at Rheims.

◆ 8. VE (Victory in Europe) Day. Extensive celebrations throughout Allied countries.

★ 8. German forces in Norway surrender to recently returned Crown Prince Olaf.

■ 3. Allies agree on boundaries of British, French, US and Russian zones of occupation in Germany.

PACIFIC & FAR EAST

★ 2. American attack on Shuri, Okinawa, driven back with heavy loss.

★ 3. British–Indian army captures Rangoon.

★ 5. Japanese counter attack at Shuri, Okinawa, defeated.

★ 10. Americans cross river Asa, Okinawa.

★ 14. Americans launch firestorm raid on Nagoya, Japan, destroying 36 sq km of city.

★ 21. Japanese withdraw from Shuri, Okinawa. Heavy rain halts US attacks.

★ 3. Japanese defenders on Okinawa now restricted to Oroku Peninsula.

■ 6. Brazil declares war on Japan.

★ 10. American 24th Corps launches attack on remaining Japanese positions on Okinawa.

★ 22. Americans declare Okinawa to be secure.

EASTERN FRONT

★ 2. Russians capture Berlin.

★ 7. Siege of Breslau ends after 82 days.

★ 8. Formal German surrender ratified in Berlin by German Field Marshal Keitel and Russian Marshal Zhukov.

THE MED & MIDDLE EAST

◆ 4. US General MacArthur announces final liberation of the Philippines.

★ 10. Raid by over 1000 B29 bombers pounds Tokyo area without loss.

■ 12. Japanese Prince Konoye in Russia asks Stalin to pass on request to USA and Britain for peace terms. Stalin refuses.

▲ 16. First atomic bomb tested at Alamogordo, New Mexico, USA.

★ 24. Most of Japanese fleet sunk at Kure.

★ 6. Hiroshima hit by first atomic bomb to be used in action. About 80,000 die instantly as 12 sq km of the city is destroyed.

★ 9. Nagasaki hit by atomic bomb. About 40,000 die as 4 sq km of the city is destroyed.

★ 9. Russia invades Japanese-occupied Manchuria.

■ 14. Japan surrenders. The formal surrender document is signed on board USS *Missouri* in Tokyo Bay on 2 September.

Index

S

Acknowledgements

The publishers would like to thank the following artists whose work appears in this book:
Peter Dennis, Alan Hancocks, Mike Saunders, Mike White

Maps by Chris Moore

All other artworks are from Miles Kelly Artwork Bank

The publishers would like to thank the following picture sources
whose photographs appear in this book:

p.27 John Frost Newspapers; p.28 Topfoto; p.31 www.pictorialpress.com; p.32 Topfoto;
p.35 www.pictorialpress.com; pp. 41, 42, 44 Topfoto; p.47 John Frost Newspapers;
p.51 www.pictorialpress.com; p.58 Topfoto; p.61 www.pictorialpress.com; p.64 Topfoto;
p.67 www.pictorialpress.com; pp.73, 76 Topfoto; pp.78, 83, 86 www.pictorialpress.com;
p.89 Topfoto; pp.101, 102 www.pictorialpress.com; pp.107, 113 Topfoto;
p.115 John Frost Newspapers; p.120 Topfoto; pp.123, 125, 126 www.pictorialpress.com;
p.129 Topfoto; p.130 www.pictorialpress.com; p.137 John Frost Newspapers;
pp.138, 140 www.pictorialpress.com; pp.142, 145 Topfoto; p.146 www.pictorialpress.com;
p.149 Topfoto; p.152 www.pictorialpress.com; pp.157, 158, 161 Topfoto;
pp.165, 166 www.pictorialpress.com; p.168 Topfoto; p.171 www.pictorialpress.com;
p.176 Topfoto; p.180 www.pictorialpress.com; pp.183, 186 Topfoto;
p.189 www.pictorialpress.com; pp.193, 194 Topfoto; p.197 John Frost Newspapers;
p.199 www.pictorialpress.com; p.200 Topfoto; p.203 www.pictorialpress.com; p.207 Topfoto;
pp.213, 229 John Frost Newspapers; pp.232, 235 Topfoto; p.238 www.pictorialpress.com;
pp.241, 243, 244, 250, 253, 257 Topfoto; p.263 www.pictorialpress.com; pp.265, 267 Topfoto;
p.272 www.pictorialpress.com; pp.275, 276, 287 Topfoto; p.289 www.pictorialpress.com;
pp.295, 298, 301 Topfoto; pp.303, 310, 311 www.pictorialpress.com; pp.315, 317, 323 Topfoto;
p.329 www.pictorialpress.com; pp.333, 334, 336, 338, 347, 350, 356, 359, 361, 364 Topfoto;
p.373 www.pictorialpress.com; p.375 Topfoto; p.379 John Frost Newspapers; p.389 Topfoto;
p.395 John Frost Newspapers; pp.399, 400 Topfoto

All other photographs are from Corel, ILN